Created and Directed by Hans Höfer

INSIGHT
GUIDES

Mallorca & Ibiza

Edited by Andrew Eames
Editorial Director: Brian Bell

APA PUBLICATIONS

MALLORCA & IBIZA

Second Edition (2nd Reprint)
© 1992 APA PUBLICATIONS (HK) LTD
All Rights Reserved
Printed in Singapore by Höfer Press Pte. Ltd

ABOUT THIS BOOK

There are countless publications about the Balearic islands, but few good ones. The challenge facing the team who compiled *Insight Guide: Mallorca and Ibiza*, was to dig behind the hackneyed image portrayed in the mass-market publications, and find out why these islands have attracted so many distinguished visitors.

Project editor **Andrew Eames**, after contributing to *Insight Guide: Great Britain* and editing *Cityguide: London*, is no stranger to Apa's philosophy, which first attracted him while he was working as a journalist in Singapore. Eames is a freelance writer and editor now living in London. He is the author of *Crossing the Shadow Line*, his travel autobiography, a novel and a cartoon book. In recent years he has worked for *The Times* in London and as a magazine consultant.

Invaluable for their ideas, writing and photography were **Don Murray** and **Ana Pascual**, on their boat *The Travelling Desk* in Palma. Ana Pascual, who was born in Palma, studied in Barcelona and Madrid before returning to Mallorca to teach Spanish language and literature. Seven years later she turned to journalism, at times by herself, and at times in collaboration with Murray, a partnership which has produced one bestselling book and countless articles.

Don Murray, a Canadian, arrived in Mallorca in the late 1970s, at the invitation of Ana Pascual, whom he met on a film-making expedition in Alaska. He started taking pictures while a pilot in the Canadian Air Force, and began to write when an editor said he would buy his pictures if he wrote something to go with them. Murray insists that one day he and Pascual are going to untie his boat and disappear off quietly into the sunset; meanwhile they continue to enjoy farewell parties.

The Travelling Desk produced essays on architecture (with **John Matthews**), gardens, modernism, windmills, Cabrera and the British Influence, as well as substantial numbers of photographs and invaluable assistance on ensuring that the text was consistent in its place names, all of which are in Catalan.

The essay on the islander, a difficult subject, was tackled by **Pedro de Montaner**, the son of a Mallorquin nobleman. Montaner has been a philosophy lecturer, Director General of Culture of the Balearic Islands and is now the chief archivist and librarian in the Palma City Hall.

From *Insight Guide: Spain*, Eames recalled **Gil Carbajal**, a Californian of Iberian background who now works for the Spanish World Service in Madrid and contributes cultural and historical articles to the local English press; Carbajal wrote the sections on the old city of Palma and the islands' nightlife.

Ray Fleming (chapters on the Mallorcan Plain and Issues in the News) retired to Mallorca after a career in media with the United Nations. He first visited Mallorca in 1968, on a £29 holiday package which included air fare, apartment, maid services and car, and returned frequently thereafter. The timelessness of everyday life on the island is what appeals to him about Mallorca, the "Biblical" scenes, the annual rituals, the landscapes.

Since 1963 **Ben Roth** (essays on Jet-setters and Xuetas) has written his own column in the *Mallorca Daily Bulletin* under the pen-name of Benito. Roth, a Hungarian of Jewish descent, spent his early years in America, where he was at times pilot, physical training instructor, physiotherapist, interior designer,

Eames   *Murray*   *Pascual*   *de Montaner*

truck driver and salesman. Now 71, he claims that his continued health is the result of "taking everything easy and avoiding all arguments".

Dr William Waldren (Prehistory chapters) is an American archaeologist who lives and works for part of his year in Deià, in a house which he created and designed during the years when he was a sculptor. During the winter he is research fellow at both Oxford and Cambridge universities. Waldren (pictured on page 79) describes his life as "going from one ivory tower to another. In this I feel one of the luckiest and happiest men in the world." His wife, **Jacqueline**, did her doctoral thesis on the coexistence of foreigners and locals in Deià, about whom she also writes in this book.

Completing the list of resident contributors is **Bob Norris**, who first came to the islands in 1977, as a manager in the hotel industry. Norris, born in Brazil of English and Brazilian parents, has spent much of his life travelling. He completed the exhaustive and exhausting task of compiling the Travel Tips section of this book. Aside from writing, his other ventures include real-estate, translation, a bar, and import-export.

The history chapters of this book were the province of **Felipe Fernandez-Armesto**, a fellow of St Antony's College, Oxford. His books include *Before Columbus* and *The Spanish Armada*. He first saw the Balearics when he was one year old, and has been studying them almost ever since—but principally from an armchair. "I detest travel," he writes. "The only journeys I like are made in the imagination."

By contrast, **Robin Neillands** is an indefatigable 50-year-old Englishman who regularly walks, cycles or canoes distances that would make a car sigh, and has written some 40 books under various pen-names and on various topics. From his second home in Puerto Pollença, Neillands researched the essays on Expatriates, on Pollença and the guide to the Sierra.

Vicky Hayward (chapters on Ciutadella, Formentera, food, cheese and art), has made something of a speciality out of writing about places and things Spanish. A history graduate from Cambridge, she lived for a while in the South Pacific. Of the Balearics she confesses to have been "struck by the curious acceptance of tourists as the last in a long line of colonisers. What will happen to the islands when the fashion for sunbathing dies away?"

Music, not sunbathing, is **Pol Ferguson-Thompson**'s passion. A career which started with the study of philosophy and comparative religion led into a tour of Spain with a pop band; by several circuitous routes since then he is now producing television programmes in London.

For writer, photographer and teacher **Mike Mockler**, travel is an opportunity to seek out beautiful countryside, interesting animals and exotic birds, a fascination he communicates in his chapter on birdwatching.

The illustrations are primarily the work of **Bill Wassman**, **Don Murray**, **Jaume Gual** and **Kim Naylor**. Special mention is due to **Neil Menneer**, who spent four weeks on the islands with his cameras, only to suffer the theft of all his film and equipment from a car in Palma; it still gives him nightmares.

This book could not have been completed without the assistance of the Balearic tourist authorities, particularly **Eduardo Gamero** and **Anna Skidmore**. Thanks are also due to the **Auscher Lindquist** family of Formentera, and to **Air Europe**.

Roth   *Norris*   *Fernandez-Armesto*   *Hayward*

23 A Closer Look
—by Andrew Eames

25 Warehouses of Prehistory
—by William Waldren

31 From the Moors to the Christians
—by Felipe Fernandez-Armesto

37 Greatness and Decline
—by Felipe Fernandez-Armesto

49 Tides of Change
—by Felipe Fernandez-Armesto

59 The Islander
—by Pedro de Montaner

60 Xuetas and Judaism
—by Ben Roth

69 Mallorca as it was
—by Neville Waters

75 Jet-setters, Past and Present
—by Ben Roth

81 Expatriate Existence
—by Robin Neillands

93 The Archipelago
—by Andrew Eames

97 Palma
—by Gil Carbajal

109 The Mallorcan Sierra
—by Robin Neillands

112 Deià, Portrait of an Artist's Colony
—by Jacqueline Waldren

121 Cabrera, Island Wilderness
—by Don Murray and Ana Pascual

127 The Mallorcan Plain
—by Ray Fleming

130 **Famous Sons: Junipero Serra**
—by Ray Fleming

132 **Famous Sons: Ramón Llull**
—by Ray Fleming

136 **Windmills**
—by Don Murray and Ana Pascual

145 **Mahón and Eastern Menorca**
—by Andrew Eames

150 **Mahón Cheese**
—by Vicky Hayward

154 **Prehistoric Menorca**
—by William Waldren

159 **Ciutadella and Western Menorca**
—by Vicky Hayward

168 **The English Influence**
—by Don Murray and Ana Pascual

175 **Ibiza, White Island**
—by Pol Ferguson Thompson

178 **The Hippy Era**
—by Pol Ferguson Thompson

180 **Doing the Paseo**
—by Pol Ferguson Thompson

186 **Las Salinas**
—by Pol Ferguson Thompson

195 **Formentera**
—by Vicky Hayward

207 **Issues in the News**
—by Ray Fleming

215 **The Pulse of Pollença**
—by Robin Neillands

221 **In Search of a Speciality**
—by Vicky Hayward

227 Nightlife
—by Gil Carbajal

235 Birdwatch
—by Mike Mockler

243 Old Houses, New Houses
—by Don Murray, Ana Pascual and
John Mathews

253 Island Deco
—by Don Murray and Ana Pascual

259 New Art
—by Vicky Hayward

265 Traditional Gardens on Mallorca
—by Don Murray and Ana Pascual

MAPS

 93 The Balearics
 94 Mallorca
 98 Palma
147 Menorca
148 Mahón
160 Ciutadella
176 Ibiza
179 Elvissa (Ibiza Town)
195 Formentera

TRAVEL TIPS

GETTING THERE
274 By Air
275 By Sea
275 By Rail
275 By Road

TRAVEL ESSENTIALS
276 Visas & Passports
276 Money Matters
277 Health
278 What to Wear
278 What to Bring
279 Animal Quarantine
279 Porter Services
279 Reservations
279 Extension of Stay
279 On Departure

GETTING ACQUAINTED
280 Government & Economy
282 Geography & Population
282 Time Zones
282 Climate
282 Culture & Customs
283 Weights & Measures
284 Electricity
284 Business Hours
284 Holidays
284 Religious Services

LANGUAGE
285 Useful Words

COMMUNICATIONS
286 Media
287 Postal Services
287 Telephone & Telex

EMERGENCIES
288 Security & Crime
289 Loss
289 Medical Services

GETTING AROUND
290 Maps
290 From the Airport
290 Domestic Travel
290 Water Transport
290 Private Transport
291 On Foot

WHERE TO STAY
291 Hotels

FOOD DIGEST
294 What to Eat
295 Where to Eat
300 Drinking Notes

THINGS TO DO
301 City
301 Country

CULTURE PLUS
302 Museums
302 Art Galleries
303 Concerts
303 Ballets
303 Opera
304 Theatres
304 Cinema
304 Architecture

NIGHTLIFE
304 Pubs & Bars
308 Gambling

SHOPPING
308 What to Buy
308 Shopping Areas
309 Shopping Hours
309 Export
310 Complaints

SPORTS
310 Participant
311 Spectator

SPECIAL INFORMATION
311 Doing Business
312 Children
312 Gays
312 Disabled
312 Students
313 Pilgrimages

FURTHER READING
313 General

USEFUL ADDRESSES
314 Tourist Information
315 Consulates

A CLOSER LOOK

Qui vol peix, que es banyi es cul. (You don't catch fish with dry trousers.) — Menorquín proverb.

Every country, every region, has its old multi-purpose proverbs; the Balearics are no exception. The particular not-quite-truism above has probably had its day as a literal saying, and it is unlikely that the islanders were ever in the habit of chucking themselves, fully clothed, at passing mackerel. They would never do anything in such a hurry.

Fishing on the islands has waned, but tourism has waxed to an awe-inspiring degree; fishing boats make a far better living as tourist boats, and their owners only get wet trousers when a holidaymaker spills warm beer. There are more tourist beds in the bay of Palma de Mallorca than there are in the whole of the Eastern Mediterranean, from Greece round to Algiers, and the number is still growing. Palma is the grand-daddy of mass tourism, and its children continue to produce grandchildren on the coasts of all four islands.

For decades the Balearics have been marketed as a cheap and cheerful kiss-me-quick location where the beer goes down a treat and the girls go topless on the beaches, raising the hopes of the boys.

And yet, while this industry has steamrollered its way around the island coasts, there has always been a subtler, more discreet type of tourist on the islands. The more visible of these appreciative visitors are the celebrities who have made or are still making regular appearances. These include Robert Graves, Winston Churchill, Joan Miró, Errol Flynn, the British and Spanish Royal Families and many more, in whose shadow are a whole host of the wealthy, the cultured, and the artistically inclined.

They know, and a lot of quieter tourists know, that there is more to the Balearics than meets the brochure, and this book is also party to that knowledge.

These pages dig behind the hackneyed image of Mallorca, Menorca, Ibiza and Formentera, combining the elements of an illustrated lecture, a magazine, an academic text, a collection of anecdotes and a gazetteer of everything of interest, animating a group of islands which is in danger of looking like a tired hostess in a rather cheap establishment.

But, like the fishermen who don't get to catch their fish unless they wet their trousers, you don't get to fully understand the Balearics unless you go out and take a closer look.

Preceding pages: festive mood in Ibiza; lurid colours in Mallorca's Hams Caves; coastline; the ancient city of Eivissa; women farm workers. Left, a closer look.

WAREHOUSES OF PREHISTORY

Like islands anywhere, the Balearics are rare warehouses of prehistoric data and information. The prehistoric record of the islands begins more than 180 million years ago with the accumulation of micromarine organisms as fossil sediments beneath the more primordial seas of the time. Petrified by great pressures, these once living organisms became the limestone of which the island is built today.

Then, over the interim of 100 million years or so, the forces of continental drift and land movement between the continent of Africa and the land mass of Europe forced the ancient limestone sea floors upward in a buckling movement, shaping a land mass in the form of a finger-like peninsula that then jutted out into the water off the present day coast of Valencia. By stages of further land movement and rising sea levels over the intervening eons this Valencian peninsula was to become eventually the separate islands which we know today as the Balearic and Pityussae island group: Mallorca, Menorca, Ibiza and Formentera.

However, the seas of those distant times were not in the familiar shapes that we know today. The Mediterranean is a sea in a shallow land-locked basin. Over millions of years it was being emptied and refilled by climatic changes and the great glaciers that slowly and periodically covered northern and western Europe. These immense ice masses, as well as growing and storing immense quantities of the earth's water, melted, raising sea levels and emptying into the Mediterranean basin, forming the great river systems, like the Rhône, Rhine and Danube Valleys, and in turn shaping by degrees the mainland and island coastlines now familiar to us.

Migrant life: Driven southward by great weather changes in Eurasia, the ancestors of the first life forms to reach the islands probably arrived during one of these early stages of island development, some eight to six million years ago, when access was possible. Making their way during this period over

Left, a taula, evidence of early man. Right, the Ses Paisses prehistoric village.

land bridges formed by the lowering of the Mediterranean sea-level, these migrant animals would have arrived during a colder and drier period hard to imagine now, when the sea's waters were frozen around the encroaching glaciers, leaving large areas of land over which they could migrate throughout the semi-dried Mediterranean basin.

Islands, as microcosms, are subject to quite separate laws from mainland areas. Because of their limited land size they can only support a certain number of mammalian and other life forms and practically none can play host, for very long, to a carnivore or meat eater, such as members of the cat and dog families, before they consume all existing prey and face mass starvation and extinction. Because of the carnivore's large appetite and continual need for fresh prey, an island would have to be able to provide food in the form of vegetation and maintain large herds of animals in order to maintain an ecological balance. Few islands in the world are large enough to do this.

Hence as a result of limited geographic boundaries, lack of predators and other ecological factors, the more docile herbivorous species that arrived and evolved on islands became very specialised, often with adaptations strangely different from mainland species. In some cases, these plant eating creatures had to develop special mechanisms and feeding habits to cope with the plant life that was available.

Species size too becomes an important survival factor on islands because of limited floral conditions. For example, the evolution of dwarf elephants and hippopotami is known on Cyprus and Crete, because no island the size of these two could feed the appetite of full grown individuals of these types over a long period. The elephant and the hippo had to regress in size to survive.

species, the *Myotragus*, arrived in the region of the Balearic Islands some six to eight million years ago. It is the appearance and survival of this particular animal, a strangely modified and oddly adapted creature, an aberrant member of the antelope family, that was to serve as both food and economy for the early human settlers, with which the prehistoric habitation of the Balearic Islands of Mallorca and Menorca begins.

First discovered and described by the British paleontologist, Dorothea Bate in 1909, the *Myotragus* was thought to have become extinct some 20,000 to 40,000 years ago during one of the great glacial periods, probably as the result of over-specialisation

Under such conditions smaller individuals would be more apt to out live the ravages of mass starvation principally because they need less food.

First cattle: One important mammalian Super Family, the cattle family or *Bovidae*, the cloven hoof animals as they are known today, evolved in Eurasia some 20 million years ago. Many species of this Super Family migrated southward some eight to ten million years ago, driven probably by changing weather patterns, and some made their way to the African continent. Others moved elsewhere in Southern Asia and Western Europe. From fossil evidence we know that one

and inability to further adapt to its environment. Discoveries, however, by the author in 1962 in the Mallorcan Cave of Muleta along the coast of the island's Northern Sierra demonstrate that it survived until the late date of 4000 B.C. Here, also, the Muleta cave produced in the same levels, human skeletal remains, establishing a coexistence between man and *Myotragus*, as well as demonstrating human presence on the islands at a much earlier date than hitherto attested; thus opening a new page in the human prehistory of the Balearics.

As an insular evolved species *Myotragus* had developed frontally placed eyes, the result of living without predators, and an adaptation more suitable for seeking food in the inhospitable rock crevices of mountainous slopes. Changes in the teeth of its lower jaws are demonstrated by fossil remains of several species of *Myotragus*, beginning with the *M.antiquus* and *M.batei* species; one which had the normal three sets of incisors, the other where the incisors became evergrowing.

In the later stages of its evolution the jaws lost two of the three sets of incisors normal to this species; the remaining one set developing into a single evergrowing, chisel-like pair of teeth in the finally evolved *Myotragus balearicus* species; an adaptation useful for

scraping bark, eating tough vegetation or even turning over stones to get at roots and lichens. Its limbs also showed great change from other similar animals. These grew short and broad and the flexible components of the lower limbs fused, resulting in slow movement, but at the same time becoming more sure footed in search of its livelihood on the craggy and difficult slopes of the islands' high mountains.

Man: Six years after the above discovery in the Muleta cave, the early date for the arrival

Left, caves in Menorca with modern troglodytes.
Above, Torre Llonet, early defensive tower.

of man in the Balearics was further extended by another 1,000 years to 5000 B.C. with the discovery of the Rock Shelter of Son Matge, located in a narrow pass also in the high mountains of the island below the village of Valldemossa. The site was also to provide us with further details of the coexistence between man and *Myotragus*.

At Son Matge, evidence showed that man had made trials at domesticating *Myotragus* by corralling and trimming the horns of the animal to prevent it injuring itself when kept in the corral.

The survival date for the animal was also extended to 2200 B.C., finally becoming extinct some 800 years after the introduction of domesticated goats, sheep, pigs and cattle about 3000 B.C.; an extinction directly and indirectly caused by man. Pottery technology has also been demonstrated to have occurred about this time. Later levels in the Rock Shelter showed that metallurgical techniques were in practice in a workshop area of the shelter by 2000 B.C. with the appearance of an enigmatic culture in the Balearics known as the International Bell Beaker Culture.

This culture, widely dispersed throughout Europe is synonymous with the Copper Age or Chaleolithic Period, around 2500 to 1400 B.C., preceding and including the Bronze Age. This is believed to be the time when Europe's first socially structured societies began and man began to accumulate wealth and surplus, through the aid of developing trade and technology.

Early life-style: The arrival of the Beaker Culture in the Balearics was responsible for construction of the first open-air settlements in such sites as the Old Settlement in the Prehistoric Settlement Complex of Ferrandell-Oleza-Mas, as well as the first sanctuaries, like the one at Son Matge, both discovered by the author in 1978, and which are found on a soil rich alluvial plain, known as El Pla del Rei (Plain of the King) near the village of Valldemossa on Mallorca.

Radiocarbon dating shows that the site of the Old Settlement was occupied some 700 years ago from around 2100 to 1300 B.C. and was abandoned only when the soils eroded so severely that they made farming the immediate area no longer viable.

As a result of findings in the Old Settlement of the Ferrandell-Oleza-Mas Prehistoric Complex, we can reconstruct the everyday occupation and life-style of these early Copper Age and Initial Bronze Age settlers. We see reflected a prosperous group who delineated their property with high, well constructed walls, behind which they could shelter their goats, sheep, pigs and cattle. They also collected wood, milked and slaughtered their animals.

They managed water with a hydraulic water system of some sophistication, bringing it in via a stone slab and clay lined water channel into the rear of their well built stone naviformed (boat shaped) houses. They farmed the adjacent fields growing grain and harvesting it with beautifully worked serrated, tabular flint blades. They constructed the beautiful, thin-walled, incised, geometrically decorated pottery known all over Europe as International Beaker Ware.

Further to the south close to the rich soils of the alluvial Plain of the King lie the Late Bronze Age and Iron Age settlement areas of the Ferrandell-Oleza-Mas Prehistoric Settlement Complex which date from around 1000 B.C. to the Roman Colonisation of the islands by Cecilius Metallus in 123 B.C. Here, man built his Talayotic mother culture. He lived and worked in stone radial buildings connected in beehive fashion to the *talayot* structures, practicing a successful combination of agriculture and basic animal husbandry.

Evidence of his burial practices also comes from the Son Matge Rock Shelter which was converted into a cemetery or burial area from around 1400 B.C. to the Roman Colonisation. Here cremation burials (Bronze Age) and inhumation in quicklime (Iron Age) represent over 6,000 individuals buried with grave goods of pottery, tools, arms and jewellery. These illustrate the wealth as well as status which these early societies had developed.

Culture clash: It was only involvement as mercenaries in the military campaigns of the classical world of the Carthaginians and Romans that brought a finish to these early societies and the prehistoric record of the Balearic Talayotic culture in general, although incipient fragments of the culture existed into the Christian Era of the third century A.D.

Known as expert slingers, it is a matter of historical record that Hannibal used 5,000 Balearic mercenaries in his Sicilian Campaign in 406 B.C. By 654 B.C., the Carthaginians had colonised and settled in the adjacent Pityussean island of Ibiza, completing a westward series of settlements extending from Carthage (modern Tunis) to Gades (modern Cádiz) that were to remain influential in Mediterranean politics and trade until their annexation by the Romans as a result of losing the Last Punic War in the second century B.C.

While islands until recently have been treated largely as backwaters of prehistoric data and information, their value, interest and importance rests in the way in which they are subject to a flotsam-jetsam arrival of the cultural developments which surrounded them in prehistory. Even today as islands they collect on their shores most of what occurs around them, either in people or in architecture. The large expatriate community on the Balearics is clear evidence of this.

Furthermore, that which arrives on the shores of these islands from abroad can be better preserved than the evidence found in mainland contexts, simply because the cultural fragments have survived the ravages of time better than in the more active areas of Continental Europe.

In fact islands are perfectly capable of giving us unique details of the past which are clearer and more complete than those which are present elsewhere. They are apt to present us with evidence of uniquely developed animal species which in turn reflect floral and climatic conditions, such as the Balearics' *myotragus*.

The archaeological richness of the islands of Mallorca, Menorca and Ibiza with their Talayotic Culture, as well as the equally rich archaeology of Sardinia with its equivalent Nuraghic Culture and Corsica with its Torreanos Culture and the presence of their thousands of prehistoric sites is proof enough of these islands' characteristics as warehouses of history. In all events, these islands are just not vacation paradises, but important places in which all nature of evolution, prehistory and history have taken place, in which the interested visitor can share. You just have to know where to look.

Right, islands (these off Mallorca) collect the flotsam from surrounding cultures.

FROM MOORS TO CHRISTIANS

Across the threshold of Calle Serra, Number Seven, a visitor to Palma steps from the sunlight of the street into a strangely dark, clammy and exotic interior. The low vaults, horseshoe arches and delicate pillars belong to an oriental bath-house—almost certainly Moorish, though Jewish origins have also been alleged, and probably of the 10th century. The building may even belong to the period of grandiose architectural self-indulgence launched in about the year 903 by al-Khaulani, the Moorish conqueror of Mallorca, who adorned the city with "mosques, dwellings and baths."

The very perfection of this curious little Moorish survival evokes a problem which puzzles every observant traveller to the Balearics: why are there so few mementoes of the Islamic past in the islands? Is it just a trick of the evidence? Or was the Moorish contribution to the formation of the Balearics as slight as the sparse survivals suggest?

Rule of Islam: The Moors were latecomers to the islands and left relatively early. The total period of Islamic domination in Mallorca and Ibiza was a little over 300 years—little more than in Sicily and less than half the corresponding period in the history of Granada, on mainland Spain.

Recent study of Mediterranean sea-lanes in the middle ages helps to explain why this was. The patterns of currents and prevailing winds ensured that in the age of galleys and cogs the islands would tend to be dominated from the north or west; though the Balearics were bound to send traffic towards Africa, the sailing season from the south was short and could be hard work. Yet whatever the religion of the ruling élite, the islands were attractive to oriental settlers; in Mallorca, especially, Moors and Jews were enduring and influential elements in the population, whose presence helped to shape some of the distinctive features of the history of the archipelago.

The post-Roman period of Balearic history is a genuine "dark age." Against a background of overlapping trade and piracy there may have been a long period of peaceful penetration by oriental merchants, but no invasion. The islands did not succumb to the Moorish conquerors of the Iberian peninsula. An appeal to Charlemagne in 798 against Moorish pirates shows that, locally, Christian rule prevailed.

Córdovan claims: In 848 the Emir of Córdova, Abderrahman II, sent a fleet, reputedly of 300 ships, apparently to suppress the islanders' reprisals against Moorish ship-

ping and to place Mallorca and Menorca under tribute. But while Andalusian control remained limited, Córdovan pretensions to sovereignty were either defied or ignored. Instead close relationships of dependence seem to have bound the islands to Catalonia, from where religious jurisdiction was exercised over the Church on the islands.

Towards the end of the 9th century, al-Khaulani is said to have spent time in Mallorca on his way to Mecca. Seduced by its beauty and convinced of its exploitability, he returned in force in 902 and turned the Balearics into a nominal fief of the Emirate of Córdova, with himself at its head.

Left, the Arab bath in Palma. Right, an Arab tombstone of 968 A.D.

For 100 years or so after his death in 912, little is known of the history of the islands beyond the names of the *walis*, or governors, who exercised effective authority, until 1014, when the empire of Córdova disintegrated and the islands became part of one of the numerous petty successor-states, known as *taifa* kingdoms, with its capital at Denia, on the Valencian mainland of Spain.

Mainland rule: Mujahid, the first ruler of this sea-straddling and diverse kingdom, established at Denia a sybaritic, cosmopolitan court. He was a self-designated literary critic, who liked to have works dedicated to him but not, it seems, to pay for them. His relatively long reign of some 30 years de-

fined features of Balearic history that would characterise most of the rest of the middle ages: fragile rule from the mainland and a tendency to seek overseas conquests.

In 1015 he launched an ill-fated expedition against Sardinia from Mallorca which failed apparently because of storms. The attempt seems to have had little effect on the security of his home bases. In about 1036, he appointed a governor, al-Aghlab, to rule the Balearics; the relationship was cemented by exceptionally strong ties of loyalty, for al-Aghlab, served until his master's death, then departed on pilgrimage for Mecca.

His successor introduced to Mallorca the

brilliant court life of Denia, without usurping the sovereign authority of the new mainland king, Ali ibn Mujahid. The latter, son of a Christian concubine and, for a long time a captive of Sardinia, was exceptionally indulgent towards Christians. He gave the Bishop of Barcelona surveillance of their rights and enjoined their prayers for himself. His reign was an era of peace until he fell victim in 1076 to the ambitions of al-Muqtadir, king of Zaragoza (the warrior-aesthete who was later to employ El Cid).

Piractical times: The Balearics then enjoyed a brief period of independence: the incumbent governor at the time of Ali's death, al-Mu'tada, issued coins of his own name between 1077 and 1093. Thereafter, the islands were an unruly outpost of the north African empire of the Almoravids—a sect of desert nomads who would now be classed as Islamic fundamentalists. The islands were equally convenient for commerce and corsairs. According to al-Maqqari they "supplied much of Africa with wood and salt". Naturally the effect of such trade was to excite the greed of would-be conquerors or raiders.

The first well documented attack of the period was made by Sigurd of Norway in 1108 on his way to Jerusalem. Sigurd made a conspicuous sideline of combining pillage with pilgrimage, and he was said to have burned the defenders of Formentera to death in the cave known as Cova d´es Fum, towards the eastern end of the island.

Sigurd was a vulture of passage but the next invaders appear to have intended to stay. In 1114 a large Catalo-Pisan amphibious force settled to the systematic reduction of the islands in an attempt to drive out the moors. For the merchants of Pisa the attractions of the Balearics were obvious: Mallorca was an ideal staging-post for growing trade with Spain and North Africa; it was a piratical base from which they would be able to harrass their Genoese rivals; and Ibiza was a major salt-producer in her own right.

The interests which moved Count Ramón Berenguer III of Barcelona to join the alliance and lead the force are less clear: Catalan commercial interest in the Balearics was still at a rudimentary stage, though the Christians of Mallorca probably looked to their parent-see in Catalonia, Barcelona, for protection. Certainly, the Count of Barcelona was charging his allies a fee for his services.

However, the campaign went badly. The count was anxious to return to his own lands, the Pisans to struggle on in the hope of recouping their investment. Exasperation inspired a policy of scorched earth and wanton massacre and Ibiza was virtually destroyed. Eventually, by March, 1115, Moorish resistance was reduced to Mallorca's citadel, the last governor escaping by swimming "like a dolphin". Yet almost at the moment of final victory the Christians were forced to flee with their booty in the face of an Almoravid relief expedition which put the desert sect back in power.

Despite its failure, this attempted conquest

"governors" or "kings", the greatest of whom was Ishaq ibn Ganiya (1115-85); he rebuilt ruins unrestored since the Catalo-Pisan invasion, and revived prosperity based on African trade. By the 1190s, Mallorca was exercising a form of protectorate over a number of coastal trading stations of mainland Africa and a Ganiyid "empire" seemed to be taking shape.

In 1202, however, a rebellion in Mallorca itself, stimulated perhaps by Islamic extremists, halted the development of that empire. A Maghribi army invaded, the last of the Ganiyids was beheaded or fled and the islands passed under the nominal suzerainty of the Almohad dynasty, which had enjoyed

had important consequences: the memory of Ramón Berenguer's exploits was kept vivid by an epic poem in Latin and vernacular versions, the *Liber Maiolichinus*, which inspired periodic further attempts to emulate him over the next 100 years.

Rulers on the isles: Throughout that period, however, while Pisan and Genoese commercial involvement increased, the islands remained politically an offshore outpost of the Arab Maghribi world. For most of the time they were ruled in effective independence by

Left, an early Arab oil lamp. Above, the Almudaina as it looked in the 13th century.

supremacy in North Africa and al-Andalus for about two generations. The result of the Ganiyids' work was to leave Mallorca both rich and vulnerable: Palma—"the city of Mallorca" as it was then called—was one of the ornaments of the western Mediterranean, with its busy quays, its 50 bakeries, its watemills and its baths. But it had run out of the physical means of self-defence and of friends to fight for it.

Jaime's rule: A new alliance, capable of exploiting the vulnerability of the Balearics, was soon to form under King Jaime I of Aragón (in power 1213-76). When King Jaime described his conquest of Mallorca, the arguments which moved him to undertake it and the experience of crossing the sea to carry it out, he revealed a vision of maritime war as a means of chivalric adventure *par excellence* which he obviously found exilharating. There was more honour in conquering a single kingdom "in the midst of the sea, where God has been pleased to put it" than three on dry land, he said.

The voyage was lingeringly and lovingly described: the numbers of ships, the sailing order of the fleet, the location of the guiding lanterns, the waiting for a wind, the cries of the watches exchanged when the ships made contact, the changes of breeze, the shortenings of sail, the heaving of the sea in a storm and the resolution and faith in God which it called forth. No moment matched the moment of making sail. "And it made a fine sight for those who stayed on shore, and for us, for all the sea seemed white with sails, so great a fleet it was."

When the king wrote, "The best thing man has done for a hundred years past, God willed that I should do when I took Mallorca," he probably meant that it was the best by the standards of chivalry, the deed of most daring and renown. It was to be an achievement of great importance for his dynasty, which began henceforth to create a network of island dominions in the Mediterranean. By the end of the 13th century, the chronicler Desclot could claim, with pardonable exaggeration, that no fish could go swimming without the King of Aragón's leave.

At first, however, Jaime's nobles were unenthusiastic about the projected conquest. They would have preferred to tackle Valencia—a lush Islamic kingdom approachable across a land frontier, without all the complications of boats. Mallorca proved an acceptable alternative partly because the king was lavish with promises of reward. When one of the greatest lords, Nuño Sanz, promised to aid the conquest with horse, foot soldiers and ships, including a hundred of his household knights, he was explicit in his demands for land and wealth by return. Jaime's response was embodied in a charter addressed to all the nobility: "We shall give just portions to you and yours, according to the numbers of knights and men-at-arms whom you take with you."

Rich pickings: As well as the work of contingents from this feudal world of give-and-

take, the conquest was the work of militias, mercenaries and ships from the commercial world of the cities. Jaime describes a great banquet on the mainland in November or December, 1228, when a leading citizen and shipowner, Pedro Martel, explained to the magnates the whereabouts of the Balearics, perhaps with an early map spread before him, and commended the islands as the richest pickings then available in the world. Jaime liked to discuss business after dinner: it was a typical social ritual of the Catalonia of his day. The account books of the city of Mallorca after its conquest show that banquets to honour great events or stimulate appetites for civic transactions were a major

source of expense, like the business lunch today. It was characteristic, too, that a nautical technician like Martel could act as host to the king and sit down with great nobles without embarrassment due to lack of social status: this feature of the Catalan social world was also transplanted to the post-conquest Balearics.

But Barcelona, alone or even in combination with the other great Catalan port of Tarrogona, could not launch enough ships to conquer Mallorca. The shipping for Jaime's expedition was in a sense a joint effort of the Catalan and Provençal worlds, suggesting that the commercial rewards promised must have been considerable.

Jaime denounced the Balearics as nests of pirates, but though a rather rough-and-ready form of exchange, piracy should probably not be too sharply distinguished from trade in this period. Most seafarers and most ships slipped in and out of both vocations without specialisation. It is reasonable to suppose that the merchants who backed the king aimed not only to suppress the pirates but also to supplant them in their more legitimate lines of business. Though many new products would be introduced by the conquerors, the islands' role in western Mediterranean trade was well established. The entrenched positions of Moorish traders, and of their ghost-writer. The conquest of Mallorca, however, did inspire passages of exceptional fervour in the king's mouth. When adverse winds made some of his company want to abandon the voyage, Jaime answered them, by his own account, "We are going on this voyage out of faith in God, and against those who do not believe in Him, and we are going against them for two purposes, either to convert or destroy them and since we are going in His name, we confide in Him to guide us." Yet even here the emphasis was on making the conquest seem legitimate rather than trying to turn it into a crusade. Jaime justified his war as a war justly waged for the recovery of usurped lands.

Above, jousting Christians and Moors. A ceiling panel from the Almudaina.

privileged partners from Genoa and Pisa, adequately explain the jealous anxiety of the Catalans and Provençals to break into the cartel, by force if necessary.

The role of faith: Crusading rhetoric justified the expedition and papal indulgences helped to launch it. Can religious motives be distinguished in the background? Pious avowals, beyond conventional invocations of Providence or assurances of godliness of purpose, are rare in King Jaime's *Book of Deeds*, which may be the work of a clerical

This is the usual context of pious allusions in western Mediterranean texts; the numinous east, where Christ trod and relics seemed to spring from the ground, was more productive of purely spiritual motives. The conquest of Mallorca was determined, and the subsequent colonisation shaped, by greed for commerce and land. It was bloody, ruthless and quick, evidence of it is scant. Today's visitor can compare King Jaime's beach-head of September, 1229, at Playa Camp de Mar, now smothered by a tourist-industry urbanisation, with the gaunt ruins of the castle of Santueri, near Felanitx, the only stronghold to resist for anytime.

GREATNESS AND DECLINE

The late medieval Balearics were genuinely a crucible of colonial experiment, in which the problems of adjusting the balance of indigenous and incoming populations, native and new elements of the economy, were tried over and over again. A pattern was established which remained influential throughout the history of western Mediterranean colonialism.

The islands, and Mallorca in particular, have never since experienced such an age of greatness: briefly, in the 14th century, they were the *mise-en-scène* of the most dynamic and economically successful society in Christendom and led the medieval "space-race"—the quest for new colonies and trade.

Division of the spoils: Until practical problems supervened, Jaime's conquistadores who set about erasing the influence of the Moors, probably envisaged a Mallorca created from scratch and thickly planted with new settlers and their crops. The division of the city proceeded house by house, and of the soil plot by plot, where detailed records survive. In fact, 150,000 acres (60,000 hectares) are unaccounted for in the surviving records; this may correspond to a portion left for the natives or may be a trick of the uneven survival of evidence. The rest was divided up by one of the most efficient and pernickety royal bureaucracies in Christendom.

Most of the large grants are known only in outline. Nuño Sanz and his followers got the biggest single domain: 13,500 hectares in Valldemossa, Bunyola, Manacor and 89 houses in the city (which he settled mainly with Catalans, southern Frenchmen, Italians and Jews). The Archbishop of Barcelona was rewarded with half the city and the coast as far as Bunyalbufar. Sóller was divided between the Count of Ampurias, the Bishop of Gerona (who quickly sold his share) and the Viscount of Béarn.

The most detailed evidence of land distribution survives from outside these magnates' portions, in the so-called royal "moiety", the *medietas regis*. After discounting

what was passed on to the Templars, the towns and the nobles, King Jaime was left with direct control of more than twice the land granted to the biggest magnate proprietor. It was a huge bonanza for the impoverished crown.

The king's half of the city went in rewards to the soldiers of his urban militias, the sailors of his fleet and the merchants who backed his invasion: 307 houses to Tarragona, 298 to Marseilles, 226 each to Barcelona and Lérida, 100 to Montpellier, and

corresponding proportions to small island communities.

The division of the island suggests a programme of intensive colonisation at every social level. The same intention is revealed by the exhortations which Pope Gregory IX distributed around the western Mediterranean basin. He made a gift to all potential settlers (with the exception of Cathar heretics) "who wish to inhabit lands newly won" of indulgences equivalent to those given to pilgrims to the Holy Land.

Enough colonists responded to make the island Catalan-speaking, with marked influence from the dialects of Ampurias and

Left, the conquistadors marked their territory. Right, King Jaime I.

Roussillon, and to saturate the place names of lowland areas with Catalan. But the extent to which this colonial population displaced the Moors is a much debated topic of Mallorcan history.

Moorish remains: The myth that the Moors were all enslaved or expelled seems to have arisen from a misreading of the chronicles, fortified by a false analogy with what happened later on Menorca. Evidence of Moorish survival is overwhelming. First, there were Moors whose autonomy in the mountains was not ended by the conquest: the largest contingent, which surrendered conditionally in June, 1232, was reckoned by the king at 16,000 strong. Then there is consid-

slavery, but it was evidently common for Moors to slip in and out of slavery for debt with little or no change in their way of life. Contracts in which slaves, who were given land to work for the purchase of their freedom, stayed on as serfs and tenants, allow us a glimpse of the means by which many lords must have exploited their land-grants.

Finally the evidence of place names is probably as good a guide as any: the poorer uplands and central mountains remained Arabic. Though we shall probably never know the scale either of indigenous survival or settler penetration, it seems that both happened. The thoroughly Catalan appearance of Mallorca in the late Middle Ages was

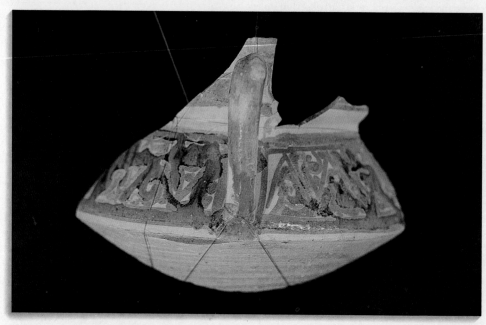

erable evidence that in the interests of keeping the island well-populated, the king and other proprietors rapidly came to look favourably on their Moorish tenants, ignoring their initial hostility.

The Templars brought "Saracens" from the mainland; the king encouraged Moors from Menorca. The large number of surviving documents of the late 13th and 14th centuries indicate the continued presence of Moors on a considerable scale, especially as artisans in the towns—smiths, metal workers, leather and textile workers, shopkeepers and even a painter.

Many of these documents are records of

a result of Catalan predominance in the main centres of population but this does not exclude other influences outside those areas.

Early expatriates: Alongside the Catalan predominance, Mallorca retained and developed, in the commercial zone, a cosmopolitan feeling, because of growing numbers of foreign residents and a lively trade in slaves of diverse nationalities.

The Genoese were one of the most important foreign communities tolerated or encouraged, even in times of war between Genoa and the Crown of Aragón. In 1233, the king granted them a trading precinct in the street that led up to the Templars' castle.

They were a valuable property, more profitable to persecute fiscally than by embargo or expulsion. Between 1320 and 1344, for instance, they paid an import tax ten times as high as that charged to the Pisans: the high level was justified on the grounds that it provided indemnities for Mallorcan goods against Genoese piracy.

The Jews were even more numerous and at least as important to the economic life of the island. At the time of the conquest, a prosperous Jewish community seems to have acted as a magnet for poor co-religionists from all over the western Mediterranean.

Ships' masters had to be deterred by royal decree, issued on the request of Mallorcan Jews, from embarking Jewish immigrants on credit in the expectation that their unwilling hosts would meet the bill at the other end. Poor Jews—or, at least, those who pleaded inability to pay taxes—remained a problem for taxpayers whose considerable burden was incurred collectively and discharged by an often painful process of mutual agreement, negotiated by elected "secretaries".

Jewish wealth: Despite pleas of poverty, however, the overall impression is of comfort. The Jews were regarded as a "treasure house...from whom the trades and traders of this kingdom in peacetime derive great abundance". Most Jewish wealth was accumulated in crafts or professions. In the 14th century Jews were active as silversmiths, silk merchants, veterinarians, peddlers, freelance postmen, armourers, cobblers, tailors, drapers, dyers, kosher butchers, carpenters, physicians, illuminators, bookbinders, soap-makers, map-makers, wet-nurses, wine merchants and millers.

Today's visitor can get a flavour of the ambience in their ghetto from the Carrer de Argenteria, its best surviving street, where the silversmiths worked. They were disadvantaged in long-range trade by fiscal victimisation and exclusion from some ports. The only routes on which they played a major role were those to Barbary, where they were too deeply entrenched for their grip to be forcibly relaxed.

They had a peculiar relationship with the crown, which, as in much of the rest of Christendom, generally worked to their advantage. They were the "king's coffers of money", generously endowed with privileges, of which the most valuable was that no Jew could be convicted by Christian or Moorish testimony. Under King Sancho (in power 1311-24) fiscal exploitation of Jews grew more abrasive; but almost throughout the 14th century Jews maintained favoured status. Despite occasional prohibitions from 1285 onwards, they continued to hold public offices up to the level of members of the royal council.

Ghettos of privilege: Growing popular resentment was their undoing. Their characteristic crimes were false coining and "dwelling in Saracen lands". The first reflects Jewish prominence in the handling of precious metals, the second their leading position in the Barbary trade. What seems most to have vexed their Christian neighbours were, first, their discharge of detested functions as moneylenders and tax farmers and, secondly, the conspicuous distinctions which set their society apart from others.

They lived in their own ghettos where they were numerous enough to do so, as at Inca and Palma. With few exceptions granted—as in the case of the royal cartographer, Abraham Cresques, for exceptional service—they wore a prescribed form of dress. They could re-marry on divorce, by royal leave, and (as is shown by a plea of 1258, made on grounds of childlessness) were allowed lawfully to contract bigamous marriages. Hebrew marriage contracts were valid without registration by a public notary. Jews flouted the Christian Sabbath and aroused the anger of other market vendors by their pre-emptive habit of early rising.

But, as their legal privileges were greater than those of Christians, so were their punishments more severe. A Jew guilty of a hanging offence was suspended upside-down—"mouth downwards"—to protract the death and aggravate the agony.

The natural resentment of a community apart was exacerbated by accusations of usury. The Jews were anyway under an ancestral cloud. Their taxes fell due at Easter. Holy Week yielded an annual crop of outrages and hard times and febrile preachers could stir popular hatred with astonishing ease. In 1374, the king had to quell demands for the Jews' expulsion at a time of famine by recalling that they had paid for relief ships. In 1370, the preaching licence of the rabid, footloose mendicant, Fray Bonanto, was withdrawn because of his anti-semitic excesses. The pogroms and forcible conversions of future generations were being prepared. In the blood-letting of 1391, perhaps 300 Jews were slaughtered in Palma.

Crossroads of trade: Most other foreigners were slaves, reflecting the islands' role as an *entrepôt*. Mallorca was a centre of re-export for the entire Aragó-Catalan world. The iron of Bayonee and Castile, figs of Murcia and Alcudia, Ibizan salt, Sevillian oil and Greek or Calabrian wine, with slaves from Greece and Sardinia, were the commodities most

often seen in the markets. They were traded to the Aragónese dominions and North Africa: about half the sailing licences surviving from the 14th century are for Catalonia, the rest divided between Valencia and Barbary.

The island of Mallorca was dependent on this re-export trade but also fostered new industries. Commerce bred shipbuilding, especially after Sancho I turned one of the Jewish cemeteries into a shipyard. Mallorcan cogs were the best ships in the sea in the 14th century, leading the way in Atlantic exploration. The remarkable arms industry, in and around the 1380s shipped literally thousands of crossbows to Flanders and England. But the greatest industrial success of post-conquest Mallorca were textiles, the most important product of the medieval industrial revolution.

The range of new commercial and industrial activity, the prodigious economic growth of the century after the conquest, made the Balearics as a whole a land of medieval *Wirtschaftswunder*, as Germany was after World War II. Jaime I expressed the kingdom's potential eloquently: it was the finest land, with the most beautiful city in the world.

In the eyes of Ramón Muntaner, writing in about 1325, Mallorca was "a goodly isle, and an honoured one", its city "of greater wealth than any ", and with "the most businesslike and best endowed people of any city there may be in the world". The concentration on "the city" is revealing.

When outsiders thought of Mallorca, they thought only of its great port, just as today they think only of the mass tourist complex, on the same coast, centred on the same city. Muntaner also perceived the conditions that enabled Mallorca's economy to thrive: the economic freedom and low taxation that accompanied a sustained effort to draw settlers to the island.

Slump: In the generation after Muntaner's praise, Mallorca's economic miracle seems to have run out of steam. Between 1329 and 1343, for instance, the hearth-count (number of houses) in Palma fell from 5,256 to 4,124. The loss of autonomous status for the islands, and re-absorption under direct Aragónese rule, may have helped to bring the pioneering era to an end, to remove a source of incentives and to make Mallorca a less stimulating place to live in and operate from.

Yet if expansion was halted, and if dynamism subsided, complacency prevailed. The municipal accounts of 1349 tell the story of the pursuit of bodily delights of the city fathers in the very year of the Black Death. Theirs was a world of status linked to consumption, measured in costly feasts and ostentatious displays of loyalty to the Aragónese dynasty.

At least 76 decorators were employed—some Moors, some Greeks—to adorn the city chambers for the banquets. Two "painters of altarpieces and battle flags" decorated hangings to celebrate the obsequies of the mainland queen. And the large sums spent on defence against island separatists included the pay of 11 surgeon-barbers to serve the fleet. A society so abundantly supplied with quacks and craftsmen must have wallowed in surplus wealth.

Top-heavy society: The government of this era presented problems which Aragónese kings found hard to resolve and historians hard to classify. Devolution of power in the regions to municipal communities and lords was combined with a bureaucratic layer of royal or seigneurial representatives called *batles* and two central representative institutions: the *jurats* (nominated by the king) to advise on policy and administer justice; the *Consell* (elected partly by the *jurats* and

under Sancho and a total of 63 by the end of the 14th century.

Unreliable kings: The Kingdom of Mallorca was typical of the Aragónese medieval dominions in the vagueness with which its place in the monarchy was defined. Like most other areas of Aragó-Catalan expansion, it was often hived off to local rulers whose loyalty, secured only by oath, was generally unreliable.

The first of these was that extraordinary mercenary-cum-gigolo, Don Pedro of Portugal, who entered Aragónese service in 1228 to become the husband of the discarded royal concubine, Countess Aurembiaix. She saw him as a means of vengeance on her erst-

partly by syndics in the localities) as a representative assembly.

Because so much of the great nobility was based in mainland Spain, and represented in the islands by administration trained in the law, both institutions had a deceptively bourgeois air. The potentially conflictive division was between the representatives of the *part forana*, from outside the city, and the élite of Palma: the numbers of the former grew from three after the conquest to 10

Left, a llaud, a descendent of the early shipbuilding industry. Above, Palma city voting box.

while lover, but in a secret deal with the king, Don Pedro accepted the lordship of Mallorca as a pay-off. He ruled the island (and, for a time, part of Ibiza) in the fitful intervals permitted by his mercenary commitments elsewhere, until his death in 1256.

Thus, when the firstborn of the royal dynasty died in 1260 and the patrimony was prospectively divided between the king's other heirs, there was a recent precedent for Mallorcan anatomy which from Jaime I's death in 1276 would be precariously sustained, with attenuations and interruptions, until 1343.

Mallorca became the treasury and granary

of a kingdom of enclaves and islands—the Balearics, Roussillon, Cerdagne and Montpelier—on the fringes of the Aragó-Catalan world. At times, its kings could break their oaths and defy the senior line, but it was never viable as a wholly independent state. Its manpower was made up of Catalans, who retained habits of loyalty to the historic dynasty; it was dependent on peninsular trade; its magnates were for the most part peninsula-based.

Its king, King Jaime, was powerless to resist Pedro III's demand for homage in 1279 or to oppose the Aragónese invasion of 1285. Jaime's restoration in 1299 was made in the interests of the dynasty as a whole by the decision of the King of Aragón.

When the ambiguities of the relationship between islands and mainland were finally swept away by the definitive Aragónese conquest of 1343, the operation took a week. The invaders were welcomed almost everywhere and there was little or no support for the schemes of *revanche* of the pretender Jaime III, who died in a hapless invasion attempt in 1349.

Beyond Mallorca: Ibiza and Formentera were also conquered by "crusaders" but, unlike Mallorca, by crusaders working on their own initiative. The crown played no part, except as a source of legitimation. Don Pedro of Portugal and Nuño Sanz, on his Mallorcan expedition, were granted a right of conquest which they failed to take up.

It was therefore re-allocated, with their agreement, between December, 1234 and April, 1235, to Guillermo de Montgrí, sacristan of Gerona cathedral. He was acting on behalf of the Archbishopric of Tarragona, which had got little out of the conquest of Mallorca. For a while, however, he was to rule Ibiza unchallenged. Don Pedro and Nuño were to hold their portions of Ibiza town in fee from him and perform homage.

Despite the exalted language in which the Pope exhorted the conquerors "to snatch the island (of Ibiza) from impious hands", the conquerors' bargain was quite explicit: as in Mallorca, their investment would be recouped from the spoils of conquest.

When Ibiza castle and town were taken by storm in August, 1235, it seemed as if the partners would have a free hand. Montgrí, who had provided the biggest contingent, appointed himself governor of the principal castle and took half the land. Pedro and Nuño divided the rest equally. Gradually, however, the crown's right to possession of strongholds was enforced. Pedro's fief passed to the crown; Nuño sold out to the see of Tarragona. After about a generation, the island thus became governed by a royal-ecclesiastical coalition.

The society of post-conquest Ibiza resembled Mallorca in miniature, save that sub-letting of territory was rare. The big exception was Formentera, granted away by Montgrí in fee perpetual, with exemption only of Don Pedro's share and a few sites intended for a hospice and hermitages. The lord was to receive a quarter of the profits of justice and a tenth of wheat and meat "according to the custom of Ibiza", in addition to the dues owed to the church. In colonised areas, the seigneurial economy evidently relied on ecclesiastical dues.

Settlers, sin and salt: Throughout Ibiza, settlers were at first difficult to attract, to such an extent that in 1237, the Pope authorised the Bishop of Tarragona to readmit to Communion those who had commited arson, profaners of sacred persons and suppliers of illicit arms to the Saracens on condition that they settled in Ibiza in person or by proxy. Like Mallorca, Ibiza relied on the survival or reintroduction of Moors, many of them brought in by Pedro of Portugal.

Nothing better illustrated the difficulty of attracting settlers and the narrow economic base of the island than the failure of the lords to increase revenue from salt. Their efforts lasted for eight years before they yielded to the necessity of exercising liberality in allowing settlers use-rights. Apart from slave-trading and piracy salt was the only available economic activity of promise, and the only "perk" that would attract colonists.

Despite the early preponderance of Moors, the fragile economy and the hesitant colonisation, Ibiza was remarkably successful—reflecting, perhaps, the glow of the tail-light of Mallorca's "take-off". By the late 14th century, there was an island council of 250 members, a large élite for a small island. The scale of the institutions seem to belong to a solidly established society, with deeply rooted settlements. Yet in the same period the insecurity of life on small islands in corsair-infested seas was starkly illustrated by the abandonment of Formentera. By

1403, there was nobody left on the island.

Menorca: The second island of the Balearics suffered the most ruthless form of Aragónese imperialism. At first, it was left undisturbed, save for nominal client-status and token tribute, as a Moorish vassal-state: this was a common solution in the Iberian peninsula for Moorish states which could not be practically or profitably absorbed by Christian kingdoms. In the 1280s, however, Menorca assumed a new importance on the way to further conquests in Sardinia and Sicily. It was an island of invitation to potential commercial rivals, Pisan and Genoese, as well as an embarrassment to the Aragónese kings' crusading propaganda.

Shortage of the means of life was chronic: every cornbearing ship that called was compelled to offer its cargo for sale.

Nor were the means of civilisation in greater abundance. In 1358, a governor of the island was killed by a blow from a candlestick in a brawl at the high altar of the island's main church. Such was the tenor of life in this showpiece-conquest of Aragónese imperialism.

Decline and fall: Historians are now revising the notion of a "decline" of the Catalan world in the 15th century. In the case of the Balearics, however, the evidence seems incontrovertible. The population in the early 16th century was still about 20 percent less

Thus it was that Menorca offered an opportunity for a young king, Alfonso III, to demonstrate his mettle. His conquest of the island in 1287 was the most brutal in the history of the Aragónese monarchy. Departing from the practice evolved in Mallorca and Ibiza, Alfonso aimed at a radical extirpation of the native population. A century after the conquest, the wreckage remained. In 1370, houses abandoned by the Moors and never reoccupied were in a state of collapse.

Above, 15th century painting with the port of Palma in the background.

than before the Black Death. The formerly renowned Mallorcan shipping fleets almost disappeared, and the islands' dwindling trade fell into the hands of foreign carriers. The unreliability of grain supplies (which condemned the islands to chronic shortages), high tax demands from the mainland and the depredations of pirates, were the major external influences on decline.

The inhabitants did little to help themselves. Exacerbated by economic failure, the divisions between port and hinterland became increasingly violent, especially in Mallorca, where a virtual civil war raged from 1450 to 1453.

The apparently insuperable combination of problems was exemplified by the experiences of Governor Aymerich in the 1490s. He arrived at his post to find a simultaneous plague and famine decimating the population; yet his counter-measures were so resented by the islands' élite that they temporarily suspended their own squabbles in order to denounce the governor to the king.

The introduction of the Inquisition in 1484 was a timely means of relief for local tensions: it was a cheap tribunal, in which one could denounce one's neighbour on irrational grounds: it began with a brief burst of fire and bloodshed in which 85 penitents were burned between 1484 and 1512.

Carnival riot: The social unrest of which these figures are a symptom seems to have abated with equal suddenness; after 1517, the Inquisition was virtually inert for over a century and a half. This is an indication, perhaps, that conditions were already beginning a modest improvement when the bloodiest conflict in Mallorca's history erupted in 1521. On Carnival Day, traditional excess overspilled into riots when seven leading guildsmen were gaoled.

These circumstances, which launched a revolt known as that of the *Germanía* or "brotherhood" of rebels, who bound themselves by common oaths, have created the myth that this was an attempted social revolution, launched by a worker or *sans-culotte* class against feudal oppression. In reality, it seems to have been a protest to do with the economy: the guildsmen's main demand was for the alleviation of taxes. It was also animated in part by anti-clericalism and in part by desperation at grain shortages.

Although the mob got out of hand and raised cries like "Let's have the merchants' heads!" and "Let no lawyer stay alive!", it seems clear that for much of the time, and certainly in the early stages, the rebels were manipulated by factions of the local élite, whose pride of ancestry—vividly depicted by Pere Nissart's paintings of their forebears "coming over with conqueror", in the Diocesan Museum—was offended by the growing power of royal servants.

On 16 April 1521 the governor was forced to flee to Ibiza. The guildsmen, still professing loyalty to the crown, took the Castle of Bellver by storm and massacred the garrison. As has so often happened in the history of such revolts, an exploitative demagogue rose to the fore and only in the spring of 1523 was the bloody dictatorship of Joanot Colom brought to an end by the combined efforts of crown and aristocracy.

The revolt gave the aristocrats a means of explaining the moral decline by which they felt increasingly surrounded. In 1539, the conservative *jurats* complained of "how much respect for God and His Majesty the common people have lost since the *Germanía* and how much our difficulty in confronting crimes has increased."

Coastal raiders: Insecurity and insufficiency remained the keynotes of island life. The three enemies of recovery were pirates, bandits and famines. Visitors to Balafi on Ibiza can see what life in the shadow of coastal raiders was like for a population huddled in fortified villages; even a relatively large and developed place like Santa Eulàlia, also on Ibiza, retains the configurations of a communal refuge from predators.

The effort Charles V and Philip II invested in the protection of their subjects is evident in the surviving fortifications of Eivissa (Ibiza Town), initiated by the Italian engineer Calvi in 1554, and those on Mallorca of 1575. Mahón's Fort San Felipe dated from the same period, after the town had been destroyed in two major Turkish raids.

The chronic shortage of grain arose not only from threats to transport but from problems of supply which afflicted the entire western Mediterranean. A particularly bad famine in 1674 coincided with renewed persecution of the descendants of Jews. Between 1675 and 1698, 236 were penanced and 63 put to death.

Yet, though life was laborious and precarious, it was possible to prosper in the islands. Joan Mir, who had been a creditor of King Philip III, had shown that by becoming a very successful man. The growing number of religious communities in the 17th century may be another indication of prosperity, and the fortunes of some great dynasties were being laid by a recovery of trade in the last third of the century. The general renewal of prosperity, however, had to await recovery from a new trauma: the War of the Spanish Succession.

Right, the painted gate, or Puerto Pintada, of the city of Palma.

44

La Sommissione di MAIORCA,
Isola Balearica nel Mare Mediterraneo.

Maiorca nominata cosi, per esser la più grande delle Isole Balearice, sul Mare Mediterraneo vicino à Spagna, ha frà esse la preferenza, et da molti Anni in qua governata da un Vice Rè di Spagna. Essendo arrivato l'Amiraglio Inglese il Cavaghero Leake, con buon numero di Vasselli attorno la sodetta Città Capitale, fu essa, dal medemo Amiraglio ricercata, à rendersi à Devotione di Sⁱ Mᵗⁱ Cᵗ il Rè Carlo III. mà quel Vice Rè con altri affettionati alla Francia inclinavano alla Diffesa. Fecè il Cavaghero Leake gettar delle Bombe, li Cittadini non consueti di tali trattamenti obligoronto il Vice Rè, a richieder una Capitulatione, et à rendersi senz'altro Indugio al Rè Carlo III. Fu ratificato subito un'Accordo, et con cio quest'Isola, con tutte le sue Città et Castelli, senza perdita veruna, sotto missa à Sᵃ Mᵗᵃ Cᵗᵗ augmentandosi di molto le sue forze marittime.

Cum Grat. et Privileg. S. C. Maj.   Ieremias Wolff excud. Aug. Vind.

TIDES OF CHANGE

The Balearics sided firmly with the losing side in the War of the Spanish Succession. As in other lands of the Crown of Aragón, most of the élite wanted a traditional, even a contractual monarchy, which would devolve power into local hands—an aspiration which seemed best represented by the cause of the Habsburg pretender, Charles III, rather that the French-style absolutism threatened by the Bourbon Philip V.

Mallorca thus welcomed Charles's representative, the Conde de Zavellá, with enthusiasm, sabotaging the Bourbon governor's guns. Mallorquíns were instrumental in beating the Bourbon blockade of Barcelona. And in July, 1715, when the entire mainland had fallen, Mallorca was the last outpost to surrender to Philip V.

Menorca never did so. Seized in 1705 by Charles III's British paymasters with the collusion of most of the population it was retained under British sovereignty at the end of the war and became the key point in the new Mediterranean naval strategy which Britain was to sustain throughout the following century.

Occupational hazards: Thus both main islands of the archipelago ended the war under armies of occupation, yet for both the long-term effects of occupation were favourable. Menorca smarted under redcoat rule. Welcomed as liberators, the English were resented as rulers. The local clergy encouraged contempt for the Protestant heretics and terrorist outrages against British personnel were commonplace.

In Mallorca and Ibiza, Bourbon rule also had the semblance of foreign occupation. The traditional status and privileges of the kingdom were abolished; the functions of the *jurats* or local magistrates, who by now had become a hereditary oligarchy, were transferred to a court of royal nominees. Both regimes, however, tempered severity with conciliatory acts.

Menorca was particularly favoured by the

Preceding pages: Junípero Serra, Mallorca's missionary, in America. Left, the English navy off Palma. Right, a typical 17th-century knight.

changes of fortune that befell the occupiers. In 1756 the English were driven out for the duration of the Seven Years War by a French task force in an encounter that supposedly gave the world *mayonnaise*—said to have been concocted by the French commander's chef—and led to the execution for negligence of Admiral Byng, *pour encourager les autres*. In consequence, the island, which already had the benefit of the model British garrison town of Georgetown (now known as Villacarlos), acquired a French successor

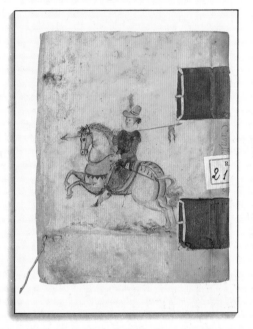

at San Luis. The improvements made by the British to the roads were continued by the French and contributed the infrastructure of Menorcan prosperity in the next century, and are still visible today.

The most enlightened British governor, Richard Kane, had already embellished Mahón, which owes its status as the island's chief town to the occupiers' choice: the well preserved old-world charm of the displaced capital, Ciutadella, is a by-product of the decision. In Mahón the sash windows of Hanover Street are a memento of Georgian supremacy.

Mallorca, too, benefited from the policies

of its new rulers. The island was able to thrive, as a garrison and naval base, from the renewed activity of the Bourbons in the Mediterranean. Though politically repressive, the new regime was economically successful and a mood of *enrichissez-vous* gripped the island élite. There was more new enterprise and more new building than at any time since the 14th century, and the embellishments of the parish church of Santa Cruz in Palma betray the wealth of its early 18th-century parishioners.

The elliptical cloister of San Antonio Abad is only the most startling of the ornaments of Baroque Mallorca. The painter Mesquida, who was active in his native is-

land at this time, was one of the most accomplished in Spain.

Inner debates: Island society remained introspective. Between 1749 and 1777, for instance, the entire community was divided by a dispute over the status of the cult of the Blessed Ramón Llull, the great mystic, missionary and proverbialist who was one of the island's greatest sons, and who, before his supposed martyrdom in Barbary in 1314, established himself as a leading influence in late mediaeval intellectual tradition.

At one level, it was a conflict between Llull's own order, the Franciscans, and the Dominicans. At another, it was a vow be-

tween supporters and enemies of the enlightenment, the former anxious to degrade a candidate for sanctity (Llull) whose works reeked of irrationalism, the latter equally keen to vindicate a traditional cause. But it spread and mobilised hostile factions, waging war by street violence and pulpit-thumping iconoclasm. In the end the cult of Llull survived and the only long-term casualty was the advanced-thinking Bishop Díaz de Guerra, who was driven out of the diocese.

The enlightenment was, however, probably as thoroughly received in Mallorca as in any part of Spain. The libraries of the palaces of Campofranco and Vivot bear witness to the aristocratic patronage of new ideas and the accessibility on the island of texts which had previously been banned.

A division of principle between sympathisers with new ideas, including rationalism, constitutionalism and liberalism, on the one hand, and clericalists, traditionalists and absolutionists on the other came to characterise the political history of the island. The left hand constantly disagreed with the right, and vice versa.

Between 1773 and 1786 royal decrees emancipating the descendants of Jews provoked bitter controversy; the great geographer Bauzá wrote his works in the palace of Vivot but later died in exile in London; the Junta that seized power in the islands in defiance of Napoleon's peninsular take-over dreamed of reviving the ancient kingdom of Mallorca, but the most distinguished exile from the peninsula, the economist Jovellanos, used the island to launch his elegant *apologia* for enlightened resistance to the French; French prisoners were propagators of revolutionary ideas, but 5,000 of them were left to die on the offshore islet of Cabrera; the Bishop of Mallorca was a supporter of the constitutionalist assembly which met in Cádiz to create a modern government in the wake of French defeat, but his fellow-bishops, who were exiles from the war on the mainland, were unanimous in rejecting it.

In 1812 the new street lighting in Palma seemed to symbolise the end of the oppressive traditionalists, but ten years later an absolutist rebellion had to be bloodily suppressed in Campos and Llucmajor. The tomb of the ringleader, Don Joaquín Obrador, who was buried in a Franciscan habit, can be seen in the church of Campos.

Liberal zeal: By the mid-1830s moderate liberals predominated in the island but remained wary of the abiding strength of the rebellious reactionaries. Most islanders stood aloof from the constitutional conflicts of the next 40 years, drifting with the wind and concentrating on self-enrichment. They voted for the ruling party in the minority of Isabel II; responded so enthusiastically to the government's anti-clerical policies that the arch of the Almudaina was almost knocked down along with redundant monasteries in an excess of liberal zeal; swamped the polls with votes for the Liberal Union when its leader, O'Donnell, was in power; celebrated

new theatre in Manacor, a new newspaper, the first steamship sailing to the mainland and the foundation of a company to invest in the growing opportunities for oceanic trade.

Perhaps as a result of the consequent increase of wealth, the islands' reputation for being politically progressive waned. Under the First Republic, two-thirds of the adult population subscribed the petitions of the right-wing Unión Católica, which was led in the islands by the revered figure of J.M. Quadrado, the Balearics' most renowned intellectual and most distinguished historian. The restoration of the monarchy on the mainland in 1875 was enthusiastically received on the islands.

the proclamation of a "democratic monarchy" in 1868 by burning the house of a famous reactionary hero of the 1822 rising; and made a virtue of necessity when the First Republic was declared by hoping for increased Mallorcan autonomy.

Meanwhile economic activity grew apace. The atmosphere of the period of the war against Napoleon, when Mallorca and Menorca were full of refugees, seems to have stimulated projects and ideas. 1834 was an *annus mirabilis*, which saw new roads, a

Left, the Grand Hotel, precursor of modern tourist buildings. Above, the Almudaina today.

Meanwhile, however, republic policies had promoted important material effects, such as laying a railway system and enlarging the harbours. With the restoration, the paddy-like Albufera marshland was drained for pig-farming.

1902 was another *annus mirabilis*: the city walls of Palma were destroyed in an extraordinary orgy of destructive progressivism; and an electricity station and a "Grand Hotel" were under construction; Palma unveiled an opera house with a capacity for 3,000; and the island got its first soccer team. Tourism was beginning to grow with improved communications and in 1905 a society was established to promote it.

Industrialisation was also taking off. There was a locomotive factory by 1901, a car factory by 1922; and for most of the First World War Mallorcan and Menorcan manufacturers supplied the French army with soldiers' boots.

But the sudden rise of an industrial proletariat created only containable social tensions, thanks in part to the paternalistic influence of the self-styled "capitalist worker", multi-millionaire Juan March, (the gardens and his summer residence are open to visitors in the northeast of the island) who employed many of them.

A spate of food and fuel riots occurred in

1918-19, as the favourable war-time conditions came to an end, but did not last. There was a large potential left-wing vote waiting to emerge with the fall of the Primo de Rivera dictatorship in 1930, but monarchists easily predominated in the elections of 1931. Menorca, where the fragile industrial base suffered most from the economic fluctuations of the period, began to part company politically from her sister-islands and remains the most reserved of the Balearic archipelago.

Islands at War: When the Spanish Civil War began in July, 1936, Mallorca and Ibiza were strongly nationalist, Menorca republican. In August 1938, a republican invasion of Mallorca from Menorca was aborted when the expected rising in its favour failed to materialise.

The nationalist build-up of air superiority turned Mallorca into a sort of permanently-anchored aircraft-carrier for the duration of the war, but it was not until the republican cause was evidently hopeless, in February, 1939, that Menorca finally surrendered, partly as a result of an internal *putsch* by lieutenants and NCOs of the republican garrison.

In the Franco era the islands were transformed by a last conquest: the coming of mass tourism. Tourism had been significant previously—with perhaps 40,000 visitors a year just before the civil war—but it had been decorous and rich, symbolised by the clientèle of the German-Argentinian Adán Diehl's luxurious Hotel Formentor, which was a renowned plutocratic spa and watering-hole of the late 1920s and early 1930s.

The airborne invasion of the 1950s boosted annual numbers of tourists from 98,000 in 1950 to 400,000 by the end of the decade and some 10 million today.

This was the era of what Spaniards called *turismo pobre* (poor tourism) which defaced the landscape with cheap development and threatened to swamp traditional culture with foreign trash. The hippie culture of Ibiza in the late sixties seemed to sum up Franco's failure in his self-appointed role as guardian of traditional Spanish values.

However, by the early 1970s, Menorca, measured by the usual trivial standards of car and refrigerator ownership, had the fourth highest standard of living in Spain. Spain's transformation by consumerism and materialism was nowhere better exemplified than in the Balearics.

In the 1980s, the rational limits set to development, the revival of traditional culture and the restoration of some threatened sites has been partly the result of a fashion for nostalgia, and partly the work of the regional government established under Spain's devolutionist constitution.

The islands have been saved temporarily from becoming a mass resort, and, like the girl on Keat's urn, they are forever warm and still to be enjoyed.

Left, testing gin on Menorca. Right, Palacio Vivot, a symbol of the enlightenment.

THE ISLANDER

A Ciutadella es cul no els hi quep dins sa barcella. (In Ciutadella their bottoms don't fit on a tray.)

A Maó mostren sa panxa per un boto. (In Mahón they show their bellies for a button.)

Islands and islanders always have plenty of individual peculiarities; look at the British, the Japanese, the Tongans, the Fijiians…at least all these groups have a collective name. The people of the Balearics do not even have that; they are either Mallorquíns, Ibizencos, Menorquíns or Formenterans, and they don't always see eye to eye with each other, sometimes even on the same island, as the above proverbs from Menorca demonstrate.

Of course the islanders as a whole share many general characteristics with other inhabitants of the Mediterranean basin. The traits common to all of these seaside populations (particularly reserved hospitality and a marked respect for tradition) are the consequence of a history of the symbiosis of a primarily agricultural economy with seaborne trade.

Like the islands of Corsica and Sardinia the Balearics as a whole have avoided becoming too dependent on this sea commerce, largely because a large part of the population has always lived completely ignoring the sea—surprisingly, at times, never leaving the island's interior even as far as to venture into the capital (invariably the major port). At the same time the *marineros* and fishermen who inhabited the littoral of the islands seldom ventured into the interior. Consequently the relationship between the two groups—the traders and the farmers—was merely commercial in nature.

But beneath the geneal characteristics of Mediterraneans are other more specific traits at a family by family level. Today, with tourism having almost totally displaced the islands' maritime commerce and agriculture, the present generations are rapidly losing the individual traits that distinguished

the *campesino* from the coast dweller, and island by island the populations are more unified than they once were. Nevertheless throughout the archipelago there do remain important distinctions.

The Mallorquíns: The inhabitants of the principal island are difficult to characterise primarily because of their own lack of strong character, marked temperament, or extreme behaviour. The Mallorquín doesn't like exaggeration or haste. He moves with a calm that can enervate other people.

The soubriquet *Isla de la Calma* given to Mallorca by the Catalan painter Santiago Rusinol was so apt that it has become a cliché over the course of time. The present reality is that the island, with its seething coasts in the summer, its excess of cars and its overcrowded airport, has lost a great deal of its traditional calm, but the islanders haven't changed the quiet way in which they march through life, disliking the unexpected and the improvised.

They see an ally in time itself; to put an idea into practice or to take a decision is often a matter of considerable length. The answer to the question "when?" is normally "next

XUETAS AND JUDAISM

A personal account by Ben Roth

The word *Xueta* (also spelt Chueta) is the name given to the group of descendants of the Conversos, Mallorcan Jews converted to Catholicism during the Inquisition, who still constitute a distinctive group of people on the island.

Some say that the word derives from the old Mallorcan word for Jew, *Xuhita*, which translates literally as Jew-ette; others suggest that it comes from the word *Xua*, which means porkchop, because these converts used to eat porkchops on the street to demonstrate that they were really Catholic, and did not follow Jewish dietary laws.

Much has been written about the Xuetas, and, depending on whether the writer was Xueta, Mallorquín or otherwise, many texts differ on how they were converted and whether there was religious or racial discrimination against them.

Until the time of the conquest of Mallorca by King Jaime I in 1229 the Jews and Muslims (Mallorca had been dominated by Arabs) lived together in peace. The Muslims were largely driven out by the conquerors, but the Jews were allowed to stay because of their knowledge of arts and crafts, map-making and commerce. As a group they earned the island an enormous amount of foreign trade, particularly with Africa. They were bankers to the crown, which gave them certain privileges, including a decree that no Jew could be convicted and imprisoned by Christian or Moorish testimony.

During the harsher economic periods on the island this ethnic group, who lived apart in ghettos particularly in Inca and in Palma, suffered at the hands of rioting Mallorquíns; 300 Jews were slaughtered in the streets of Palma in 1391.

During the Inquisition the Jews were given the harsh choice of converting to Catholicism, being burned at the stake or leaving the island. Those that chose to stay and who thus became Xuetas were still discriminated against to the extent of not being allowed to leave their ghetto, to hold office, or to marry outside their community. It wasn't until fairly recent times that Xueta priests were allowed to hold Mass in the cathedral.

Despite their conversion the Jews stuck to their old customs; many publicly practised Catholicism and privately held their own Jewish services, and it wasn't until the end of the 17th century that the label "Xueta" was truly earned and the whole community was properly Catholic. Then, as now, a Xueta could be instantly recognised by his or her name, of which the 14 most recognised were Aguiló, Bonnín, Cortés, Fuster, Forteza, Martí, Miró, Picó, Pomar, Segura, Tarongí, Valentí, Valleriola and Valls.

The Calle de Platería, or street of the silversmiths, which runs nearby, was inhabited by Xuetas, and still houses their descendents.

Despite being completely Catholic by the beginning of the 18th century there was still some discrimination against the Xuetas, and relatively few married outside their own community. The situation today is better. There are Xuetas in the government and they hold positions of trust in all kinds of business. They are even considered desirable because of their innate talents as bankers, businessmen and stockbrokers. Despite their unshakeable Catholicism today's Xueta still retains some Jewish traits, including very close family ties and deep respect for elders, who are kept in the family homes until they die.

There have been attempts to recover them for the Jewish fold. In 1966 Dr Israel Ben Zeev, the president of the International Organisation of the Propagation of Judaism, came to Mallorca at the request of one person who claimed that the Xuetas wanted to re-convert. He arranged for 24 people from five different families, none of whom were Xuetas, to visit Israel with a view to settling there. The person who invited Ben Zeev to come was not included amongst the visitors. When they arrived in Israel these would-be Jews found that jobs and housing were very limited, and swiftly returned to their old lives in Mallorca.

The recent rebirth of practising Judaism on the islands has been inspired by outsiders, particularly from the US and UK, who have come to settle. The first public act of religious worship was held 20 years ago, and the community secured a charter which started a legitimate Jewish community that incorporated American, African, Turkish and British Jews. The new legal footing allowed the community to purchase land and for the first time in half a century orthodox Jews could be buried in the ground rather than in cement crypts.

In 1987 the community converted an ex-Christian Scientist church into the first synagogue on the islands since the others were destroyed during the Inquisition. Other evidence of Jewish presence on the islands is scant: the most noticeable is the rose window of the cathedral, in the form of the Star of David, and the Jewish Baths in Palma (which are still considered by many to be Arab). In some parts of the island *crespell* cookies are still made in the form of a six-pointed star, and you can get the braided bread eaten by Jews on the Sabbath.

But despite the fact that once again there is a legitimate Jewish community on the islands it still has no Xueta members, and it probably will never do so: the Xuetas are, by now, far too far away from their origins and it is doubtful whether they will ever consider themselves as Jews.

week" or "next month" or even "next year." This doesn't mean that the Mallorquín is allergic to work (in fact he is very industrious), but he is lazy and sceptical of new projects and novelties that threaten to alter his daily routine.

A Mallorquín is accommodating and self-contented, with an inbuilt prudency that avoids any risk. In an island where everything is at hand the islanders seldom experiment with that which is not known. There is always time to start or finish anything without fear of the unexpected or of rapid change. As a permanent presence the sea slows one down, allows one to not rise too early, permits one to go slowly.

The impression of a tourist-visitor will always be superficial. A bit of patience and respect is enough to penetrate into the depths of the Mallorquíns and benefit from their devotion towards their guests. The Mallorquín warms to those who are capable of understanding this.

The Menorquíns: The brotherhood of character between the Mallorquíns and Menorquíns is visible in their affability and their quietness. But in spite of these common profiles they cannot be confused as twins.

The Menorquíns are people of an easy smile and of a happy temperament, but the context of the islands makes them vastly different from the extrovertedness dis-

Foreigners passing through the island usually conclude that Mallorquíns are very closed, idiosyncratic and are full of complexes. This judgement is the result of their frustration at not being able to introduce themselves easily into island society. They are quite right in their diagnosis—but it is one that applies to any small community with a long history of being forced to live by itself as is the case with all three of the Balearic Islands.

Above, Mallorquíns making *sobrasada*, the local minced sausage.

played, for example, in the south of the Iberian Peninsula.

Their nature is to be happy. The fatalistic scepticism of the Mallorquín is converted into clever well-meant irony in the Menorquín. The island's society, ever relaxed, doesn't invite uproars, irritations or envies. The balanced prosperity of recent times and the somehow general well-being have educated the Menorquíns.

Perhaps it is this desire for well-being which inspires their dislike of the ugliness of disorder or dirtiness. Their neighbours, in Mallorca, admire their love for order. It is easy to see the influence of the utilitarian values and appreciation of good taste brought and cultivated during the British domination—a period of Menorcan history looked upon most affectionately.

The old quarrel between the two "capitals" of Menorca, located at either end of the island—Mahón, proud of its port and dominating the traffic with the continent, and Ciutadella, bastion of the island's tradition and aristocracy—blemishes, ever so slightly, the perfect balance of Menorcan society. It is said that this rivalry has to do with the unrelenting memory of Ciutadella at the total lack of help offered by Mahón during the punishing seige by the Turkish pirate Red Beard in 1558.

Ibizencos: If the Mallorquíns and Menorquíns can be considered as brothers in character, the Ibizencos are hardly even distant cousins. The island has suffered from the effects of isolation throughout its history. This island, the only one without a Roman name, has been bypassed by time itself. Even being situated between two very important capitals—Alicante, on the mainland and Palma in Mallorca—and being in less treacherous waters than those which surround Menorca, the Ibizencos have developed an introverted life and culture.

Despite being rather stand offish, Mallorquíns and Menorquíns try hard to open and adapt themselves to their visitors. The Ibizenco, on the other hand, is not nearly so flexible. To bend his thought, his will or his behaviour is impossible. To insist is useless. His life marches on parallel to that of the numerous foreigners, with little interconnection. And accordingly the Ibizencos have maintained a pure and singular character in the midst of the cosmopolitan human traffic that today lives on the island. No other islanders would probably tolerate such unusual expatriates.

Of course this refers to the "traditional" Ibizenco—those of the countryside. Society on the island had always been primarily rural, with austere virtues, honour codes and silences, all more seemingly appropriate to a character of mythology than to a flesh and blood human being. The Ibizenco looks as if he has escaped from an unwritten book, and the only thing easily identifiable about him is the fact that he is Mediterranean.

Right, Ibizenco in folk costume.

MALLORCA AS IT WAS

A personal recollection by Neville Waters

I will never forget the day that I first arrived on the island of Mallorca. It was late in the month of November 1958.

I had motored from Copenhagen in a little Morris Minor, down across a freezing Europe almost entirely covered in snow. I came to Barcelona to catch the midnight ferry, and I do not recall that I saw the sun throughout the whole journey. The wind was strong in Barcelona, and icy cold. My car was hauled up and lashed to the deck of the boat.

The next morning at dawn, after a rough night, I could see the island of Mallorca across a calming sea, bathed in the rays of the rising sun. I watched with interest as all the many white and stone coloured houses, the church towers and spires of the city of Palma came more and more clearly into view. The great Gothic cathedral at the end of the harbour looked like an immense old galleon come to rest with all its sails furled.

The hotel where I spent my first night was comfortable and clean, with a private bathroom to each bedroom. The room, with three meals and wine and coffee, cost a pound.

The following morning I visited a Spanish lawyer whose name I had got from the British Consulate before leaving Scandinavia. I told him I intended to buy a house and hoped that he would act for me, although I expected to take six months before deciding where to live. He commended my common sense.

"Many people," he said, "come here on holiday, think that they would like to live here, and buy a house at the end of their summer holidays. They have no idea what it will be like in winter, and are rarely satisfied as a result."

Later that morning I noticed a cluster of white houses and a church up on a mountainside, and by the afternoon I was back in the lawyer's office to confess that I had bought a house! For the past 30 years I have lived in that same hillside village.

Customs in the *casa*: The first morning that I opened the front door of my new home it was to discover plates of green figs on my

doorstep. A welcome from my neighbours.

In those days it was the custom to leave one's front door key on the outside of the door if you were leaving the house as an indication to any caller that you were not at home. Collectors came round with bills for gas, electricity, house and car insurance, etc. You did not keep such people waiting on your doorstep, but invited them in and offered them a glass of brandy with the words *mi casa es su casa*, my house is your house. This practice meant that you had at all times to keep a sizeable sum of ready cash about the house. In those days it was quite safe to do so; house-breaking and burglary were virtually unknown.

Fairly early on in my residence on the island I was informed that, "Northern Europeans are slaves of the clock, we, in Spain, regard the clock as our slave." *Mañana*, tomorrow, can mean the day after tomorrow, or next week, or month, or indeed whatever is convenient to the person using the term. All too often one still waits for the electrician, the plumber, the carpet-layer who have told you most emphatically that they will be with you *mañana*. But in this use of *mañana* Spaniards are telling you what they think it will please you to hear. It is not meant as a guarantee. In 99 percent of the cases it doesn't really matter whether you get a letter today or tomorrow.

My much esteemed friend was Jaime the postman. If you needed your garden walls or your cellar whitewashed, he would dump the bag of undelivered letters in the entrance hall, take off his coat and start work. If the work took longer than he anticipated he would, on leaving say, "Ah well, they can have this lot tomorrow." Postal deliveries are still slow and unreliable, but not because the postman is whitewashing my cellar.

Language, food and church: I did not speak any Spanish when I first arrived and my Italian proved of no use at all. Words in Spanish that sound familiar are more of a trap than a help. I remember one dignified Spanish señora informing me that she was very *constipada*. The lozenges I gave her can have been of no help, for today I know that she was informing me that she had a cold.

When I arrived on Mallorca it was not possible to buy tea, and butter was available in only one shop on the island, where it was heavily salted and kept in a tub. The shop was nicknamed Fortnum and Masons by expatriates, for though it was only a small grocer's shop one could buy things unavailable anywhere else, particularly at Christmas time.

In those days if you were Church of England you attended services in a converted soda-water factory, in a slight atmosphere of persecution. Services could not be advertised, and armed Civil Guards frequently came into the church to stand, arms akimbo, usually during the sermon. It was enough to make one fidgety.

The law of Religious Liberty was passed during the last years of Generalísimo Francisco Franco's dictatorship, and today, through the efforts of the English and American residents, we have a church and chaplaincy house.

Evening habits: In my early years in Mallorca the pavements of the towns and villages were lined with women fanning charcoal in the early evenings of winter. All types of basins and dishes were used to hold the charcoal, basins of enamel, copper, brass, or whatever they had. The breeze and a newspaper fan having well ignited the contents, the bowls were carried indoors and put beneath a special table, known as a *camilla*. It was circular and draped with a cloth that came down to touch the floor all the way around. If going to read, write, play a game, eat, or just sit, you picked up the cloth, inserted your legs beneath, dropped the cloth and allowed the comforting warmth to rise to where it was most needed. Sadly *camillas* are no longer in use.

The *serenos* have also gone. They were a sort of vigilante who roamed the streets of the towns at night calling out the hour and that all was well. As burglary was almost unknown their duty was mainly directed to seeing drunks home, helping them up the steps and getting the key in the keyhole.

City dressing: Palma is a provincial capital city with a magnificent Gothic cathedral, two palaces, many streets of noble mansions, elegant shopping thoroughfares, avenues of trees and fountains. Thirty years ago people dressed as you would expect them to be dressed in so beautiful a city. Almost all heads were covered, all taxi-drivers wore caps, and on a Sunday, after mass, Spanish señoritas, holding their missals, would slowly parade up and down the main avenue, the Paseo el Born, with their *dueñas* beside them, and the sibilant sound of *piropos* filled the air. It was gracious and lovely.

A *piropo* is a compliment paid by a young man to a passing girl or girls. Though quite clearly heard by the young woman for whom it was intended, she was supposed never to acknowledge it in any way. Not even by the slightest inclination of the head, or the flick of an eye. These *piropos*, now alas gone, were always in good taste, and any woman up to late middle-age who had not received one as she walked about the streets of Palma, would see to it, when she returned home, that almost every item of her wardrobe was immediately renewed.

The Spanish gentleman was ever gallant, and I heard of one *piropo* paid to an elderly spinster with few if any attractions—"Señora, I would die for that elbow."

Nowadays English youths on holiday walk through the streets of Palma dressed in the briefest possible shorts, often patterned with their country's flag. Girls in the smallest possible bikinis try to gain entrance to the cathedral. Theirs is a display which should be confined to the beaches.

A distinctive era: Modern times have brought often unhealthy changes, too. Mallorca used to be advertised as *La Isla de la Calma*, the island of peace, but all publicity has dropped that particular phrase. It was a peaceful island when I first came to it, but today there are aeroplanes flying over every few minutes, noisy trucks at all hours, and worst of all are the *motos*. Spanish youth seem to think that their masculinity is increased in proportion to the noise their motorcycles make. The new high rise apartments which line the coast have often replaced something much older; between 1900 and 1902 the City Fathers of Palma pulled down the immensely strong, thousand-year-old walls of the city. Even so, there was one place that everyone believed they would not dare to touch, however much they longed to: the Puerta de Santa Margarita was the gate by which King Jaime the Catalan conqueror of Mallorca had entered the city to receive its surrender, and almost as sacred as a church. But in 1910 the desire for progress became too great for the gate, and at midnight on a moonless night down it came.

I understand that Alcudia took a leaf from the Palma authorities' books, selling the remains of their city's Roman walls in 1928 as builder's material. The present day walls of that town, variously described to the tourist as Roman or Arab, depending on your guide, were largely built on top of the 14th century foundations during the time I have been living on the island. Fortunately, the present City Fathers of Palma seem keen on making green places and placing trees where there were none. Good for them!

Thirty years ago Mallorca was a place of windmills. The journey from the airport was enlightened by hundreds of them, variously led down into enormous cisterns built below. Despite the new pipes most of us still prefer to go on pumping up the water from these old cisterns. No chlorine, no salt.

Transports of dismay: Then there is the traffic. Almost none when I came. A few 1920 boat-backed Fiats and other museum pieces, but mostly donkey carts, mules and bicycles, the latter adorned with colourful bags across the handlebars, bags that had once been thrown across the backs of donkeys. But the lanes by which it was once possible gradually to discover Mallorca have been turned into four lane motorways, and all roads are at all times heavy with traffic. Thanks be my village street is too narrow, and those

coloured, twirling merrily, pumping up water for the fields. Mass tourism has necessitated a vast increase in the use of water, and as the water table sank the water itself became salty, useless for irrigation. Accordingly the windmills ceased turning and fell into decay.

My village, which is less than three miles from the centre of Palma, was in recent months given piped city water and a piped sewage system. Prior to these modernisations every drop of rain that fell was caught upon the roofs and terraces of our houses and

Above, shepherd and his dog.

coaches that have tried to use it get stuck, loaded with tourists, like a cork in a bottle.

I have seen all too many changes to the island and the coasts are almost totally ruined. Inland, however, away from the touristic areas, Mallorca is still supremely beautiful, and there are still areas of great peace.

It is a long time since I came, a homeless bachelor in my late forties, to live on an island I have grown to love. Now I have a house, a loving wife, two English stepdaughters, two Spanish sons-in-law, six Anglo-Spanish grandchildren, and four step-great-grandchildren!

What Zorba called "the full catastrophe".

In the Balearic summer season—a moveable feast which seems to include most of spring and all of autumn as well—barely a week goes by without one or other of the newspapers mentioning the arrival of someone significant at the airport and the departure of someone else.

Arabs, artists and aristocrats, screen and singing stars who have made money, society figures who have inherited it, and beauties who have married it—the jet-setters of these islands are no different to anywhere else in the world, but here, in these small areas, they are noticed and their presence makes the islands proud. The less important have wild parties; the more important slip in and out virtually unnoticed.

The tradition of just dropping in for a couple of weeks of sun was started by people like Frederic Chopin and his common-law wife George Sand, who came to spend a winter in Mallorca because the weather would supposedly be good for the composer's health. Unfortunately the monastery in Valldemossa is cold and damp in the winter and Chopin almost died; moreover George Sand disliked the island and its people, who for their part didn't view her with much favour either.

By contrast Archduke Salvador of Austria, who arrived on his yacht *Nixe* in 1869 and stayed for 22 years, loved the locals and they loved him. He blazed a trail which many have followed. His palace near the village of Deià is now a museum; Deià itself has become a nest of people who think they should be recognised, and a lot of today's jet-setters come and go by yacht.

Royalty: Most significant of all jet-setters are the two best-loved Royal Families in Europe, the British and the Spanish.

King Juan Carlos of Spain, with Queen Sofía and their three children, spend the month of August in the Royal Palace in Mallorca, which was renovated for them by the local government. It is the former home of the Greek painter Juan Saridakis, once

Preceding pages: trappings of the rich pour out of marinas. Left, King Juan Carlos. Above, a memorial tablet to famous visitors.

known as quite a jet-setter himself.

The family sail around the island on the Royal Yacht the *Fortuna* and compete in regattas. Princess Elena takes part in horse-jumping competitions and the King often plays golf with his father Don Juan, the Count of Barcelona. One of the King's sisters, Princess Pilar, the Duchess of Badajoz and her husband the Duke of Badajoz, have a villa on Mallorca which they often visit.

In the mid-eighties the British Prince Charles and Princess Diana also became

regular visitors as the guests of the Spanish Royal Family, and in 1988 the Queen herself, with the Duke of Edinburgh, arrived on the royal yacht *Britannia* and stayed for an informal visit of three days after an official visit to the Spanish peninsula.

Venues: Evidence of the early boom of elegant living on the islands is still very much visible in the Hotel Mediterraneo on the seafront in Palma, which retains some of its colonial atmosphere. The hotel boasts Ava Gardner, Richard Nixon, the Shah of Iran, Errol Flynn and even Agatha Christie among its guests, although other establishments outside town have since taken over the

mantel as the host hotel for the *glitterati*.

The luxurious Son Vida estates (and nearby Bendinat) are filled with titles, including such unpronounceables as the Prince Zurab Tchokotua.

When the Son Vida Hotel was inaugurated in 1961 Prince Rainier and Princess Grace of Monaco were guests of the management, as were many famous names from society and show business, some of whom have returned and purchased property here. The hotel itself is one of only six in Spain to be rated *Gran Lujo*, above five-star.

At the other end of the island the Hotel Formentor, discreet and colonial, has played host to Winston Churchill, Douglas Fairbanks, Charlie Chaplin, Christopher Plummer, the Prince of Wales, the Prince and Princess of Monaco and countless others. At the Formentor everybody thinks they are somebody; have a drink at the bar and pretend that you too have a title, or a fortune.

In Ibiza the lure is more for those who make their money young: a recent party for a film entitled *Ibiza 1992* (to coincide with the Barcelona Olympic games) boasted several princesses and Roman Polanski as guests, and Maradona and Harrison Ford also showed up. The island has several small hotels of "character" which do not publicise their telephone numbers and discourage children, who might disturb their anonymous important guests.

Residents: Bruno Kreisky, ex-Chancellor of Austria, has a home on Mallorca, as does Joanna Hearst, who reputedly gives fabulous parties. King Faud of Egypt used to come to Mallorca, as did Haille Selassie, the Grand Duke Vladimir of Russia, Queen Faridah and many others who like the weather and central location of the islands.

Writer Faye Emerson was on Mallorca when she died, film director Guy Hamilton is a more or less permanent resident, as is French film star Dany Robin and her husband and agent Michael Sullivan and singer Bonnie Tyler. Virgin's Richard Branson has a house in Menorca and film producer Hal Prince spends the summer in his villa in Pollença, Mallorca.

The Balearics have also been recognised as a prime site for property investment by

some of the most gilt-edged speculators in the world. In the mid-eighties an Arab prince purchased a large area of land on the coast a few miles from Palma on which he built an elegant *urbanización*. He hired the French architect François Sperry to design the various elements, which include a golf course, luxury apartments, and the seaside resort called the Anchorage Club, which has attracted many other VIPs to Mallorca.

New image: In the last decade Arab interest on the islands has increased enormously, indicating the credibility level that the islands have achieved. Properties have been bought for investment and development, and the number of expensive restaurants and famous label boutiques has increased. Yacht clubs are expanding their marinas and new ones are being built.

Where jet-setters go they must have their places to play. Favourites of the Royal Family are the Peppone Italian restaurant and the Ole Sevilla Andalucian restaurant in Palma; the cousin of the owner of Peppone's is married to the King's sister. Royalty has also been seen at the Shangri-La Chinese and the Mediterraneo 1930 restaurants. The discotheque of the Club de Mar is a favourite haunt of the young prince and princesses.

Favoured by the faster set of residents are Wellies in the Puerto Portals yacht club (recently at the centre of a drug smuggling scandal) and Tristans, which earns a top rating in the Michelin guide but which has punitive prices to match.

On the beach at Palma Nova are La Baraka Tunisian restaurant, Ciro's seafood and shellfish restaurant, and Bertorelli's, run by the same family who own and manage the chain of that name in the UK. Big-name discos like B.C.M (opened by Samantha Fox) are more for the upwardly mobile than for those who've already made it.

The image of the islands has definitely gone upmarket. Yachting, golf and various watersports are being emphasized by the promotion authorities, and events such as the classical music festival in Pollença have stamped a cultural credibility on Mallorca that Samantha Fox could not endow upon it. Nevertheless the constant stream of VIPs through the Balearics has always been applauded by the locals; in themselves these visits are quick and easy steps to free publicity for the islands.

Left, Prince Felipe is a keen yachtsman. His sister competes in horse-riding competitions.

EXPATRIATE EXISTENCE

Everyone has an image of life in the sun. It is a pleasant picture, sitting on the shady terrace, looking out beyond the orange trees to that distant glint of warm, blue sea, living in a soft, warm climate, far from the cold, dreary, northern winters, in a place where the money goes further than it might do at home, and the company largely consists of like-minded friends. We may not want to work there, and it may even be a little dull, but as somewhere to retire to, to finally put one's feet up, it sounds ideal.

The Balearics measure up to this picture quite well. In the past 50 years or so, they have attracted a great quantity of expatriates, all of whom live at least part of the year on the islands and regard them as their main place of residence, if not actually as *Home*. The attractions are broadly those outlined above, but the expatriates themselves now vary widely. There is no one type, no dominant nation. They come from all countries and classes and with tastes that vary from the extravagant to the spartan. Even the common image of the "expat" as necessarily retired is not accurate; not all expatriates are elderly or pensioners. An increasing number have come to the islands to work, and with Spain's entry into the EEC, this number can be expected to grow.

New breed: In the main, the new breed of expatriate works in the tourist trade, which is now the principal industry, or by serving the many needs of the growing expatriate community. Expatriates run the local offices for tourist or holiday companies, act as guides or resident representatives, run hotels or bars or restaurants, and work in such places as full-time staff or, increasingly, running their own service industries.

Looking after flats, houses or gardens while the expatriate owner is abroad, handling lettings, liaising with local builders for construction work, maintenance or repair, running estate agency offices, letting, buying or selling property, or offering much the same services to boat-owners in the harbours

or marinas—these are the occupations of the newer and younger expatriates.

Some are married to islanders, speak Spanish and can sometimes manage local dialect and, having decided to make their homes on the island, have come to terms with the fact that the pace of life there is not so much slower than in other European countries—indeed, it can be considerably faster—but it is certainly very different, a fact that many of the older expatriates find difficult to take. If you ask a number of these

working people why anyone should pay quite substantial sums for their services, a large proportion will state, "knowledge of island ways," and "ability to get on with the locals," as the two main justifications.

For these younger expatriates the Balearics are their future. Their lives are not unlike those of colonial officials in the days of empire, although the comparison is not one they would care for. However they have no servants and will usually work quite hard. Their children tend to be educated at local nursery schools to begin with, but will then be sent to a bilingual establishment in Palma before being sent off to secondary schools in

Preceding pages: the lifestyle has its appeal. Left, OK for two weeks, but for a lifetime? Right, Dr Waldren, archaeologist, in Deià.

America, England or Continental Europe. Few expatriates of any age are fully integrated with island life.

Races apart: The second, and larger part of the expatriate community, fits into a more traditional mould, though here again, not all of them are necessarily old or retired. Many are in some sense refugees, fleeing to the islands to escape the weather or declining fortunes, or war and insecurity at home.

Every world upheaval provides the islands with a number of expatriates; the Iranian community has grown in numbers in recent years, and as Hong Kong begins to wind down towards re-integration with China, there has been a perceptible increase in the

by their own younger relatives who are now starting to take up residence.

Becoming an expatriate resident of any country requires careful consideration, even after the legal and financial problems have been sorted out.

The weather is usually given as one of the principal reasons for leaving the north of Europe, but Mediterranean weather is not always benign. There are storms from September onwards, and winter weather can be bleak, with fires or central heating essential from November into March. The cost of living, which once drew many pensioners, is no longer a strong attraction, for the Balearics, while cheaper, are no longer exactly

number of Chinese restaurants operating on the islands.

The majority, however, are still relics of the Second World War or the decline of empire in the post-World War II period. Mallorca contains great numbers of old soldiers who were unable to settle down in Britain, and a good percentage of people, British, French and Dutch, who used to live in India, Indonesia, Algeria and Indo-China, who find the weather and ambience of the islands more to their taste than the egalitarian state of their native countries. As this generation grows older, it is being replaced and increased by the first kind of expatriate, and

cheap and inflation seems to be rampant. Nonetheless the local people are friendly, medical services and hospitals are surprisingly good, social life is good and many expatriates claim it is even better in wintertime, when all the summer visitors have gone and they can socialise among their island friends in peace.

Flat or *finca*: Where to live will depend on personal preferences, but the basic choice usually boils down to one or the other. A flat can vary from a small *pied-à-terre* in a sidestreet of Palma to a luxurious coastal apartment with a boat dock at the marina, while a *finca*, though by tradition a small farmhouse, is now a term used by expatriates to mean a house in the country; perhaps a modern villa in a new development, perhaps an old farmhouse set among the olive trees. The choice here usually depends on the amount of use envisaged for the property. Those who spend long summers on the islands go for flats or apartments, while those who live there all year round tend to favour houses with some sort of garden.

Flats have the advantage that owners can close the door and walk away, with the disadvantage that the other surrounding flats may be let out throughout the summer to holiday companies and filled with tourists and their noisy children. *Fincas* have gar-

cope with local builders, who are a race apart. One expert suggests that the best way to get what you want from local builders is to sit by the works with a chequebook in one hand and a whip in the other.

Even so, with all the inevitable problems and culture clashes that expatriates inevitably encounter, most residents seem happy on their islands. They enjoy the weather and the lifestyle, the rounds of drinks and dinner parties, and avoid insularity with a constant stream of visitors from abroad, and by keeping the ear pressed to the BBC World Service or—increasingly—by erecting a dish for satellite television. Many have boats, or enjoy their gardens, and take advantage of the

dens which must be maintained, many lack water during the dry summer months and are beyond the reach of electricity and telephone lines. In either case the property intended for year-round use must be insulated against the winter chill and made secure against increasing numbers of burglars themselves attracted by the foreigners.

The heady days when a beautiful old farmhouse could be picked up for a few thousand pesetas are now long gone, and those who decide to go ahead and build, must learn to

Expats on the isles; some are here to walk (left) and some to work (above).

excellent communications with the peninsula of Spain and the rest of the world. As a rule most expatriates have few islanders as friends, although all declare that the natives are friendly.

The main causes of separation in those marriages that take place between locals and expatriates are that few expatriates speak more than shopping Spanish and fewer still Mallorquín, while the island people are often insular, as tend to be, keeping their socialising within the wide boundaries of their own families. Even so, few Mallorcan birthday parties, or *santos*—saint days—are without a handful of expatriate friends.

THE ARCHIPELAGO

The family Baleares in the Mediterranean consists of three brother islands and one sister island.

The eldest and biggest is Mallorca, (population 530,000) with the loudest voice, the most money, the keenest sense of responsibility and the most diversity in landscape. Mallorca is a miniature continent, with beaches, mountains, railways, flat agricultural lands and a major and beautiful historic city, department stores, boutiques and restaurants with Michelin stars where royalty dine.

Everyone thinks they know Mallorca well, but there is far more to Mallorca than is commonly supposed. Serious claims, on a world level, are made about the turnover and scale of the port and airport; serious art, on a world level, is active in the hills and on the plain; serious money, on a world level, is holidaying or investing here.

If Mallorca is the biggest and loudest of the three brothers and Ibiza the youngest and trendiest, Menorca is the quiet one in the middle who actually proves rather interesting if you draw him into conversation. Menorca (population 56,000) is an understated, under-appreciated island with two surprising cities and a landscape that at first sight might seem monotonous, but which requires a

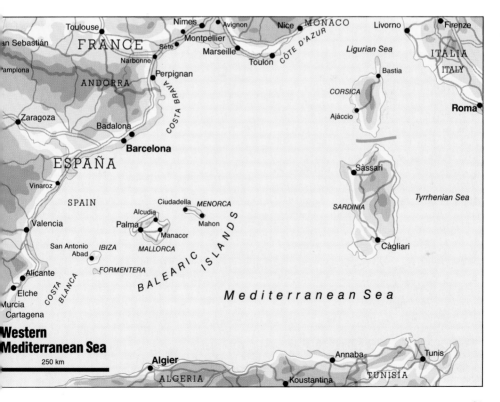

keener, gentler eye, and consequently attracts a quieter, older visitor. The island's enormous quantity of prehistoric stone edifices make it a warehouse of ancient history.

By contrast, after centuries of struggling to make ends meet, Ibiza (population 50,000) has done well to become as successfully young and trendy as it has. The island is a summer mecca for ravers, clubbers, and music-lovers, and frankly there's not much else to see or do; the landscape, although hilly, is rather unkempt where the farming community has abandoned it to concentrate on tourism.

Here originates the Balearic beat, a disco mix which is concocted in the clubs at the height of the summer and which is heard in discotheques throughout Europe by the autumn. Rock and pop stars holiday here, in a surprising number of exclusive hotels that have no need to advertise their existence. In Ibiza it is the night that matters.

Formentera (population 4,000), the little sister of the family, trailing along holding Ibiza's hand, is of quite different character but is not strong enough or independent enough to be firm about her own identity. Holidaymakers from the bigger brother island, revved up and raring to go, cross the two-and-a-half mile (four km) strait that separates the islands and go tearing around Formentera, looking for something that really grabs them and not finding it. This, after all, was where the police made their first drug raids on the Sixties hippies on bicycles, or later in a hired taxi. Formenterans have the longest life expectancy in Spain.

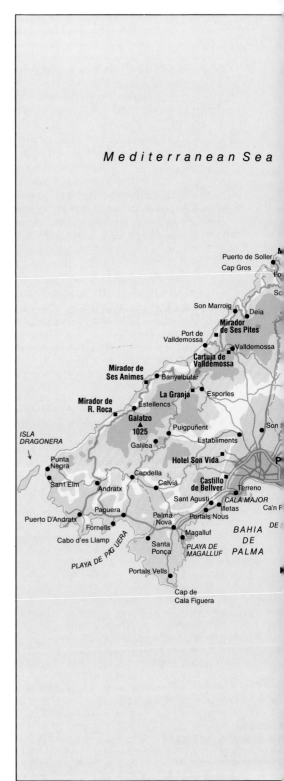

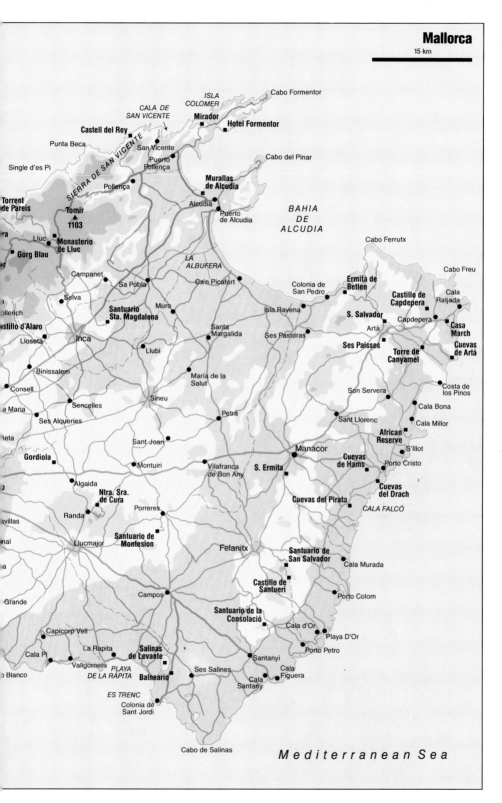

Mallorca

15 km

Cabo Formentor

ISLA
COLOMER
CALA DE
SAN VICENTE
Mirador
Hotel Formentor

Castell del Rey

Punta Beca
San Vicente
Cabo del Pinar

Single d'es Pi
Puerto
Pollença

Torrent
de Pareis
Pollença
**Murallas
de Alcudia**

Tomir
1103
Alcudia
Puerto
de Alcudia

Lluc
Llubi
**BAHIA
DE
ALCUDIA**

**Monasterio
de Lluc**

Gorg Blau

Cabo Ferrutx

LA
ALBUFERA
Cabo Freu

Campanet
Ca'n Picafort
Colonia de
San Pedro
**Ermità de
Betlen**

Selva
Sa Pobla
**Castillo de
Capdepera**
Cala
Ratjada

llench
Muro
Isla Rayena
S. Salvador

castillo d'Alaro
**Santuario
Sta. Magdalena**
Capdepera
**Casa
March**

Lloseta
Inca
Santa
Margalida
Ses Pastoras
Artá
Ses Paisses
**Cuevas
de Artá**

Llubi
**Torre de
Canyamel**

Binissalem
María de la
Salut
Costa de
los Pinos

Consell
Son Servera

a Maria
Sencelles
Sineu
Cala Bona

Ses Alqueries
Petrá
Sant Llorenc
Cala Millor

eta
Sant Joan
**African
Reserve**
S'Illot

Gordiola
Montuiri
Manacor
**Cuevas
de Hams**
Porto Cristo

Algaida
Vilafranca
de Bon Any
S. Ermita

**Ntra. Sra.
de Cura**
Porreres
**Cuevas
del Drach**

villas
Randa
Cuevas del Pirata
CALA FALCÓ

nal
Llucmajor
**Santuario de
Montesion**
Felanitx
**Santuario de
San Salvador**
Cala Murada

a
**Castillo de
Santueri**

Grande
Campos
Porto Colom

**Santuario de la
Consolació**

Capicorp Vell
Cala d'Or

La Rapita
**Salinas
de Levante**
Playa D'Or

Cala Pi
Santanyi
Porto Petro

Blanco
Vallgornera
PLAYA
DE LA RÁPITA
Balneario
Ses Salines
Cala
Figuera

ES TRENC
Cala
Santany

Colonia de
Sant Jordi

Cabo de Salinas

Mediterranean Sea

PALMA

There is no better way to approach Palma de Mallorca than by sea. Over a thousand years of history are etched in various parts of its skyline, crowned by a Gothic cathedral.

Nestling at the foot of the cathedral is the Royal Palace of the Almudaina, built by Moslem rulers and remodelled by Christian kings. Separated from the waterfront by a broad boulevard known as the Paseo Marítimo is the medieval merchants' stock exchange called La Lonja. Next to it is the 17th-century, Renaissance-Baroque structure built to house the Consolat del Mar or Sea Tribunal. Standing sentry above the port on an overlying hill is the circular 14th-century Castle of Bellver, and puncturing the city's skyline elsewhere are the spires of Palma's ancient churches.

By a stretch of the imagination it is possible to blot out the 20th-century spread of Palma and imagine what the city was like just over 150 years ago when Frederic Chopin and Aurore Dupin, Baroness Duduvent (alias George Sand), sailed into the bay to spend a winter in Mallorca. In a book of the same title, George Sand prophesies: "The day will come no doubt when those seeking rest, and even beautiful women, will be able to go to Palma with not greater fatigue and trouble than that with which they now go to Geneva."

The thousands of regular and charter flights that land in Palma's airport each year are a fulfillment of Sand's prophecy. Palma de Mallorca has not only become a haven for sun-hungry visitors but it has also become the summer haunt for the wealthy, the aristocratic, and the famous. The complex of hotels, highrises, restaurants, bars, clubs and discotheques is similar to resort areas throughout Spain, but what makes Palma unique is its old city with narrow and ancient streets.

Ancient quarter: The oldest part of Palma fans out from around the cathedral. Medina Mayurka, as the city was known in the Moslem world, was bounded approximately by the present Miramar and Morey Streets and the Plazas Santa Eulàlia and Cort, from where it extended to the Paseo d'Es Born. This boulevard was built on what used to be the bed of the Sa Riera river, which served as a moat to the western walls of the Arab city. Palma's port formed around the estuary of this river. In the complex of walls below the Almudaina Palace there is an Arab arch called the **Arc de la Mar**, which once crossed a canal which connected the river estuary to a royal inner harbour.

The **Almudaina Palace** is on the site of the citadel of the Roman city. The fountains of the present structure were laid out by the Arabs. Indeed, *Almudaina* means "citadel" in Arabic. This palace was remodelled at the end of the 13th century at the command of Jaime II. The work was carried out according to the plans of the master builder, Pere Salvá, who set about converting the Moorish castle or *alcázar* into a residence for Christian kings according to the Gothic style of his time. He added

the chapels of Santa Ana and San Jaime, the Patio de la Reina (Queen's Courtyard), the Sala Mayor (Main Audience Room), the Patio de Armas, (Military Courtyard), the Hort del Rei, (King's Garden), the King's Palace and the Queen's Palace. Today the Almudaina serves as the military headquarters for the Balearic Islands and is also used for official functions when the King of Spain is in Palma.

Although Medina Mayurka was one of the most important cities of Moslem Spain, there are few traces of it left today. There is the arch on Almudaina Street, which once marked the limits of the *alcázar*, and the Arab baths on Serra Street. The other relics of Arab culture are to be found in the **Museum of Mallorca** and the Almudaina Palace. The former, located on Portella Street, has a variety of ceramic pieces as well as architectural remnants in the form of capitals and the intrados of an arch dating from the Almohad period.

The Arab foundations of the Almudaina Palace may still be discerned in the towers that flank its entrance. Within the palace are the intricately carved, wooden ceilings laid out in arabesques, some splendidly sculpted stone lions, and stone faucets sculpted as animal heads.

Gothic majesty: Palma's **cathedral** stands on the ground around which Medina Mayurka's main mosque once stood. At the command of Jaime I its construction was begun in 1230, soon after the Christian conquest of the island. The work began with the levelling of houses around the mosque which was converted into a Christian church.

The cathedral was more than three centuries in the making, and finishing touches were made as late as this century. In the first third of the 14th century the Chapel of the Trinity and the vault of the central nave were completed. It took another 50 years to complete the second part of the great nave, and at the end of the century work on the magnificent sea-side portal known as the Mirador was begun.

The original mosque, which had not

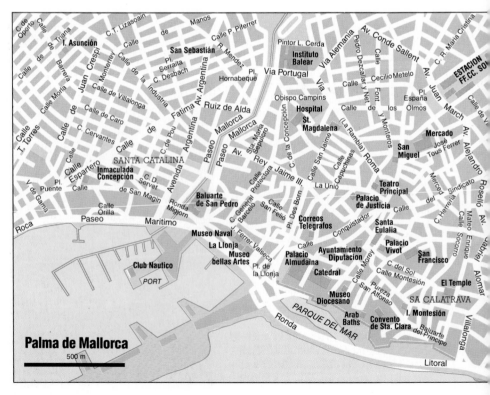

Palma de Mallorca

500 m

quite occupied half of the main nave, was torn down in 1412, and by the end of the century the three naves extended beyond the lateral doors. These were completed in the 16th century. The cathedral was considered finished with the completion in 1601 of work on the Great Door facing the Almudaina, but an earthquake in 1851 necessitated the remodelling of this façade which is strongly criticised for not blending properly with the rest of the building's Gothic design.

George Sand called the cathedral a starkly severe "imposing mass, which rises from the edge of the sea." It has also been called "a great stone organ", or "a thick wall of pikes and lances that pierce the sky in pacific combat."

Whatever impressions this majestic, Gothic conglomerate may inspire, it is clear that it was meant to be admired from the sea. Like a beautiful woman conscious of her better profile, Palma's cathedral faces the world with a wall of pinnacled columns and buttresses. The pinnacled columns are not reproduced on the cathedral's northern side. Perhaps no Gothic cathedral in the world has such a spectacular situation, set as it is over the city walls, completely dwarfing surrounding buildings.

The architectural focus of the cathedral's seaward side is the **Portal del Mirador**. Here are enshrined the main aesthetic and religious tenets of the Middle Ages. Its ogive arches are lavishly ornamented with geometric and vegetative motifs and gargoyles. The central Christian mystery portrayed here is the Last Supper. Cast as supporting statues are angels, prophets, and apostles. The original plan of master builder Pere Morey was to have 36 more saintly figures set in what are still empty niches in the stone.

Inside the cathedral 14 slender columns soar up to sustain the weight of the roofs of the high central nave (143.5 ft, 43.7 metres) and the lower lateral naves. The first pair of columns were completed in 1368, but so insufficient was their 4.8 ft (1.48 metres) diameter that they began to curve. When the time

came to raise the second pair in the first years of the 15th century, the builders increased their width to 5.5 ft (1.68 metres), still very narrow when compared to the columns of other Gothic churches. Chartres, for instance, has far shorter columns 9.2 ft (2.8 metres) wide.

The bright Mediterranean sun filters through the stained glass of the cathedral's 35 windows. The rose window suspended above the apse has a diameter of 41 ft (12.51 metres) making it one of the largest in the world. Its 1,236 pieces of red, green, yellow, blue and grey glass combine to form an enormous Christian mandala in which the Star of David is formed by 12 of a total of 24 triangles intersected by red and yellow flowers.

The art within: More than a masterpiece of Gothic architecture, the cathedral is also a museum of the history of art. The 17 side chapels are lavishly embellished with statues, reredos, and decorations in the Gothic, Renaissance, and Baroque styles. In the **Vermells**

Sacristy, located in the ground floor of the Belfry, there is a collection of gold and silver reliquaries, statues, books and other artefacts dating from the 12th to the 15th centuries. The **Gothic Chapter Hall** has a splendid collection of Gothic paintings. The **Baroque Chapter Hall** entered through a sumptuous portal contains reliquaries, monstrances, and candelabra from the 16th to the 19th centuries.

At the beginning of this century the great modernist architect Antoni Gaudí remodelled the interior of the cathedral. The most conspicuous of his innovations was to hang an enormous *baldoquino* over the main altar. In natural light it looks like a gigantic spider-web caked with centuries of dust. But once its 35 lamps are lit, this modernist sculpture made from brocade, cardboard, nails, wood and cork becomes a symbol illustrating Eucharistic mysteries. Another conspicuous touch by Gaudí was to gird the columns with candelabra. He also placed the Renaissance-style Gospel and Epistle pulpits in their present loca-

The interi‹ columns a remarkabl slender.

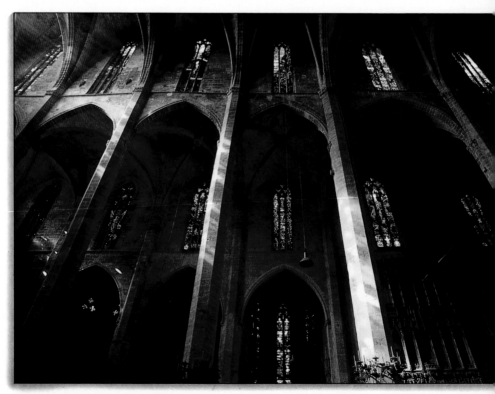

tions within the cathedral.

Surrounding three sides of the main altar are the elaborately carved walnut choirstalls. The *cátedra* or archbishop's chair which dates from the year 1269 divides the stalls and is set immediately behind the altar. Above the *cátedra* there is an opening onto the **Trinity Chapel**. This is the oldest part of the cathedral and contains the sarcophagi of Jaime II and Jaime III.

On the street: A good place to begin a walking tour through old Palma is on Mirador Street which borders the sea side of the cathedral. Across from the cathedral apse is the **Archbishop's Palace**. The oldest part of this building is the Chapel of San Pablo which is entered through a Gothic portal. The rest of the palace was remodelled in the 17th century. The museum housed here has a *potpourri* of articles collected by generations of archbishops. The finest piece of art is a sculpture of the Virgin Mary which was once enshrined above the Portal del Mirador of the cathedral and a reredos depicting St George and the dragon with medieval Palma depicted in the background.

Continuing down Palau Street to Zanglada Street you come across the first of Palma's numerous mansions, famous for their courtyards. The *patio* or courtyard of the **Casa Colom** dates from the 18th century.

Straddling the narrow Almudaina Street is an arch that was once part of the wall of the Arab citadel, and on the same street is the **Casa Oleo** which has a Gothic-style courtyard and stairway. In Morey Street is the **Casa Oleza** which has a 16th-century plateresque façade and a courtyard remodelled in the 18th century. On Pureza Street is the **Museum of Mallorca**, housed in the 17th-century mansion of the Counts of Ayamans. It is a treasure trove of Gothic sculptures, paintings, Arabic ceramics and other artefacts produced by the Moslem and Christian cultures.

Behind the **Museum of Mallorca**, on Serra Street, are the **Arab Baths** whose ceilings are sustained by columns with horseshoe arches. The curious lack of

patio,
a Oleza.

uniformity among the capitals of the columns is due to their having been salvaged from the ruins of other buildings. These baths have two chambers. One, the *calderium*, could be used for steam baths. The other, known as a *tepiderium*, was for lukewarm baths.

Around the corner on Santa Clara Street is a **convent** of the same name which has its original 13th-century cloister and an 18th-century façade. The entrance to the chapel is in the Baroque style.

At the other end of Viento Street is the superb Baroque church of **Montesión** on the street of the same name. It was constructed in the 17th century by the Jesuits. Of special interest inside is a 16th-century reredos depicting scenes from the life of the Virgin Mary, one of the best examples of late-medieval Mallorcan art.

Craft ghetto: This church was built on the site of a synagogue, for this area was laid out as a ghetto during the reign of Jaime II. Under the Moslems the **Jewish quarter** centred around the present Santo Domingo street.

The Jews later moved to two areas: one behind the Lonja and the other between the Plaza Cort and the Plaza Mayor. In the ghetto around Montesión Street they were obliged to wear distinctive garb; their main occupations were handicrafts, medicine, and usuary.

Some of the most important trades practised in this neighbourhood were the manufacture of navigational instruments and cartography. A map of the known world in the 14th century was drawn up by the Jewish cartographers, Abraham and Jafuda Cresques, father and son, at the command of King Pedro the Ceremonious. It was given as a gift to the King of France. After the sacking of the ghetto in 1391, Jafuda Cresques converted to Christianity and took the name of Jaime Ribes. He ended his days working for Henry the Navigator, Prince of Portugal.

On Sol Street is one of the most impressive of Palma's mansions, the **Casa Marqués del Palmer**. It was built in the 16th century and boasts a splendid Plateresque façade, protected from the rain by long, protruding eaves. This street ends in the **Plaza del Temple**, once the site of a monastery-castle of the Knights Templar. Before their suppression in the early 14th century these military monks provided a service for moving money from one part of the Mediterranean to another, a service vital for Palma's success. All that is left of the Templar's redoubt are two Romanesque side-chapels in an oratory. They can be seen by asking the oratory's doorkeeper.

Church of sages: From the Plaza del Temple you may walk up Ramón Llull Street. On the right is a large building which houses the **Archives of the Kingdom of Mallorca**, rich in documents that reveal the history of the Western Mediterranean from the 13th to the 15th centuries. This street ends in the **Plaza de San Francisco**, named after the church that stands on it. Before the church is a statue of Junípero Serra, founder of most of the California missions. He lived in the convent attached to the **church of San Francisco** before

Stone carvings of the church San Francisco.

travelling to the New World.

The foundation stone of the church was laid on 31 January 1281 by King Jaime II. The property was at the time outside the walls of the city, still basically Arab in format. The original façade, part of the nave and two side chapels were demolished by a lightning bolt in 1580. The present façade is a masterful blend of the sheer, stark and massive frontal wall with the exquisitely wrought florid friezework of the portal, completed in the year 1700. Its centrepiece is a great fluted shell harbouring an image of the Virgin surrounded by attendant cherubs. On either side of the Virgin are the great Franciscan Theologian, Duns Scotus, and the local sage, Ramón Llull, holding an open book. The neoclassical pediment flanked by two turrets on the top of the façade is a 19th-century addition.

Inside the church are eight side chapels decorated in the Renaissance and Baroque styles. Of special interest is the Gothic funeral monument to Ramón Llull located in the **Chapel of Our Lady of Consolation**, to the left and behind the main altar. It consists of an alabaster sarcophagus with the sculpted image of the great philosopher raised above seven niches. The statues representing the seven liberal arts meant to fill them were never made; nor were the statues representing theology and philosophy meant to stand on either side of the sarcophagus.

The Baroque main altar is the fruit of a wholesale remodelling of the church in the late 17th and early 18th centuries which replaced the then unfashionable Gothic artwork. On the right side of the nave, facing the main altar, there is a doorway closed by a curtain. It gives access to one of the most marvellous architectural experiences of Palma: a Gothic cloister constructed and elaborated between the 14th and the 17th centuries. A pillared attic was inaugurated as recently as 1960. From one corner of the cloister, the church's main tower looms up, like a minaret.

Skirting what were once the confines of the Moslem city, a small street leads

*eggar
its for
ange on
church
ps.*

from the **Plaza San Francisco** to the **Plaza Santa Eulàlia**. Here stands one of Palma's oldest churches, constructed in the years immediately following the Christian conquest. It was later remodelled in the 14th and 19th centuries.

Best of the *casas*: In the adjoining **Plaza Cort** stands a building completed at the end of the 16th century, although its façade was restored in 1675. It is overhung by eaves supported by wood carvings of caryatids and atlantes, the work of a naval carpenter accustomed to carving the figureheads of ships. Among the valuable paintings in this building is a Saint Sebastian attributed to Van Dyck. Originally constructed to house the autonomous institutions of the Kingdom of Mallorca, this building served its function for a relatively brief time since autonomous rights and usages were abolished in 1715 by the Bourbon dynasty which won the War of the Spanish Succession the year before.

Some other great mansions to look into are the 18th-century **Casa Vivot** on Zavella Street, the **Casa Marqués** on

Apuntadores Street, the **Casa Weyler** on Paz Street, the 17th-century Casa Belloto on San Feliu Street, the Casa **Montenegro** on the street named after it, and the **Casa Sollerich**, which has an impressive Baroque façade, on Cayetano Street.

The most impressive of Palma's buildings dedicated to civilian purposes is **La Lonja** constructed in the 15th century. It was designed by Guillem Sagrera, the master builder responsible for designing the Portal del Mirador of the cathedral and for remodelling the Castel Nuovo in Naples. Seen from the port its four crenallated towers give it the appearance of a castle, but the martial elements in its architecture are merely ornamental. This Gothic building embellished with gargoyles and geometrical motifs served as the stock exchange for Palma's enterprising and prosperous merchants. Inside, the striated heads of the lithe, twisted columns merge with the vaulted roof. The effect is suggestive of a palm grove.

Separated from La Lonja by a small garden is the **Consolat del Mar**. This building was constructed in the 17th century to house the special court for trying disputes among merchants and shipowners. It was a tribunal which helped develop international maritime jurisprudence and was originally located in La Lonja. Its most salient architectural feature is a portioned gallery. The Consolat del Mar is now the seat of the autonomous government of the Balearic Islands.

Nearby are remnants of the walls and fortifications raised around Palma at the end of the 16th century, overlooking the intersection of the **Paseo Marítimo** and **Paseo Mallorca**. But the outstanding military structure of Palma is the **Castle of Bellver**, designed by the same master builder, Pere Salvá, who remodelled the Almudaina Palace. King Jaime II, learning from his father's conquest of Palma from its western approaches, had Bellver built to prevent a repetition of the feat by a foreign invader. Bellver was completed in the first years of the 14th century, and its circular construction is unique in Gothic architecture.

Left, La Lonja. Right, a moment o◀ quiet.

104

THE MALLORCAN SIERRA

The landscape of Mallorca has been likened to an unrolled scroll, and after a brief glance at a map of the island, it is easy to see why. The island has the shape of a rough rectangle, with the Arta mountains rolled up on the southern rim, the flat plain of the *llano* occupying the centre of the island from Palma through to Alcudia, while to the north the upper roll of the scroll is provided by the mountains of the Northern Sierra.

Bushes, boats and bicycles: These mountains regularly surprise first-time visitors to the island. Anyone who explores the Sierra will discover that it is far more than a picturesque backdrop to the plain. These are real mountains, soaring up to 4,740 ft (1,445 metres) at the Puig Major, torn with *arroyos*—or gulleys—carpeted with thorn bushes, tough country for walking, with rock too friable to climb, but ideal for bird-life, for plants and for large numbers of feral goats. Here are small towns and attractive villages, very different from the tourist developments and the coast.

To explore the Sierra you need a car, or better still a bicycle, or better still— if time permits—a stout pair of boots for walks into those regions which are and will remain impenetrable to any form of wheeled transport.

Beyond the dubious delights of **Magalluf** the three resorts of **Paguera**, **Santa Ponsa** and **Puerto de Andratx**, are just far enough from Palma to avoid the worst of the summer crowds. Here are sheltered coves and beaches and adequate bays providing objectives and moorings for the offshore yachtsman, combined with elements of history. The troops of Jaime I of Aragón landed on the beach at Santa Ponsa when they took the kingdom of Mallorca in 1229.

Somewhere different, a hint of what is to come, is the sheltered harbour of Puerto de Andratx, in an almost completely enclosed bay. This is a real touch of old Mallorca, and like Puerto de Pollença in the north, was once the fishing port and harbour for the old town of

Andratx which lies three miles inland. From Andratx there is a short but pleasant drive west to the headland at **La Mola**, north to the little hamlet of Sant Elm, or **San Telmo**, a road marked with green on the Firestone map to indicate a picturesque route. Sant Elm, the Mallorquín name, is the most western resort on the island and has good views out to **Isla Dragonera**, an uninhabited island that is the focus of arguments between ecologists and developers.

Heartlands: The main route across the Sierra is the C-710, which runs as close to the coastal cliffs as possible. Inland, the back country has been opened up by a scanty but adequate network of minor roads, all narrow, lined with stone walls, very winding and steep on the mountainous sections, perhaps not a good choice for large cars or nervous drivers. One of the most winding of these roads runs from Andratx through Sa Coma to **Capdellá** and then turns north-east towards **Galilea** (rapidly becoming an artist's colony) and **La Granja**, which is partly Moorish and

once belonged to the Cistercian monks. This road skirts the side of the Puig de Na Bauçá, which rises to more than 2,000 ft (614 metres) at the Bauçá peak, and therefore twists and turns relentlessly up and over to the road junctions at Son Net and Puigpunyent.

From this last point there is a short, one-mile (two-kilometre) walk north up a narrow track to the 17th-century mansion at the aptly named **Son Forteza**, on the slopes of yet another steep-sided mountain, the Puig Galatzó, (3,362 ft, 1,025 metres) which skirts the road to the left all the way down to La Granja and the large village of **Esporles**, which has a 13th-century church and straggles along both sides of a dry stream bed. The country house at La Granja is open to the public and provides a fascinating cross-section of what life on this baronial scale must have been like.

Headlands: A circular route, combining the outward journey on the road described above with a return to Andratx on the C-710, incorporates a truly delightful route along the coast. To achieve this, turn left at the junction with the C-710, towards **Banyalbufar** through the pine forest, or—and this too would be ideal—take the small road directly ahead down to the little *puerto* of **Canonge**, which is quite tiny and as yet untouched by tourism. Then, back on the main road, head west through Banyalbufar and along this swinging, winding road, well supplied with coaches, to Estellencs. Here and there are *miradors*, or viewpoints, each with a parking lot, each offering great views out to sea and along the coast.

Banyalbufar itself is set among green terraced fields and has several restaurants and bars and a pleasant beach. A little west of here lies one of the older *miradors*, the **Mirador de Ses Animes**, which has a tower and was once a place from which the local people kept watch for pirates and the Barbary corsairs who raided their islands relentlessly until the early years of the 19th century. This tower can be climbed and gives good views along the coast.

Weatherwo
door.

West of **Estellencs**, which lies among orange groves at the southern foot of Puig Galatzó (climbable with a guide or good directions), the road resumes that winding, rising and falling motion, which should be taken as the norm, there is yet another *mirador*, the **Mirador de Roca**, and therefore more great views to either side before the road finally descends to the shelter of Andratx in the valley of the Rio Salmet, which is usually dry as a bone in the summer months but a real torrent throughout the other seasons.

Here, in the western end of the Northern Sierra there are more spider's web-like roads to follow, skirting the northeastern suburbs of Palma through the village of **Calvia**, the administrative centre of the enormously prosperous tourist coast below, climbing up and over the hills to **Establiments**, where George Sand and Chopin lived before moving to Valldemossa. They lead to nowhere in particular, but they take the traveller to small Mallorcan villages which are light-years away from the urban delights of Palma or the modern tourist developments around the coast.

Key route: The second foray into the Sierra takes in some larger and more popular places, but here again there is a choice of route and plenty of possibilities for circular journeys. Beginning in Palma the C-711 leads out through **Bunyola** (literally "small vineyard") in the foothills of the Sierra, past the exotic Moorish gardens of Alfábia. This road marks the eastern boundary of this journey, climbing over the hills from the Bunyola junction to the town of **Sóller**, which has a 16th-century church and many pleasant squares and side streets and claims along with several other places to be the birthplace of Columbus.

Those who dislike driving in the mountains (and this requires great concentration) can make this journey by train from Palma, a very agreeable excursion, especially when combined with the tram ride from Sóller down through orange groves to the fishing port and harbour at **Puerto de Sóller**, three miles (five km) away. Having a

ie Sóller
am (left)
nd
astline.

DEIA: PORTRAIT OF AN ARTIST'S COLONY

The village church and cemetery of Deià rise above the valley on a hill called Es Puig, 692 ft (211 metres) above the sea. Tile roofed, stone houses, with wooden shuttered windows, arbours of grape vines, bougainvilleas and morning glories, surrounded by palm, olive and almond trees are clustered together along the hill-side, bordering the main Palma to Sóller road and descending into the valley down to the sea and cove below. As long ago as 1878 a guidebook noted of Deià that, "One of its chief characteristics is its collection of strange and eccentric foreigners." It still is.

British poet and writer Robert Graves was the main figurehead of the artist's colony that gathered at Deià from 1929 until his death in 1985. His prolific writing attracted poets and writers who bought or rented houses. Poetry readings and theatre productions were organised and presented in the small amphitheatre built into the hills below his house.

In the early 1970s a number of British hippy bands settled in Deià and added a new dimension to the foreigners.

Deià is the home or holiday spot for internationally known writers, artists, and actors from other parts of Mallorca, mainland Spain, England, Germany, Austria, France, the Americas, Australia, New Zealand and China. Narcis Serra, the Spanish Minister of Defence has spent his holidays in Deià. Archaeological excavations have added a prehistoric dimension and the Deià Music Festival organises a series of concerts for international audiences throughout the summer season.

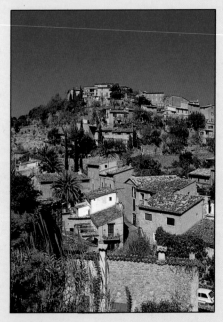

The rock star Kevin Ayres still lives in the village and teams up with local and foreign musicians to bring a bit of live music to the bars on Saturday nights. Other well known pop musicians have become regular visitors since Richard Branson of Virgin Records bought an interest in the Hotel La Residencia. But no single name or activity has given Deià and its residents, local or foreign, a new direction or personality to replace Robert Graves. Even in death Graves continues to draw admirers to Deià and his simple burial place

in the local cemetery has fresh flowers put on it by family and visitors almost every day.

Mallorquín or English is the *lingua franca* of Deià's foreign colony. Locals and foreigners can be found drinking side by side at any of the three bars. Some local men sit at Paco's Bar playing *truc* or *tutti*, the two most popular card games in Mallorca. The village mayor, a young man in his late twenties, sometimes plays opposite his political rivals. Local political opinion is based more on family associations than on party platforms and the majority of Deià voters support the families that have always been in power.

The Deià of today is only a romantic illusion of the agricultural village of the past where peasants welcomed foreigners and accepted their eccentricities without question. Since 1980, Deià prices have tripled each year. Foreigners are competing to buy houses with sea views and few modern conveniences for £150,000. Increased house prices have altered the inheritance patterns, the community structure and the social relations between locals and foreigners. Local people can no longer afford to buy a house in their native village, and nor can struggling artists afford to live in Deià any more.

The setting is the same but the magic is harder to find. In its place there is a show of flamboyance, fashion and frivolity. Everything in Deià during the summer season is expensive, crowded, colourful and slightly exotic compared to other areas of the island. The small quaint *pensions* and the two four-star hotels are completely booked and every empty house is rented. On the week-ends the rock and pebble covered cove is filled, cars line both sides of the street from the beginning to the end of the village, the nine restaurants are packed and the cafés brimming with people.

Long-term foreign residents see progress only as destructive to the idyllic setting they so admire. Locals want to open the village to more investment which will produce jobs, housing and livelihoods for their children and grandchildren.

Visitors may confuse long-term foreigners with natives. The latter are the ones who wear skirts or shirts made of local "vichy" materials, *espadrilles* (rope-soled shoes) and straw hats while the locals wear Levis, Lacoste and Gucci.

car will allow a visit to the village of Biniaraix, east of Sóller, a charming little place, quite unspoilt by tourism.

The custom of having the town inland and the harbour on the coast, as here at Sóller and Puerto de Sóller, common in Mallorca, is caused by two factors. Firstly, the inland site is flatter and therefore permitted the development of a larger town than the cliff-surrounded harbour, but more important in the time of the town's foundation were the activities of the Moorish and Barbary corsairs, who kept the inhabitants of the Balearic Islands on the defensive for centuries. It was simpler and safer to build a town some distance inland, away from the dangerous coast. Puerto de Sóller occupies one side of the perfect harbour, a compact bay almost completely encircled by mountains, which is now a popular tourist resort, full of small hotels, bars and restaurants, with villas dotting the slopes of the surrounding hills and plenty of smaller roads and tracks leading out to the **Mirador de la Atalaya**, another viewpoint, or the lighthouse on the Cabo Gros to the west.

Artists' quarters: West along the coast is the small town of **Deià**, an artist's and writer's town, most famous as the home of Robert Graves. On first sight, and indeed on closer acquaintance, Deià seems a rather strange town to find in Mallorca, for it has a distinctly French, even a Provençal feel about it, which might explain why Miró enjoyed coming here. The main road through the middle acts as an artery to a score of narrow, winding streets, some cobbled, all steep, with geraniums in window-boxes and everywhere the sight or sound of water. There is a small but interesting **archaeological museum**, and Robert Graves lies buried in the churchyard on the hill. From Deià there is a track to the sea at the Cala de Deià and once up and round the main bend, a narrower track between the C-710 and the sea, which runs out to the rocky peninsula at Grutas, the location of the dramatic **Na Foradada** cave. At **Son Marroig** the old estate of the Archduke Luis

Salvador of Austria is now a museum combining the Archduke's own collection and Mallorcan crafts; the temple in the garden was for the better enjoyment of the Mallorcan sunset.

This section of the C-710 is designated as a picturesque route, well supplied with viewpoints and parking places, each with its little bar or café, all the way to **Valldemossa**. **La Cartuja** was a monastery owned and largely built by the Carthusians. When the monkish orders were expelled from Spain in 1835, the new owners began renting rooms to travellers, which is how Chopin and George Sand came to spend the winter here in 1838-39. Coaches pile in every day, bringing tourists to visit their apartments, which contain Chopin's piano, his death-mask and some original manuscripts and scores. That apart, the monastery is a beautiful building, set among orange groves. Chopin and Sand together eclipse the fact that Mallorca's Saint, Catalina Thomas, was born here. Sand herself is not particularly well-liked on the island thanks to the unflattering picture of the place she painted in *A Winter in Mallorca*. It rained a lot (reflected in the fact that it was here Chopin composed *Raindrop Prelude*) and she considered the Mallorquíns a lot of country idiots. For their side they disliked her for her long trousers and her cigarette smoking, and because she was living with a man who was not her husband. Chopin felt ill a lot of the time.

Birds and botany: The real attraction of these journeys through the Sierra remains the mountains themselves, and the third leg of these travels takes the visitor into the hills again, up to the east of the island, from Sóller to Lluc and Pollença. On this leg of the journey the mountains reach their highest points, at Puig Major (4,740 ft, 1,445 metres), now topped by the great, round golf-balls of the radar tracking and communications centre, Puig de Tossals (3,438 ft, 1,048 metres), and high over Pollença towers the great hump of Puig Tomir. This is the great walking, bird-watching and botanic area of Mallorca,

for the mountains hereabouts are seamed with old tracks, often mule tracks, and littered with abandoned farms, providing perfect habitat for a whole range of plants and birds.

The faithful C-710 veers inland after Sóller, and begins to climb into some very wild and rugged mountain country. Two places worth a diversion here, are the **Mirador de Ses Barques**, which gives stunning views over Sóller, and the beautiful village of **Fornalutx**, which is even prettier than Deià and hardly visited by tourists. There are, as usual, plenty of stopping places and viewpoints, but as the road enters the highest point, the Sierra de Torrellas, it cuts so deeply into the hillside that here and there it requires tunnels. The high point here is the **Coll de Puig Major**, a pass at 3,399 ft (1,036 metres) which is followed by the great reservoir or *embalse* of **Cúber**, a great place for birds and birdwatchers.

Beside the lake a track climbs away to the south, to the *finca* of **Comasema** and eventually via **Sollerich** rejoins the C-710 a little east of the starting point at **S'Estret**, a good full-day excursion for a healthy and suitably-shod walker.

From the lake, which tends to dry out somewhat in summer, the road forges east past yet another great dam, the **Embalse de Gorg Blau**, built in 1971, from where a minor road swings off north on one of those more necessary excursions down to the beaches at **Sa Calobra** (noted for its Mallorcan cuisine) and **Cala Tuent**. Mallorca is full of breathtaking places but few can match and none exceed the beauty of the beach and rocks at Sa Calobra at the seaward end of the gorge of the twin-streamed **Torrente de Pareis**, and it is more than probable that anyone who has come this far to Sa Calobra, driving gingerly over the road from Gorg Blau, will decide to stay here for the rest of the day, and may even return tomorrow. It can be crowded.

Pilgrimage: East of the Sa Calobra turn, the road plunges into the hills again to the monastery at **Lluc** (literally "sacred forest"). Lluc owes its origins to a seventh-century miracle, when a shepherd saw an image of the Virgin in the sky, and the image later appeared on the rock of Lluc, where a chapel was built to contain it. Interestingly the Virgin of Lluc, a statue dating from the 14th century and known as La Moreneta, is dark-skinned. The Virgin's crown was stolen a few years ago but recovered from the sea by fishermen. The present monastery dates from the 17th and 18th centuries, and the church was only finished in 1724. It is possible to stay overnight in the monastery, and even today, pilgrims flock to the Virgin of Lluc, often making the journey on foot overnight from Palma to arrive at dawn. 50,000 made the pilgrimage in 1987. Lluc has its own resident community of a dozen priests, 50 boys and 30 employees; the boys are members of Los Blauets choir and give regular concerts.

From here on the C-710 road, though outstandingly beautiful, is rather too full of cars and even worse, coaches. Get off this too-well-beaten track by following the road from Lluc towards

Inca, crossing the Sierra from north to south, down to the town of Selva, a fine little town on a hill. From here, pick minor roads to explore this section of the Sierra, driving through **Lloseta**, which lies in the southern foothills, and then round to the little mountain village of **Alaró**, which is rarely visited but quite unspoiled and rather beautiful. A narrow road runs out north of Alaró in a great sweep round the hills past the old castle, the **Castillo d'Alaró**, to the village of Orient, and so eventually back to Bunyola. The Castillo was defended by as few as two people during the 1285 Conquest of Mallorca by Alfonso of Aragón. When they were finally captured they were killed slowly and horribly by the angry king, and consequently now rate as great figures in Mallorcan history. It is a 45 minute walk to the plateau on the top of the Castillo.

Enclosed within this circuit of roads is the central Sierra and it would not be fair to leave this area without stressing how excellent it is for hill-walking and birdwatching. The terrain is rough, so boots are essential, but the rewards, in spectacular views, rare birds and empty hill-sides, more than make up for the effort. The best way to complete this journey is to return via Inca to the monastery at Lluc and pick up the C-710 from there. Just past Lluc, near the 17 km stone, a road leads up into the hills to the mineral springs at **Binifaldó**, where a factory bottles the water for the island bars and restaurants. There is parking by the spring and from there a steep, scrambling path leads up to the domed top of **Puig Tomir** (3,619 ft, 1,103 metres), from where a great panorama of the island lies all about, from Inca to the Cabo del Pinar.

Northern tip: Back on more or less level ground, the road continues to **Pollença**, on the Torrente Sant Jordi, the river of St George. From Pollença there are many good walks, but one easy excursion by road is to the little resort of **Cala San Vicente**, and from there to the ruins of the Castell del Rei, once a stronghold and refuge of Mallorcan kings, although little remains today.

Lluc monastery

The mountains hereabouts are now sharp, serrated peaks, a relic of the Jurassic period, and look very striking as they thin out towards the long stem of the Formentor Peninsula.

Puerto de Pollença has changed a great deal in the last twenty years, from a small fishing port with a few hotels and a small number of select villas with an art-orientated population, to a major tourist town, well supplied with apartment blocks and an ever-growing number of bars and restaurants. At one time (1922) the British navy concentrated in this port, and today many of the yachts are British and German.

From Puerto de Pollença a narrow road sweeps up the northern side of the bay to yet another *mirador*, the **Mirador d'es Colomer**, and winds down past the little island of Colomer to the sprawling and famous **Hotel Formentor**, one of the world's great hotels. It was first opened in 1926 and announced the fact to the world at large with flashing advertisements on the Eiffel Tower. Since then it has been visited by all the great and the good, Winston Churchill, Grace Kelly, Aristotle Onassis and the like, and appeared in at least one feature film. It is possible to reach the beach of the Hotel Formentor by ferry from the harbour in Puerto de Pollença, a journey which makes a popular excursion for summer visitors.

The Playa de Formentor is a classic spot, with a sandy beach for the beautiful people, a large cluster of expensive yachts moored offshore, and a hillside dotted with exclusive villas. From the Hotel the road forges on, up and over, through the pine forest to the very tip of the Sierra at the **Cabo Formentor**, where there is a large lighthouse and a small souvenir shop.

From Puerto de Pollença a wide road sweeps around the Bahia de Pollença to **Alcudia**, an ancient, even antique town, with Greek origins, Roman ruins and medieval walls. Alcudia was a successful port from the second century B.C. until the sixth century A.D., when it was destroyed by the Vandals. There is a good market on Sunday mornings and occasional fights in the old bull-ring. From here another road probes into that rocky peninsula that forms the southern shore of Pollença bay, out to the **Cabo Pinar**, with a side-road leading up to the Ermita de la Victoria, which was a monastery and is now a popular restaurant. In the resort area of Puerto de Alcudia developers have created a more interesting than usual collection of architectural styles.

Back: The best return route to Palma is along the straight and dangerous main road, the C-713, from which there is one final diversion to the great caves at **Campanet**. These are full of stalactites and stalagmites, lit with coloured lights, a very different sort of scene from that one can enjoy elsewhere in the hot yet breezy mountains of the beautiful Northern Sierra.

If time is short, the essential places are inevitably the popular ones: Valldemossa, Sóller, Deià, Sa Calobra, Lluc, Pollença, Alcudia, but to really get to grips with the Sierra, the smaller places, La Granja, Biniaraix, Alaró, Bunyola, simply have to be seen as well.

e
rmentor
ninsula
ar Es
Iomer.

CABRERA, ISLAND WILDERNESS

It seems that the interval between Cabrera's appearance in the headlines keeps getting shorter as the debate about its future gets increasingly heated. The arguments have little to do with the island's history, and the few tourists and sailors who reach the archipelago's unspoilt shoreline find it hard to imagine that this, one of the few untouched areas in the Mediterranean, was once an authentic inferno.

Until the beginning of the 19th century, the history of Cabrera and the dozen islets which surround it had been like that of most other Mediterranean islands lying in the shade of a much larger sister island. In good years the island was occupied by various generations of farmers who cultivated its fields and shepherded flocks of goats and sheep for the island's owners. It was the destination for fishermen who came to its fertile waters to fill their nets, and it also served as a base for pirates planning their pillages of Mallorca as well as those trying to protect her coasts which lay a few scant kilometres to the north.

Prison island: The early years of the 19th century were difficult ones in Europe. Napoleon marched towards the four corners of the continent followed by a proud army unprepared for the humiliation of their first full-scale defeat at the hands of the Spanish at the Battle of Bailén.

In 1808, the defeated soldiers were confined in eight prison ships anchored in the Bay of Cádiz. Weakened by disease and threatened by a hostile local population, plans were made to transfer them to a safer keep. The original idea was to transfer them to Mallorca but the island had no facility for the large contingent of thousands of officers and men. A year later, they stepped ashore on the tiny uninhabited island of Cabrera.

What actually happened to "Prissonier N130 1810", who carved this inscription high on a castle wall, and his 9,000 Napoleonic companions will probably never be truly known. But we know that upon their arrival on this harsh island their first inventory must have been no more than a short list of one or two ploughed fields, a small pine forest, a few goats and fig trees, a well with little water, a *burro* (donkey) and a ruined castle.

The castle, which was constructed in the 14th century to fight against pirates, became the centre of their first improvised camp. At first no one thought of Cabrera as being home for more than a short stay. Charles Frossard, an imprisoned officer, tells of how "we lived in grottos and caverns" until crude barracks were erected.

Rats for tea: Their plans looked ahead only as far as the next provision boat which arrived from Mallorca every four days carrying sparse rations. Eventually rats and robbers made it necessary to distribute the rations immediately upon their arrival. As was to be expected, the hungry undisciplined soldier ate the meagre food supply of one pound of bad bread, one-quarter ounce

of beans and a half ounce of oil, within hours of its arrival. The officers fared slightly better with an additional half pound of goat meat and a quart of wine. An account by chronicler Abate Turquet tells of how in the desperation for food "a mouse could be bought for seven or eight beans, a rat, for 25 or 30."

The officers began to make contact with the British who arrived on vessels escorting the food boats. It gave them the "courage to carry on a little commerce, selling hand-carved wooden cutlery to the Spanish," explained Turquet. In the following years communication with the English and Spanish grew but the hunger and starvation continued. Because of the poor rations and with almost no water, officer Frossard wrote that, "sickness became the biggest enemy. We hoped for a remedy (by drinking) salt water. But the cure is worse than the disease, and those who drink it die quicker." The death toll was immense.

In May of 1814, five years after they had arrived, the 3,600 men who survived out of the original 9,000 were taken by boat to the south coast of France. Most of them remained in Marseille until their deaths, unwanted by a French government embarrassed by both its debacle at Bailén and its own lack of care. Thirty years later a monument was erected on a pine-covered hillside overlooking Puerto Cabrera in rememberance of the more than 5,000 prisoners who never returned. It reads: "A la memoire des Français Morts à Cabrera" and is signed "His Royal Highness the Prince of Joinville."

The tragedy of the prisoners of Cabrera is all but forgotten, lost in the island's more recent history. In 1916 the islands were expropriated by the Spanish government and converted into a military zone. In the 1980s the maintenance of a small garrison of soldiers on Cabrera is out of touch with modern strategic necessity and the Mallorquíns have lobbied long and hard for its return to once again become a part of the local patrimony.

Rarities in isolation: Cabrera is a small

Puerto Cabrera.

island. The highest point is a hill called Picamoscas (meaning fly's bite) of 564 ft (172 metres). And apart from the good-weather flotilla of yachtsmen who anchor in any of its four or five safe anchorages during the summer weekends, the only inhabitants are a few soldiers and an army of black Lilford lizards *(Lacerta lilfordi)*. Because of its *zona militar* status which keeps the developers and tourists at bay, three subspecies of the reptiles which are not known to exist anywhere else in the world have survived on Cabrera.

In the unpolluted skies over Cabrera fly such species as the peregrine falcon and an important colony of the near extinct Audouin gulls. Near the sky-scraping cliffs of the islet l'Imperial, off the southeast coast of the main island, patience may even bring a sighting of a rare Eleanora's falcon.

Submarine biologists believe that the state of preservation of the underwater environment around the islands is such that species which may be found at depths of 65 ft (20 metres) off the main-land coast of Spain are often encountered here in only six or nine feet of water. Biologists have been searching for traces of the once common monk seal with long-term thoughts of trying to reintroduce the species.

Park proposal: The same idea has been reiterated recently in a Mallorcan parliamentary proposal to convert the islands into a national park. Its proposed preserve status will guarantee the island's future for everyone, and everything. Basically the plan calls for immediate cessation of all military activity, severely limiting fishing rights to a few professional "artisan" fishermen (no sport fishing will be allowed), opening the large island to controlled scientific and historically orientated tours and limiting the number of sailing and pleasure craft allowed within the surrounding waters at any one time.

It is surprising that the proposal is for Cabrera to become a "national" park and not a provincial one. The official reason, says Sr Joan Mayol, the parliamentary member of the drafting political party and chief of the Balearic government's wildlife unit, is that the Cabrera Archipelago is too important to be only a provincial entity. The unofficial reason is that the large budget needed to support the plan is far too ambitious.

Wilderness status: For the first time in many years the island's future shows a hint of a silver lining. With its pending status as a national park, its importance as one of the last remaining wilderness areas in the Mediterranean is finally being declared. The years of environmental misuse by the military have a chance of being rectified. The proposal, which still is awaiting detailed administrative planning, will assure that both the residents and the visitors will have access to an area which has been off limits to us all for more than half a century. In one respect the Mallorquíns have regained their island. But, maybe more important, because of the persistence of a few interested local people, the world has gained another place where man is not allowed to run rampant with his bulldozers.

**proaching
e prison
and.**

THE MALLORCAN PLAIN

The island of Mallorca is formed like a half-rolled rug: at the northwest edge the Mallorcan Sierra is the roll that never fully unravelled, while the plain—the well-trodden carpet—stretches out from the foothills across to the eastern shore.

Pricked with dilapidated windmills which look from above to all intents and purposes like angry, broken stings from some giant wasp, the Mallorcan plain is the agricultural and industrial heartland of the island. At first sight it is not just geographically, but also visually plain.

The towns contain few houses of quality, few fine courtyards, and the prevailing vistas are of long, narrow streets with doors and shutters closed. However, there are many occasions where the spare elements of street, church and plaza come together in a memorable way.

This is the land for the impact of the seasons. In mid-February the blossom of seven million almond trees covers the island in a delicate, low-lying white cloud. Jacaranda, oleander and bougainvillea dominate the summer colouring, and are joined in autumn by flowering vines and pampas grass.

Dominating the plain are four high points, each with a hilltop sanctuary which has played a significant part in Mallorcan history and which provide natural focal points for this chapter. These are the Santuario de San Salvador near Felanitx; the Santuario de San Salvador within the Almudaina at Artá; the Santuario de Santa Magdalena near Inca and the Santuario de Nuestra Señora de Cura at Randa.

East Coast: The bulk of the bluff and the massive building of the **Santuario de San Salvador** near Felanitx are best seen from the Manacor road, and equally impressive are the views from the sanctuary, particularly towards Porto Colom. Menorca is visible on particularly clear days. The building was started in 1348 and continued up until the 1930s, when the immense statue of

Christ was completed. In the chapel a magnificent Gothic carved stone altarpiece is, unusually for Mallorca, lit by a helpful spotlight.

It is not easy to penetrate to the centre of **Felanitx** through its one-way system but the effort is justified by the sight of the church of San Miguel (12th and 17th centuries), built of golden Santanyí stone. Unlike most churches of inland towns this one is normally open and the interior, which boasts a spectacular organ, is cathedral-like in concept but retains the feel of a parish church. Outside, a memorial tablet commemorates 414 people who were killed by the collapse of a wall in 1844.

The distinctive pottery of Ceramics Mallorca is made and hand-painted in Felanitx. For some reason the company does little to attract custom: their smart modern showroom and adjoining factory (which may be visited) are located in a nondescript new estate. Ask for directions, as this fine pottery is unique to Mallorca. Miguel Barceló, one of Spain's most successful young artists,

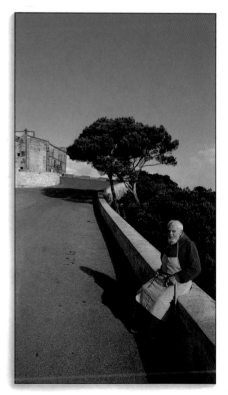

eceding
ges:
ntuiri, in
central
in. Left, a
nple
urtyard.
ght, the
nctuario
San
vador.

was born in Felanitx and still maintains a studio here.

Manacor is the nearest thing Mallorca has to an industrial town. Busy, prosperous and unattractive, there is really only one reason for stopping here: pearls. The principal manufacturer is the world-famous Majorica who have an excellent modern showroom on the main road into Manacor from Palma. The sales staff are helpful, and the best of these simulated pearls are a high-quality product at a high price. At the peak of the tourist season four or five thousand people visit the nearby Majorica factory every day. Not surprisingly the company does not give away any secrets of pearl manufacture—said to be based on "natural essences extracted from marine species of the Mediterranean warm waters", otherwise claimed to be made from powdered fish scale—on this perfunctory tour, which can easily be omitted.

Coastal coves: The east coast of Mallorca is rightly renowned for its coves and inlets and even the most general map will identify 50 or more. Many have small developments of little character which meet the needs of short-stay vacationers, but there are also some locations on the coast that have historical significance. **Porto Cristo**, an ancient fishing port, was the site of the island's only Civil War action. In August 1936 the Republican battleship *Jaime I* landed some 12,000 men here; they took the town and advanced six miles (10 km) inland but the Nationalist forces already in occupation drove them back with the help of Italian warplanes which were based near Palma. After three weeks it was all over.

Nearby two sets of caves attract quantities of summer visitors. The **Cuevas del Drach** are well-presented and impressive. A visit includes a boat trip across the large underground Lake Martel (named after the Frenchman who first surveyed these caves in 1896). The **Cuevas del Hams** are notable for their colourful formations.

South of the insensitive hotel developments at **Calas de Mallorca** are nu-

Pearls, produced industrially in Manacor

merous walking tracks to tiny rocky bays, some with pocket-handkerchief beaches. **Porto Colom** has retained much of its character and prettiness. Old houses and fishermens' huts face the harbour and often are reflected in the mirror-like water, so well protected is this port from the open sea. Controlled tourist development is contained near the attractive beach of **Cala Marçal**.

Unfortunately **Cala D'Or** has not survived so well. Once a charming small resort, its natural resources have been developed beyond their absorbtive capacity, yet the construction mindlessly goes on. Finally **Porto Petro**, from where the golden Santanyí stone was exported to Italy, has a restorative effect because it retains something of the air of a small fishing port.

Artá Peninsula: The second of the four sanctuaries on the plain is built above the town of Artá, on Moorish foundations. To the northwest is the Ermita de Betlem standing at 1,247 ft (380 metres) atop the Serra de Llevant, a modest sanctuary reached only by a tortuous road from Artá. **Betlem** itself is a small urban development whose main feature is an imitation English bowling green on astro-turf.

The Artá peninsula differs from the rest of the island in that farmhouses are fewer and more substantial. The land is pleasantly varied with valleys, plains and semi-mountainous heights, and is intensely cultivated under vineyards, fig, almond and carob trees.

In **Artá** itself the streets, spangled with small squares and dotted with fine town houses, are serried against the massive rock on which the original Moorish fortification was constructed. In one of the squares, the Plaza España, stands the Town Hall and, in a building of great elegance, the **Museum of Artá**. The archaeological exhibition inside is well displayed but appallingly annotated. The principal exhibits are said to be alternatively five or three second-century bronze statuettes, depending on the informant, but when this author visited there were only two.

The Catalan-Gothic bulk of the par-

**aterfront,
rto Cristo.**

FAMOUS SONS: JUNIPERO SERRA

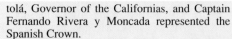

Miguel José Serra was born in 1713 in a humble house in Petrá, Mallorca, which still exists and may be visited. He was baptised in the nearby parish church and began his religious studies at the Convent of San Bernadino just across the road from his birthplace. From this constrained background—a visit to Palma, 22 miles (35 km) away must have seemed an adventure—came the man who pioneered the settlement of large tracts of California, the man whose statue the State of California chose to stand in the American Hall of Fame on the Capitol in Washington D.C.

Serra was received into the order of St Francis in 1730 and changed his name to Junípero. For a time he was Professor of Theology at the Llulliana University of Mallorca. His application to become a missionary was granted and he arrived at the port of Veracruz in Mexico on 7 December 1749. A 300-mile (480-km) trek brought Serra and his companions to Mexico City where they celebrated Mass on New Year's Day 1750.

Serra spent about 18 years preaching and converting at the Mission of Sierra Gorda and in Mexico City and its dioceses. He was 54 when he was given the task that would occupy him for the rest of his life and which led, in effect, to the creation of the State of California.

Britain, Spain and Russia had all become interested in the west coast of the North American continent. In the 16th century Sir Francis Drake had piloted the *Golden Hind* along parts of this shore and named the land New Albion; Cabrillo and Cermeno had surveyed it for Spain and in 1603 Sebastián Vizcaino had discovered the Bay of Monterey and named the settlements of San Diego and Santa Barbara.

None of these early explorations was consolidated but in 1768 Carlos III decreed that Spain should establish herself in these territories. The well-tried formula of the Cross of Christ and the Crown of Spain—missionaries and military working together—was again employed. Father Serra carried the Cross and Don Gaspar de Por-

tolá, Governor of the Californias, and Captain Fernando Rivera y Moncada represented the Spanish Crown.

The expedition suffered appalling privations, sickness and death, it is probable that, but for Father Serra's profound and unshakeable faith, it would have been abandoned.

The journal of the travellers testify that this Franciscan father from Mallorca was unwilling even to contemplate the possibility that his faith would not enable him to succeed—and he was eventually proved right. Between 1769 and 1782 nine Missions, from San Diego de Alcalá to San Francisco de Asís were founded and established under Serra's presidency; 12 more were built after his death in 1784. But by 1822 California was part of Mexico, and both had been lost to Spain. The Crown had not triumphed but the Cross most certainly had. Today the Missions and their influence remain.

There is still a question mark over Father Serra's attitude to the Californian Indians he sought to convert to Christianity. It was undoubtedly paternalistic (in both a religious and non-religious sense—they were taught simple agricultural and construction techniques as well as the Bible) and it was probably also insensitive and even cruel in that he apparently gave little importance to the Indians' indigenous culture and beliefs. But this is a judgement of hindsight; we can scarcely condemn an 18th-century priest for attitudes in missionary work that are still persistent and troublesome throughout the modern world and at the end of the 20th century, in both political and religious contexts.

Walking today in the same streets of Petrá that Miguel José Serra knew 250 years ago, one wonders how much his parents, or his friends and other Franciscans of his generation, heard of his activities in the New World. Even if news did travel from California to Mexico City to Madrid and to Mallorca, it is doubtful if anyone in Petrá at that time could have understood the size and significance of Serra's achievements. Even today it isn't easy to comprehend them.

Serra's beatification was achieved in 1988 and no doubt owed much to the advocacy of the American Catholic Church.

ish church of the Transfiguration, further up the hill, is impressive from a distance but not attractive at close quarters. Steep steps lead to the Almudaina, a 14th-century fortress which protects the church of San Salvador and a hermitage rebuilt in the 19th century. Among the interesting pictures within is one of the death of Ramón Llull at the hands of a Muslim mob in North Africa, although there is now evidence that he simply died of old age in Mallorca.

Old stone, new stone: Nearby is the well preserved prehistoric (circa 1000 - 800 B.C.) village of **Ses Paisses**, and the **Cuevas de Artá** are on the coast to the east. The latter are probably the most spectacular of the caves along this seaboard and have a place in history. During his 13th-century conquest of the island Jaime I found 2,000 Arabs hiding in the caves with their cattle. Celebrity tourists such as Alexandre Dumas, Sarah Bernhardt and Victor Hugo wrote about them in the 19th century, and they are said to have inspired Jules Verne to write *Journey to the Centre of the Earth*.

Near Artá the crenellated walls and towers of the medieval fortress of **Capdepera** stand largely intact. At the highest point is a small 14th-century oratory, and the fortress walls offer a good view of **Cala Ratjada**, a tasteful resort-town popular with German tourists although its best restaurant, Ses Rotjes, offers authentic French cuisine and is one of the few in Mallorca to receive a rosette from the hard-to-please Michelin inspectors.

Nearby, among the hibiscus bushes in the grounds of what was once one of the homes of Mallorca's richest son, **Juan March**, are placed outstanding examples of modern sculpture. Artists such as Hepworth, Moore, Caro, Chillida, Corberó and Berrocal are represented here, and there is also an orchid house ablaze with vivid colours. (Visits by arrangement with Cala Ratjada tourist information office).

The sizeable beach at **Canyamel**, to the south, is prettily set in a bay backed by high cliffs. However Canyamel's impressive 14th-century tower, once a

FAMOUS SONS: RAMON LLULL

Ramón Llull's claim to be considered Mallorca's most famous son is based equally on his profound scholarship and his zeal for the conversion of Arabs and Africans to the Christian faith. He studied and wrote extensively, mastered the Arabic language, founded a School of Oriental Studies near Valldemossa and journeyed great distances through Europe, through the Middle East and in Africa.

When one considers that these activities belonged to the 13th century and to a man who was not called to his faith until his fortieth year, the immensity of his achievement comes quickly into focus.

For the first part of his life Ramón Llull was just a rich young man-about-town whose father held office at the court of Jaime II of Mallorca. He married and had two children but then scandalised Palma society by falling in love with a married woman and, so legend has it, pursuing her on horseback into the Church of Santa Eulàlia, in the old part of the town, where it still stands.

It is not reliably established what caused his sudden commitment to the Church but once the decision was made he implemented it with vigour and clear-minded determination. Having decided that the conversion of infidels and unbelievers should henceforth occupy his life, he began systematically to prepare himself. He visited many holy places in Europe, spent time at the universities of Montpellier and Paris and then returned to Mallorca—to a hermitage on the Puig de Randa—to study the Arabic language with the help of a Moorish slave he had bought specifically for that purpose.

At the age of about 60 Llull considered himself ready for his great work and began a series of journeys to the Middle East and to Africa as far as Ethiopia and the Sudan. It is believed that, some 20 years later in 1315, on one of these missions, he was stoned to death by a Muslim mob near Tunis in North Africa and his remains were brought back to Palma by a Genoese merchantman. However more recent evidence suggests that he in fact died in Mallorca of old age.

It is not altogether clear from accounts of Llull's life (or, at least, from those translated into English) precisely what he accomplished during his two decades of travelling and conversion, or how deep-rooted and long-lasting any success proved to be.

What is not in doubt, however, is the richness of the legacy he left in his writing. His 6,000 proverbs ran to 460 pages when translated into Spanish and printed in 1978, and his novels charted urban middle class life in Mallorca and are interesting for their social history.

Somehow, in his busy life, he found time to study and write on "…metaphysics, logic, rhetoric, grammar, dogmatics, ethics, geometry, astronomy, physics, chemistry, anthropology, law, statecraft, navigation, warfare and horsemanship, in Latin, Catalan and Arabic". This listing of the range of Llull's scholarship comes from Havelock Ellis's book *The Soul of Spain*, first published in 1908. Ellis concluded that Llull's "…keen and penetrating intelligence placed him at the head of, and even in front of, the best available knowledge of his time."

The tomb of this Mallorcan polymath may be found in the 14th century church of the Convent of San Francisco in the centre of Palma, close to the church of Santa Eulàlia which he desecrated as a young man. Ramón Llull's imposing statue stands on a small traffic island on the Paseo Sagrera at the main entrance to Palma from its great bay. Behind him is one of the loveliest complexes of ancient buildings in the world—the 13th century Almudaina, the 14th century cathedral, the Arab baths and the exquisite gardens, all now complemented by the boldly conceived 20th century Parque de Mar, an artificial lagoon which restores to the old buildings the proximity they once had to the sea.

Llull's statue properly belongs to this remarkable Mediterranean setting for he was, indeed, a remarkable man of whom Mallorca is rightly proud. Professor Allison Peers, who has studied the great man's life and work, writes that: "In his own country Llull receives the simple homage of a Saint." Llull is beatified already, but sainthood is still to come.

museum of sorts, is bolted and barred and its surrounds uncared for.

Mass tourism at its most impressive or depressive, according to your point of view, rears its head at **Cala Millor**. A magnificent stretch of sand is backed by innumerable hotels, appartment blocks, restaurants and shops, all done with conviction and a certain style.

Near the small town of **Son Servera** is the **African Reserve**, a drive-through safari park fairly well-stocked with contented looking creatures which provides a family outing when the back burns, the beach palls or the sky clouds. Keep your car windows closed against the attentions of the inquisitive.

Central Plain: The views from the **Santuario de Santa Magdalena**, four miles (6.5 km) north-east of Inca, are breathtaking. In the distance is the spine of the Sierra, with the Palma bay to the south and the Pollença bay to the north. Closer at hand are the rich agricultural lands of the central plain. Here are some of the twelve "new towns" which were created by Jaime II after the re-conquest in 1300. They were laid out neatly on a grid system, and each settler had to build within six months, undertaking to remain for at least six years. Unfortunately the original streets of towns like **Sa Pobla** are now too narrow for the fork-lift trucks, tractors and lorries laden with vegetables which are a feature of the area.

Northwards the landscape quickly changes at the perimeters of the nature reserve **La Albufera**, where over two hundred species of resident and migratory birds live or lodge in thousands of acres of reed and sedge. In the mid-19th century a British company tried to drain the area but went bankrupt after building 250 miles (400 km) of irrigation channels and 30 miles (50 km) of road with many bridges, most of which remain. Today it is a haven of quiet patrolled by bird-watchers. Access to La Albufera is from the Alcudia Bay coastal road. The changing nature of the landscape emphasises how necessary it was for the government to acquire La Albufera in 1985 to safeguard it from

icultural ds of the tral plain.

the ever-extending concrete jungles of **Puerto d'Alcudia** and **Ca'n Picafort**.

The Catalan Gothic church (rebuilt in the 16th century) dominates the town of **Muro**, which has an air of prudent prosperity. The delightful Mother and Child above the main door dates from the late 18th century. In a substantial town house which belonged to the Alomar family is part of the **Museo de Mallorca** (the main part is in Palma). The museum houses furniture and equipment of a typical country house, old agricultural equipment, and a display of *siurelles*, the distinctive Mallorcan whistles made out of plaster and fashioned into all manner of curious shapes.

One could be forgiven for driving through **Petrá** without realising its significance in the history of the United States. This was the birthplace in 1713 of Fray Junípero Serra, who founded the Californian missions, including those of San Francisco and Los Angeles. An attractive modern museum illustrates his life and work. Nearby are the house in which he was born and the Convent of San Bernadino (under repair) where he trained as a missionary. If the museum is closed the keys are available from a lady who lives up the road.

Plantations of pine and the frequently changing colours of the soil make the road to **Sineu** an attractive drive. The track of the narrow-gauge railway that once ran from Inca to Petrá threads its way alongside. Sineu was declared by 14th-century King Sancho to be the centre of Mallorca, and Jaime II built a palace here which was later given to the community of nuns and remains a convent today.

The tiny hamlet of **Ses Alqueries**, to the southwest, has been largely taken over by foreign residents who have restored the old houses with care. Ses Alqueries has no shops, no café, no video library and as the Mallorquíns move out for the want of these facilities so the foreigners eagerly move in for the lack of them.

The beaten track: By 1992 the motorway will be extended, bypassing many traffic-clogged areas, but until then

Petrá, a quiet town surprising significan

Santa Maria and Binisalem are ancient towns bowed beneath the weight of Palma-Pollença traffic. In Santa Maria the cloisters of the Convento de los Mínimos make a tranquil, perfectly kept oasis in the centre of town (look for the signs "Distillery and Leather Factory"). The convent also houses a private museum of the Conrado family, who lived here. The collection ranges from sea-shells to shotguns, haphazardly displayed and hardly annotated at all, but the document room is fascinating—letters, contracts, marriage certificates, tax demands, old newspapers, and much else, dating from the 15th century onwards. A poignant item is the 1518 bill of sale for Ali, a slave aged 22, who cost 70 *libras mallorquinas*. The town also has one of the best stocked antique shops on the island, on the left on the road from Palma. Mallorcan antiques are usually more functional than decorative, and are surprisingly expensive.

The face that Binisalem shows the passing world is indeed ugly—pull-up cafés for trucks and garish liquor shops for tourists. But the real town lies to the west of the road and has great dignity. Binisalem ranks second only to Palma in the number and splendour of historic 18th and 19th-century mansions, most of which were built from agricultural and wine-growing profits (the town has long been the centre of the island's wine production). They like to take a historical perspective of things in Binisalem: the parish church of San Jaime was begun in 1346 and completed in 1910.

The third largest town on the island, Inca, is a fairly sophisticated place. Several "factory outlets" specialise in leather goods for tourists and the Thursday morning market is probably the best-known on the island. However local produce and crafts are hard to find and the presence of the ubiquitous Senegalese with their cheap jewellery, radios and mini-computers suggests that these days Inca, Mallorca, is not so far distant from 5th Avenue, New York, or Covent Garden, London. The town has several good restaurants in former

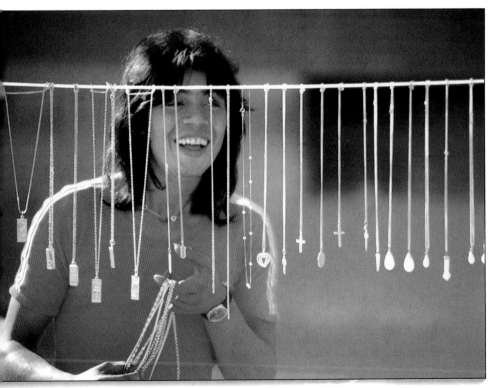

reet
arket,
ca.

WINDMILLS

Few travellers have come and gone from the island without scribbling a note or two in their diaries about the windmills on the island of Mallorca. In 1886, Charles Wood wrote in his *Letters from Majorca*: "The curious windmills of Majorca… They have six sails instead of four, which gives them a strange and unfamiliar appearance. In addition to this, a mass of ropes and cordage makes the sails look as complicated and intricate as the rigging of a ship."

Things have changed in the hundred years since then. Not only have the six-sailed windmills disappeared, but the only four-bladed ones which remain are museum restorations or skeletons decaying in the long summer sun.

For centuries the windmills have formed part of the landscape of the island, but their origin is a thing of theory. Some say that they were introduced in the 13th century, while others, who attribute their invention to Leonardo da Vinci, denounce that as impossible. Sanchis Guarner, a modern investigator, reports that they were invented by the Persians in the 7th century and widely dispersed in the eastern Mediterranean. They became popular during the Middle Ages among the Byzantines in the north and the Arabs in the south. The Moors brought the invention to the Iberian peninsula but interestingly there is no evidence that they also arrived on the island at that time. Whatever their origins they existed in Mallorca before the 1500s.

The first *molinos* on the island were used for the grinding of grain, an activity whose highs and lows were a measure of the island's economy. The normal custom was that the miller lived in the tower which both supported the wind driven sails and housed the mill stone. These *molinos de vela latina* increased to their maximum numbers in the following 200 years. The sails were eventually substituted by wooden slats or louvres, divided into six to ten sections separated by radial spokes. The inventor of this more advanced grain mill was Damían Reixach Amer, carpenter from the seaside village of Les Molinar de Llevant.

It wasn't until the 19th century that the windmill was used for the extraction of water from the subsoil. And the *molinos* which are still so prevalent today in such areas of Mallorca as St Jordi, Campos and Sa Pobla are descendants of a once ubiquitous device called a *noria*.

The *noria*, whose purpose was the extraction of underground water, was made up of a loop of jars which were lifted and lowered on a continuous belt into a subterranean well by a blindfolded mule. This device was by far the most antique system used in Mallorca and dates back to the Arab occupation of the Iberian peninsula. Primitive but effective, this method of irrigation was used for many centuries. Archduke Luis Salvador wrote that, "In the last quarter of the 19th century there were between 3,500 and 4,000 *norias* in Mallorca…"

According to one source, the first Mallorcan windmills with the purpose of pumping water were based upon the design of Dutchman Paul Bouvij. Ironically the device was built, not to irrigate but to reclaim the marshy plain of St Jordi near Palma. Later the wooden elements of the windmill were replaced by metal ones which were more efficient and far easier to manoeuvre. The newer *molinos de hierro* had the added advantage of not having to be de-sailed in a strong wind.

Recently the petrol-driven pump came close to putting an end to the picturesque windmills of Mallorca. With the rapid expansion of the island's market gardens (*huertos*) and 20th century advances in motor technology, the windmill was almost forgotten. It wasn't until the early years of the 1970s that the energy crisis resuscitated what Charles Wood had once called "the curious windmills of Majorca". Suddenly the petrol-driven pump became an expense that couldn't be justified with the relatively slow rise in market prices of the local produce. Skeletal remains of once proud windmills suddenly came to life, sporting new aerodynamically designed blades, updated interior mechanisms and new paint.

Today the multi-coloured blades, often with the red and yellow bars of the island's flag, whirl in the afternoon wind waiting to be photographed against the yellow sunset or sketched in a traveller's notebook.

wine-cellars, of which Celler Ca'n Amer, in the centre, has adventurous food and good service. The Inca train from Palma's Plaza España provides a new perspective on the countryside and avoids parking problems.

The South: There are views of the small island of Cabrera and occasionally of Ibiza from the **Santuario de Nuestra Señora de Cura** at **Puig de Randa**, but for our present purposes its field of vision is the island at its base.

The spirit of Mallorca's greatest son, Ramón Llull, pervades this place. In the late 13th century hermitage Llull began to write on a wide range of subjects, from astronomy to anthropology, from law to navigation. The Sanctuary's 16th-century grammar room contains a modest museum and many of Llull's books. Randa itself is one of Mallorca's prettiest villages and boasts an excellent restaurant, Es Recó de Randa.

In **Llucmajor**, 2.5 miles (four km) from Randa, Jaime III was defeated and killed by the forces of Peter IV of Aragón, ending the short-lived kingdom of Mallorca, and the island did not fully return to prosperity until the very different invasion of the second half of this century. A stone cross on the Campos road marks the battle site. The town itself has a quaint bandstand and Gaudí-like iron lamp standards, as well as a wide variety of architectural styles. At the north end of the plaza stands an altogether charming house of 1882 surmounted by a fantasy of an open bell tower, which is now the Town Hall.

The very beginnings of Mallorcan history are visible at **Capicorp Vell**, 7.5 miles (12 km) from Llucmajor on the Cabo Blanco road. This is the site of a settlement dating back to about 1200 B.C., excavated in 1910-20, and kept in a fair condition. It consists of five talayots (stone towers) and the walled outlines of 28 dwellings. This is a lonely, impressive place which makes the past accessible and comprehensible to the interested visitor.

Places of preservation: On the coast **Sa Rápita** and **Es Trenc**, the latter with a long spectacular white beach virtually

untouched by development, provide glimpses of Mallorcan seaside resorts before mass tourism. Commercial interests are constantly looking for a foothold here.

Near to **Colonia de Sant Jordi** are the **Salinas de Llevant**, an area well-known for migratory birds, and the **Balneario de Sant Joan de la Font Santa** (open April to October), whose hot water is considered good for rheumatism. There is an old fashioned but fashionable hotel here surrounded by tall pine trees.

The town of **Campos** is built on the site of a Roman settlement, but today the principal point of interest is the 16th-century church, whose tower and distinctive weathercock can be seen from some distance. In the church is a painting of Christ in the Hall of Pilate, attributed to Murillo. To get in you may need to get the key from a nearby house, and take a torch to see the painting.

The locals are less proud of the memorial near the imposing Baroque church of **Porreres**, a prosperous small agricultural town. In a gravelled terrace of palm trees to the right of the church façade is a memorial to the 18 men of Porreres who gave their lives in the Civil War, for "God and Spain". In other towns on the island, after Franco's death, such memorials were first desecrated then destroyed because they listed only the names of those who fought and died for Franco.

Finally, with so many locations of real historical interest available it may seem strange to recommend the modern mock-castle on the C-715 Manacor-Palma road, variously known as the **Gordiola Museum**, **Vidrios de Gordiola** and **Vidreries Siglo XVIII**. This "castle" houses an interesting glass museum, shops, and a glass-blowing workshop of ancient appearance, much used today. Gordiola blown glass, with its distinctive pale colourings, has been made in Mallorca by the same family firm since 1719, and the museum's collection is international. Every item in the display is numbered but, as so often is the case in Mallorca, the catalogue is out of print.

MAHON AND EASTERN MENORCA

Vent mestral, entra per sa porta—i surt per fumeral. The *mistral* comes in by the door and leaves by the chimney. (Menorquín proverb).

The Spanish have a partiality for christening their tourist areas with catchy names. Menorca is commonly promoted as the island *verde y azul*, although the locals know it as the windy isle. Unlike bold and brash Mallorca 21 miles (34 kms) away to the south-west (visible on a clear day), it is understated in its landscape and its people.

The island is a gently sloped plateau in the Mediterranean, 30 miles (48 kms) long and 12 miles (19 kms) wide, stitched with stone walls and laced with quiet roads. In the winter it is scoured by the chilling *tramuntana* wind, which is whipped up somewhere in the snowy peaks of the Pyrenees and thrown down onto the island, whistling through streets built narrow for protection. Even the airport, with its new £10 million terminal, points in the direction of the wind and if ever the *tramuntana* shifts planes cannot land.

Like its brother islands Menorca has been constantly swamped with invaders who have left traces behind them, particularly the British. Like Mallorca it has also been swamped with new invaders, but these tourists are not the same as the Mallorcan majority, who are often on an adventurous quest for discos and steak and chips.

The island has a reputation among Mallorquíns of being dull, and by way of retaliation Menorquíns have their own saying: *Mallorquí—lladre ff*; a Mallorquín is a fine thief. The truth is not that the island is wrong for the people who visit it, but the people wrong for the island. If Mallorca is the biggest and loudest of three brothers and Ibiza the youngest and trendiest, Menorca is the quiet one in the middle who actually proves rather interesting if you draw him into conversation.

Landscapes: The island is usually a couple of degrees cooler than Mallorca. Its northern coast is jagged and barren and scenically beautiful, while its southern coast is dotted with coves and the island's principal beaches.

Inland the landscape requires a patient eye. The impatient will miss the subtle changes from red-soiled stone-walled agricultural land to gently undulating forestland, from barren *macchia* landscape reminiscent of Scotland to pine woods smelling of Switzerland. The island is regularly likened to an open air museum, with concentrations of *talayots, taulas* and *navetas* which knock Mallorca's into a cocked hat, most of which have been discovered by farmers laboriously turning over their soil. Confusingly the island's *parets seques*—orderly piles of stones in the middle of fields—also look like prehistoric monuments.

Away from the urban or holiday areas lonely baronial *fincas* dominate the landscape, but despite the atmosphere of decay residents here have amongst the highest levels of income in Spain,

and most things are expensive. The Menorquíns prefer quality to quantity.

Industry: The first plane (a seaplane) actually landed in Fornells harbour in 1930, but it wasn't until 1960 that the tourist industry began to move. Until then the island had only one hotel and one guest house. Nowadays the resident population of 59,583 (with 1,500 resident British) is exceeded in busy months by the number of visitors. Of the 500,000 annual visiting migration of tourists 78 percent are British (Germans, the next largest group, are trailing behind at 13 percent).

But this is not the island for impulsive mid-summer visits; speculative hotel accommodation is very limited. A typical villa (swimming pool and three bedrooms) on Menorca is no longer cheap, costing roughly the equivalent of a two bedroom flat in London. Nevertheless £50 million was invested in property in 1987.

Local manufacturing is limited to shoes, gin, cheese and ice-cream, all of which keep the small container port of Mahón active, if not busy. The Caserio cheese factory makes 54 million boxes of cheese a year, or 1,000 boxes for each inhabitant (most of it is exported). Agricultural diversity is limited by the litter of stones on the fields, which prevents effective harvesting. Instead the island is home to 25,000 cows, even though forage has to be imported when the grass gets sparse in summer.

Mahón: From an aesthetic point of view the best approach to the island's capital city is the approach that it was built for: from the sea. On walls and cliffs above the extensive port, the town has a commanding position. Stairs from the port lead up to its heart, twisted with knots of small roads that are impossible to follow from any map. The best navigational point is the barn-like church of **Santa Maria** (founded in 1287) at the top of the stairs. Santa Maria is also the centre of the musical life of the island thanks to its massive organ, which was built in Barcelona in 1810 and shipped across under the protection of the British Admiral Collingwood against French pirates, and well-loved amongst European concert organists. The Chinese symphony orchestra performed in this church on their first ever concert visit to the West.

Opposite the northern end of the church is the *Ayuntamiento*, or Town Hall, with the clock presented by British Governor Richard Kane, who was much loved by Menorquíns, mounted in its façade. In the foyer there are paintings of a few English monarchs and a stone that proves Mahón (Maó in Catalan) to have been a Roman settlement.

Virtually next door, in the small Plaza de la Conquista, is the Public Library, which also has a small library museum. Mahón's principal museum will be located in the church of San Francisco at the far end of Calle Isabel II.

A visitor turning left at the top of the stairs from the port will instantly find himself in the jaws of the **fish market**, best seen relatively early in the morning. Five substantial family-owned trawlers continue to operate out of the port of Mahón.

Dominating the fishmarket is the

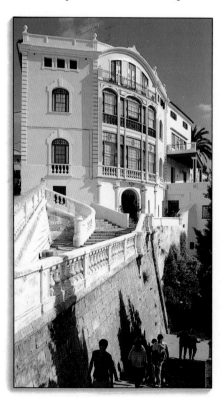

A merchant house in Mahón.

Iglesia del Carmen, dated 1751 on the front but actually much restored in 1941. Here the candles are disappointingly electric, and the round coloured glass window to the south projects its own coloured image on the interior wall opposite.

To the left of the church is the entrance to the **Claustro del Carmen**, cloisters which were part of an active convent between 1726 and 1808, but which are now in secular use as the fruit and vegetable market. This is the place to buy Mahón cheese and Menorcan sobrasada sausage (an acquired taste) though even here prices are high.

At the other entrance to the market an open doorway leads to the the **Sala d'Exposicions del Claustre del Carme**, permanent show of the collection of Don Joan Hernandez Mora, a Mahón academic (1902-84) who became the cultural leader of the island and who made it his business to gather together all historic documents relevant to Menorca, including a very fine display of maps. The music conservatory opposite is surprisingly active, as indeed is the musical life of the island: the small town of San Luis, for example, has six flautists and a violinist of all performance standard.

The main shopping street (pedestrianised) of Mahón, **Calle Dr Orfila**, stretches from near the top of the harbour stairs up to the **Plaza de L'Esplanada**, the venue for the nighttime *paseo* and the best place to catch island buses.

Mahón harbour: This, the second largest natural port in the world, has seen a lot of history. Castles have been successively built and demolished at its mouth, and the far promontories still remain military zones, to no particular evident purpose.

"The tides affect it very inconsiderably, as they observe no regularity, ebbing and flowing a foot or two, as they are influenced by the wind. The land on the north side is extremely barren...the south side assumes a better aspect, being in a good state of cultivation," wrote the cartographer to the British Admiralty in 1813. On the town side the

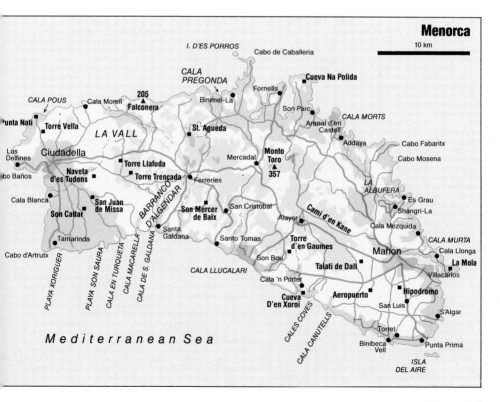

harbour is very deep, shelving to shallow water on the far side where celebrities and millionaires (Richard Branson amongst them) have their houses. There is an oft-quoted but little understood 16th-century rhyme praising Mahón attributed to Italian Admiral Andrea Doria: "Junio, julio, agosto y Mahón, Los mejores puertos del Mediterraneo son", which roughly translated suggests that the best place to be outside the summer months of June, July and August, is in the port of Mahón. Unfortunately the protection, and the lack of significant tide, means that the port remains badly polluted in comparison to other waters around the island.

Waterside: A dual carriageway under construction along the harbour edge may change things, but for the time being the road that runs around from the commercial quay as far as the oil tanks in the next bay is the best place to be in Mahón of an evening. By night the light of the clock on the church on the island opposite (part of a naval base, and much coveted by the town) gleams on water so glassy-smooth that it is hard to believe it is connected to the sea. Neon light streams out of workshop doors, with the smell of oil and the chug of idling engines. The small double-ender fishing boats are called *llauds* and are Arabi in origin and design; they are still made locally.

On the water's edge close to the ferry landing are the **Xoriguer** gin distillery and the **Aquarium**. The former, although it advertises "visits", is principally a large shop displaying the many varieties of gin it produces, and visitors are encouraged to taste and buy. At the back of the shop, behind plate glass, the stills are in use, but there's not much to look at. In the Aquarium next door there's considerably more going on behind glass, but it can be difficult to identify the fish from the labelling.

Many of the bars and shops along the waterfront here are built back into the cliff face, and the **Lora** (S'Alambic) pottery shop is no exception. In the back of the shop potters make nesting boxes for birds and pots for keeping crickets in to hear them sing.

Beyond the panelled and mirrored **Café Baixamar**, very popular with local *jeunesse*, the waterfront becomes increasingly visitor orientated and by the time the road has rounded the corner into **Cala Figuera** it is lined with foreign yachts on one side and elegant restaurants and boutiques on the other. Boat trips of the port leave from near the Club Maritime.

On the hillside above the Cala is **Disco Luis**, one of a handful of discos on the island and Mahón's major nightspot. The disco is housed in a cave which was used previously by the Phoenicians as a quarry, by pirates as a hiding place and by the English as a temporary hospital.

Brits and myths: A little further out on the left of the Villacarlos road is the **Almirante Hotel**, formerly the home of Admiral Collingwood and sometimes known (everything on Menorca seems to have two names) as Collingwood House. The hotel owner has taken some trouble to fill the elegant building with antiques and pictures relevant to Col-

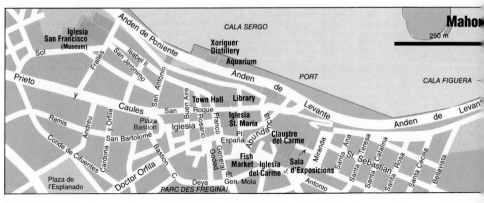

lingwood's period, including a print of the symbolic cutting off the paw of the lion of British Empire—the paw being Menorca and the culprit for its loss being Admiral Byng, who was court-martialled for withdrawing from a crucial naval engagement with the French fleet in 1756.

The French interregnum on the island was short (Menorca was returned to British control in 1763) but not before the French had supposedly discovered *mayonnaise*, claimed to have been invented by a French chef desperate for something to animate the poor fare that the island offered for his master's delicate palate. In fact the sauce had probably been in existence for a long time, but formally received its French identity at a ball in Paris to celebrate the French occupation of the island, which was called the Mayonnaise Ball, where the sauce was served.

But perhaps the greatest myth of Mahón is the legend connected with **Golden Farm**, the rust-coloured *finca* which dominates the north side of the harbour, virtually opposite Collingwood House. The debate centres around claims that Nelson and his lover Emma Hamilton spent time here in 1799, whereas most evidence now suggests that he did not. Golden Farm is full of Nelson memorabilia which is thought to have been supplied by one of Nelson's servants who returned to the island after his master's death and set up a ship's chandlery in Mahón. The house is privately owned and not open to the public; it was recently on the market for a cool £6.5 million.

The rust colouring of this and other particularly British properties is said to derive from the colour of anti-fouling paint with which every British vessel was painted below the waterline; British naval captains erected houses on the shore and covered them with the only paint readily available.

Military zones: Depending on whether you are a visitor, English resident or Catalan, the second town on the port is variously known as **Villacarlos** (after King Carlos III), Georgetown (after

MAHON CHEESE

Quite how long Mahón cheese has been made in Menorca nobody can be sure; popular tradition claims that it goes back further even than the Greeks, who called the island Meloussa after the flocks of cattle they found there. But it was christened much more recently, when the local *casa del queso*, or cheese factories, began to sell large quantities to appreciative gourmets in Palma, Barcelona and Madrid early this century.

Despite its growing renown the Menorcan product remained a purely seasonal farmhouse cheese for much of this century. Every day from September to June, twice a day after the cows had been milked, the women of the *fincas* laboriously worked the curds, squeezing out the whey from 10 litres of milk for each kilo of cheese and then pressing the curds into chubby squares. For rennet they then traditionally used the juice from *alcachofas de hierbas*, a special variety of artichoke, now replaced by bottled vegetable rennet; for moulds they used only *fogesas*, or cotton cheesecloths.

Once the cheese was shaped, it was placed in a wooden press to squeeze out the remaining whey, then unwrapped and floated in mild brine until it had sucked in enough salt to preserve it.

From this came the four types still sold today: mild *fresco*, or *tierno*, eaten after as little as eight days, smooth and white with bubbles in the centre, used to stuff Christmas turkeys and fill small, sweet pastries: *semi-curado*, sealed with yellow cheese with a creamy consistency; *curado*, matured for longer until it is firm at the edges with a deep, nutty flavour and orange rind; finally, *viejo* or *añejo*, resealed and turned for a year or more till it has a granular texture, rock hard rind and a powerful kick for the nose and throat like that of Parmesan.

Although all farmhouse Mahón shares a particular flavour from the island's salty pastures—in recognition of which it carries a *denominacion de origen* label—no two cheeses are ever the same. The local soil, warmth of the makers' hands, addition of a little goat's or lamb's milk for flavour, and the maturing process—all add individual character. An expert can judge character simply by pressing and smelling the puckered rind, but for anyone else buying a large chunk it is a good idea to taste a sliver beforehand.

Inevitably, as with nearly all other farmhouse cheeses, traditional Mahón now competes with industrial versions. First of all, unpasteurised *queso fresco* was banned from sale some years ago. More important, however, the commercial pressure for large quantities of cheap, standardised cheese recast Mahón's interesting quirkiness as lack of uniformity and offered the farms the easier alternative of selling their surplus milk to the dairies.

One of these industrial versions, called El Caserio, can only be described as a plastic, foil-wrapped travesty. The other, made by a farmers' co-operative called Coinga in Alaior, is closer to the original in taste as well as looks, but is made with pasteurised milk and by factory methods so that its taste and texture will never vary. Undoubtedly it has a blander and less distinctive flavour than the original but it has been a huge commercial success: over 1,400 tons are now sold every year, a good proportion carried away by tourists in cleverly designed boxes, but some is now also exported directly to the United States, Germany and Holland. Farmhouse cheese has even been forced to come down to nearly the same price.

Now, however, there is a third alternative: an unpasteurised cheese made traditionally, but under controlled hygienic conditions and with a mould and press to replace the labour intensive, costly work of squeezing by hand. The results, close to farmhouse cheese but with the necessary guarantees of uniform quality for commercial buyers—already 80 percent of production is exported from the island—offer a way forward not only for Mahón, but also for Spain's fifty other excellent, if little known, regional farmhouse cheeses.

If you are lucky enough to be on the spot, however, savour the taste of the really splendid genuine article. Try a chunk of well-matured *añejo* eaten the local way with red wine, figs and grapes before it is a thing of the past.

George III) or Es Castell. During the Franco years (1931-75) it was forbidden to speak Catalan on the island, but now there is a move to teach entirely in Catalan, and all place names are being changed. Villacarlos was built in 1771 by British governor John Mostyn, who needed a garrison for the troops manning **Fort Marlborough** (Spanish name Fort San Felipe) at the mouth of the harbour. Thus the main square is a parade ground and the principal buildings surrounding it still have a military function. However the fort itself has long since been dismantled by the Spanish, originally to make the island less attractive to the British as a bargaining pawn in the Mediterranean. The fort's stones were used to build the Lazaret in the harbour, a quarantine island until 1917, now used for scientific research. What remains of the fortress actually harbours a good military museum, but visitors must have a pass from the Guardia Civil in Villacarlos.

The land on the northern side of the port is altogether less hospitable. Directly opposite Mahón much of the hillside is given over to the naval base, marked by a wall which lopes around the contours. You can't get in to see Golden Farm, and a finger-wagging sentry will prevent you from driving far out onto **La Mola** promontory itself, which is a *zona militar*. Remarkably untouched by the proximity of Mahón and tourism in general is **Cala Mesquida**, at the island end of the peninsula. Here are a small village partly on an island, a single bar, a fine beach, and an ancient watchtower that looks like a castellated kettle.

Horses and resorts: The southeastern corner of Menorca, once the wine growing region until disease and labour shortage hit the industry, is dense with villas and small beaches, all of which are pleasant and none of which are particularly notable. **San Luis** used to be the seat of French government during the occupation of the island (the governor's residence was in the grand and decayed house right on the Mahón edge of town). Nearby the San Luis windmill

has been restored, with wooden cogs, to working order but is only open to the public at week-ends.

Half-way along the road from Mahón (the *talayot* and *taula* of Trebuco on small lanes to the east) is the **Hipodromo**, the Menorcan equivalent of the bull-ring (there are no bullfights on the island). Trotting races are held here on Sunday evenings. There are usually seven races in a session, some of which have staggered starts according to the horses' previous handicap. Competitors risk disqualification if they break into a gallop. The winning trotter receives around £15 per race.

The horse is a prize possession on the island and the main feature of the Menorcan festivals, which start in Ciudadela in June and end with the largest in Mahón in September. These *Jaleos* date back to crusading times, when crusaders and Knights Templar used to pass by the port of Mahón on the way to battle somewhere else in the Mediterranean. The *Jaleo* can be a rowdy affair, and small boys do their utmost to frighten the prancing horses in order to unseat their *caixers*, or riders.

Cave living: The Menorquíns are particularly proud of the exemplary resort village of **Binibeca Vell**, built on the coast south of San Luis. They are not so contented with the natural-living community at **Cales Coves**, five miles (eight kms) along the coast, where hippy groups live in some of the 150 Iron Age caves that riddle the cliffs of this quite spectacular cove complex. There is natural fresh water and evidence of Roman habitation here, and some of the multi-national modern troglodytes live in their caves all year round.

Cales Coves is accessible down a long and rather arduous track, but **Cueva d'en Xoroi**, less than a mile away, is so accessible that bus loads of tourists visit on a regular basis. The cave, sited half-way down the sheer cliff, has been imaginatively converted to house a disco (one of several such conversions throughout the Balearics) and is partly open to the night sky and the thundering sea below. Legend has it

Binibeca Vell, touri village in disguise.

152

that the cave was home to a refugee Moor, who fell in love with and abducted a local girl. The couple brought up four children in complete secrecy in the cave until footsteps in a snowfall finally drew attention to their hiding place; when they were discovered the Moor and his son supposedly jumped into the sea and died, but his wife and her other three children were re-absorbed into island life.

The largest beach on the island is at **Son Bou**, south of Alaior. Quite a metropolis centuries ago (the largest prehistoric settlement on the island, **Torre d'en Gaumes**, is nearby, and the ruins of a paleo-Christian church are in the heart of the resort itself) Son Bou was to have developed into a major resort with many more than the two hotels that currently dominate the beach, but planning permission was not granted.

The people of **Alaior** are said to keep themselves to themselves within this island of industry (ice-cream, shoes and cheese). The town's massive church, Santa Eulàlia, has a pleasant interior although it has been largely rebuilt. To the north runs the **Camí d'en Kane**, Governor Kane's original road that linked the two capitals, and since its refurbishment one of the best drives on the island, avoiding the towns and showing rural Menorca at its best.

North coast: Bearing the brunt of the wind and the sea, Menorca's northern shore has traditionally been less populated than the south and thus provided scope for grand developments such as the substantial new town of **Arenal**. Salespersons for the timeshare developers of Arenal swoop on visitors at tourist sites island-wide to persuade them to visit and buy.

While Arenal is forging ahead the **Shangri-La** development near the **Albufera** lake has fossilised. Shangri-La was the Seventies brainchild of a German developer, and a lot of investors, particularly British, bought plots of building land before the authorisation for the project was completed. Sixty-two houses, the roads and a golf course (now heavily overgrown) were finished before the whole project froze in the face of local opposition, particularly from GOB, the ecological group of the Balearics, concerned about the effect of the development on the lake's wildlife. The scheme is still the subject of much lobbying and argument, and at the time of going to press there was speculation that the houses would be bought and demolished.

Albufera itself is a freshwater lake that looks remarkably like a Scottish loch, complete with midges. It echoes with the sound of birds, the ploshes of coots and ducks, and mallard, moorhen and grey heron are here in large numbers. Undoubtedly it would have been a shame to have surrounded it with holiday villas.

Sandy dunes form a barrier between Albufera, the sea, and the village of **Es Grau**, a peaceful traditional place with a bay well-stocked with fishing boats. There's nothing special about Es Grau, but you do feel, as you sit at the bay-side café in the last of the sun, having just come from Shangri-La, that the whole area is far better for being left as it is.

Shoemaking, cottage industry in Alaior.

PREHISTORIC MENORCA

The island of Menorca is often referred to as an archaeological museum without walls. The truth of this statement becomes evident as one travels over the main roads and throughout the smaller routes of the island. One is never very long from the sight of some forms of Megalithic (large stone) prehistoric ruin, some as impressive as Stonehenge and nearly comparable in age, although at times these can be hard to identify, both because of the lack of signs and because they blend in with the stone walls of Menorca's fields.

There are an estimated 5,000 or more prehistoric sites shared between the two major islands of the Balearics. All are of prehistoric ages begin-

three to six increasingly massive stone elements, placed one upon the other.

The result of these ascending size pillar stones is the Mediterranean Pillar and the equivalent of *corbelling*, which is in turn the forerunner to the arch. In ancient times the Talayots probably served as meeting places for the elders of the community, very much like the *kiva* of the south-western American Indian.

As a comparative culture the Talayotic is believed to be most closely related in age and social organisation to the Nuraghic and Torreanos cultures of Sardinia and Corsica respectively, where similar architectural structures are to be found.

In Menorca the culture is chronologically divided into three periods: the Pretalayotic Period, culture of the caves, *circa* 2000 to 1300 B.C; the Talayotic Period, Bronze Age, *circa* 1300 to 800

ning with the Neolithic Period in Mallorca (as early as 6000 B.C.) and extending through the local Copper, Bronze and Iron Ages, circa 2500 B.C. to 200 B.C. into the Roman Colonisation of the Balearics as late as 123 B.C. Like that of Mallorca, the Menorcan prehistoric mother culture is known as the Talayotic Culture.

The word Talayotic was placed in the archaeological vocabulary at the turn of this century by two prehistorians, the Spaniard Jose Colominas Roca and the Frenchman Emile Cartaillac. It is based on the Arabic word *atalaya* meaning sentinel (watchtower) and has given birth to the name of the most characteristic local form of prehistoric architectural element, the *talayot*. The *talayot* is a circular or square building with a single entrance and a large centre pillar, made up of

B.C.; and Post Talayotic Period, the Iron Age, *circa* 800 B.C. to the Roman Colonisation in 123 B.C. This follows closely but not entirely the chronological divisions for the island of Mallorca. The larger island has a far better established chronology than Menorca thanks to the techniques of radiocarbon dating.

To understand the nature and geography of the island's vestiges of man's ancient past, it is necessary to consider a few important geographic and geological factors which account for the choice, development and preservation of the many settlements.

Smaller than its sister island of Mallorca, Menorca (271 sq miles, 702 sq km), as compared to Mallorca's 1,444 sq miles, 3,740 sq km) has none of the extremes of landscape, of mountain and plain, which characterise Mallorca. On the whole the eye meets a terrain that is rather monotonous, being continually exposed to winds from various directions, particularly the prevailing north wind. However Menorca has as many as three times the number of archaeological sites found on Mallorca.

The main highway, which divides the island geographically and geologically from north to south between the capital city of Mahón in the east and the town of Ciutadella westward, bisects the island's two broad geological formations. These are greatly responsible for the pattern of settlement of the island by man throughout prehistoric as well as modern times. It is no accident that the 5th century basilica and modern hotel are side by side on the beach at Son Bou.

To the north of the road these Secondary Formations are mainly limestone of Devonian origin. In this region, the island is completely exposed to the severity of the frequent tempestuous winds blowing in off the Golfe du Lion. In bad weather, this coast is completely inaccessible by sea for several days at a time. The best anchorage is the port of Fornells, but even this, despite its protective nature is sometimes sealed off to traffic even in summer by strong north winds. The port of Mahón is located at the eastern end of this northern Secondary Formation.

To the south the Tertiary Formations provide such shelter from the north winds as the islands offer. The south coastline is marked by *arroyos* (locally called *barrancos*) which slice the Tertiary limestone into beautiful coves and inlets, with at times, sandy beaches which run for several miles. The *arroyos* contain caves, most with fresh water sources, which pock-mark both sides of the *barrancos* by the score. Most have signs of prehistoric occupation and some are still occupied even today. It is in this southern region that about 90 percent of cave sites and Bronze and Iron Age open-air settlements can be seen.

Some of the open-air Talayotic settlements which date from as early as 1800 B.C. are very large and elaborate in their architectural features. An example of one of these, the fortified prehistoric town of Son Catlar, a few miles to the south of the modern town of Ciutadella has a cyclopian wall system with inner chambers of over 2,624 ft (800 metres) in extension. It consists of a surface area some nine times larger than ancient Troy and of roughly comparable age. Within its walls lie the entire range and variation of Talayotic architecture, including two *talayots* and a *taula*, the latter a horse-shoe shaped religious sanctuary dating from 1000 B.C., one of over 30 such religious centres on Menorca, very much like the Temples of Malta, but of considerably younger age.

Another such settlement complex is found in the Talayotic village of Torre d'en Gaumes which extends all around a large commanding ridge on the road from Alaior to Son Bou. It also consists of complex buildings, its own *talayots* and *taula*.

The *taula*, peculiar to Menorca alone, is typified by an immense rectangular and flat pillar stone, up to 15 ft (4.5 metres) high, with a tapered, huge capstone set on top. Here within the precincts of the *taula* walls, religious practices of animal worship appear to have taken place in which offerings or sacrifices of sheep, goats, pigs and cattle were made.

The best preserved examples of these remarkable prehistoric sanctuaries are those of Talati de Dalt, a few miles west of Mahón on the south side of the Mahón-Ciutadella road and the *taula* of Torralba d'en Salort several miles from the town of Alaior and mid-distance on the road from Alaior to Cala'n Porter. Here, archaeological excavations have shown the *taula* was used for ritual offerings of animals. Bronze statuary of a bull, a horse and terracotta statues of the Carthaginian goddess Tanit at Torralba, along with human effigies of foreign household gods like the Egyptian Imhotep found at Torre d'en Gaumes, and other offerings, suggest a mixed pantheon of gods in the *taulas'* latter stages of use.

Another Talayotic architectural landmark to be seen frequently is that of the *naveta*, an overturned boat-shaped building. The *naveta* is perhaps the oldest of the Talayotic architectural forms, dating from 1500 B.C., a prehistoric structure whose function both on Menorca as well as Mallorca was of dual purpose, serving at times as communal living quarters and other times as a burial chamber. Along the Mahón-Ciutadella road, a few kilometers east of Ciudadela and just off the road, is the best example of this typical and distinctive prehistoric architectural form, the Naveta d'es Tudons, which was restored in 1960. Here one can actually enter the *naveta*, gaining access to both the upper and lower levels.

There is a route itinerary available in book shops that facilitates the traveller while on Menorca (*Taulas and Talayots, What They Are and Where They Are:* Hoskin and Waldren 1988). This guide identifies several of the best routes for finding and viewing Menorca's prehistoric monuments as well as informing the reader as to what is known concerning them. Most of the monuments are open to the public, for no fee, but remember some are also on private property and permission should be asked at the closest farmhouse (*finca*) before visiting them, and this courtesy costs nothing.

Menorca is a remarkable archaeological paradise for the prehistorically informed or curiously inclined and many happy hours can be spent crawling over the many well preserved bastions and dwellings inhabited by ancient Balearic man.

CIUTADELLA AND WESTERN MENORCA

The magic of **Ciutadella** may seem to be its dense architectural beauty, but there is something less obvious, too, behind its charm: a relaxed lack of self-consciousness. The *casco viejo*, or old town, a compact mass of weathered honey-pink stone overlooking its small port, which was an aristocratic capital city for over 400 years, is today the pumping heart of a small farming town, and that is the way it behaves, paying less attention to its own beauty or the outside world than to the practicalities of everyday life.

So Ciutadella is best approached in something of the same spirit, with a relish for random exploration rather than organised culture. Nearly everything can be seen from the street, either in the old town or in the newer areas outside the ring of avenues where the walls stood until the 19th century, and is the more memorable for being part of an unidentified backdrop to everyday life. There are noisy carpenters' workshops, bakers and hardware stores doing business behind faded stone façades; a bank in a former palace and a radio station in a disused church; small front rooms with women doing piecework for shoe factories and horse-drawn carts on the edge of town.

Route march: Directions are hardly necessary. The most effective way of taking everything in is to walk around, with an accurate map but no fixed route or destination, at different times of day and night. Inevitably, you keep coming back to the **Calle Mayor**, the main street of the old town, at which all routes seem to meet.

At dusk family life spills out everywhere. Later, when night falls, the sense of history comes to the fore, with small architectural details—sundials, saints in niches, balconies and coats of arms—spotlighted by the old-fashioned street lamps. By this time the fish restaurants and bars on either side of the **port** (**baixamar**) are bustling, but if you walk back along the creek and look up at the **old wall**, you can imagine past centuries, when the gates were locked from sunset to sunrise.

Spots of splendour: Standing in front of the main cathedral steps, the town's centuries of splendour are spelled out all around. Look along to **Ses Voltes**, an arcaded alley dating back to the Moorish times, when Ciudadela became the first town of the island; gaze up at the **cathedral**, with splendid Gothic buttresses and gargoyles, built on the site of the old mosque after the 13th century Aragónese conquest; turn round to face the **Palacio Olivar**, decorated only by a coat of arms, proudly symbolic of the new aristocracy who built houses here from the 17th century; finally look down past the **Bishop's Palace** to the neo-classical **Palacio Squella**, both dating from the 18th century, when the town lost its role as capital but regained the bishopric in compensation.

There is another much photographed, but less historic, view from the **Plaza del Borne**, originally the Arab parade-ground and now a huge square with

trees and cafés. Here there is much grandiose neo-classicism packed, somewhat lopsidedly, into one end of the square. The impressive 19th-century **Palacio Torre Saura** and **Palacio Salort**, with high-arched galleries, symmetrically flank the Calle Mayor; the **Ayuntamiento**, where the police work behind elaborately carved, eroded columns, stands opposite; the **Teatro**, small and unpretentious, with a wonderful old-fashioned bar and gamesroom next door, sits in one corner. Despite all this the Borne is dominated by its central obelisk, a 19th-century memorial to the bloody but hopeless defence of the town against 15,000 Turks in 1558, after which the town never fully regained its former strength.

Elsewhere, wedged into the narrow streets, you find older buildings more satisfying for their sober simplicity: the **Palacio Ignacio Saura**, with lovely carved eaves, where you can wander through the entrance hall and gaze up the stairs on the way to an antique shop; the **Palacios Sintes** and **Martorell**, both severely plain, and the **Palacio Barón de Lluriach**, the oldest of all the aristocratic houses.

On Thursday and Saturday mornings the miniature market comes to life in the **Plaza de la Libertat**. Fish is sold under the names of the local boats in the central pavilion and meat is sold from stalls under plain, whitewashed arches reminiscent of a North African *casbah*.

Churches and culture: In contrast, the churches have an astonishingly decorative exuberance. Serpentine whirls, cherubs, fruit and flowers tumble around the Baroque doors of the **Iglesia del Roser** (closed except for the occasional concert) and **Iglesia Santo Cristo**, where there is a fine Renaissance triptych; inside the echoingly empty **Iglesia del Socors** (the radio offices keep the key) there are huge 19th century frescoes and a magnificent organ; notable in the **cathedral** are the carved *coro* with angels, the paintings behind the altar and lovely carved columns in the 18th-century domed chapel of the Capilla de las Almas.

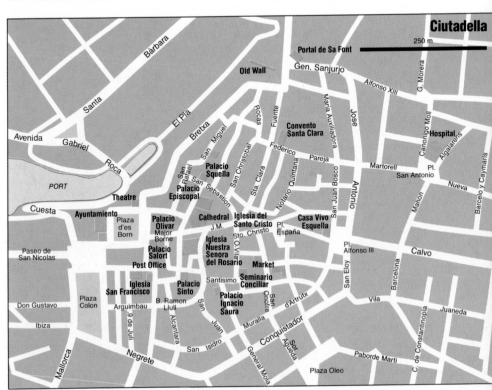

Ciutadella has little in the way of organised culture; only a tiny **municipal museum** in the Ayuntamiento, at present closed for renovation and the **Palacio Salort**, with two rooms open to the public, where there are fine oil paintings, tapestries and furniture which hint at the rich contents of the private palaces and influence of English taste in homes of all sizes. There is also a classical musical festival held in the quiet cloistered courtyard of the **Seminario Concillar** in late summer.

Fittingly, it is a street fiesta, the famous **San Juan**, which is the town's great source of cultural pride. Like any of the great Spanish fiestas it has its own vocabulary and a strict sense of ritual thought to have originated simply as a ride out to the nearby hermitage on St John's Day. It expresses above all the local passion for horses and equestrian virtuosity: the *junta* of *caixers*, or horsemen, who represent the medieval social classes, ride among the crowds, prancing and circling on their hind legs, at other times jousting, running a gauntlet of fruit and nuts thrown by the crowd and riding into houses.

Tourism: Until five years ago neither Ciutadella nor the surrounding countryside had many visitors but that is quickly changing. Along the west coast all the narrow creeks and local summer homes from **Cabo Baños** to **Son Xoriguer** have been engulfed by *urbanizaciones*, that blanket euphemism, here meaning everything from residential estates to a huge hotel run like a theme-park. Now Ciutadella is fighting to keep development away from tiny **La Platja Gran**, on the southern edge of town, hardly a beauty spot but now the only unspoiled beach on the west coast.

One other major tourist development in this half of the island, **Cala Santa Galdana**, is also depressingly out of tune with the beauty of its surroundings; the perfect oyster-shell bay with a river running in on one side, is dominated by a tall hotel tactlessly dropped, like an outsize cigarette packet, on the edge of the beach. In summer the beach is packed and the water none too clean.

ft, in
utadella's
aza del
rne.
ght, caixer
the San
an fiesta.

Search out nearby **Cala Mitjada** (down a track through pine forests just to the east) for a complete contrast.

Quiet coasting: Between Son Xoriguer and Santa Galdana the coastline still fits the image of Menorca the unspoilt island, with a handful of lovely beaches protected by the lack of easy access roads. **Son Saura** is at the end of a track which runs through six gates, several fields and a farmyard before finally emerging at the open, often windy beach; **Cala en Turqueta**, a protected cove, is popular with local families at weekends and takes you past Son Catlar, a prehistoric village; **Macarella**, the most beautiful, is also the most crowded. It has prehistoric caves—one amusingly used as a beach house—a bar and a second, largely nudist bay. From here there are good walks along hunting paths over scrubby, herb-scented headlands to both east and west.

The road to these three beaches runs past **San Juan de Misa**, an 18th-century church the size of a chapel, which is unlocked only when the horses ride out here during the fiesta of San Juan. Its square bell-tower, starkly white, stands out above walled fields dotted by farmhouses and the occasional *talayot*, crucifix, or scarecrow wearing a sombrero.

Stones and coves: North of Ciutadella, stretching towards the lighthouse at **Punta Nati** is the same open land with little obvious reason for exploration; the large 19th century villas and neat smallholdings soon give way to empty fields and the city scrap-heap strangely juxtaposed with a prehistoric village. Finally, there is nothing but earth, trees bent by the *tramuntana* wind and relentless stone walls, built into *barraques*, barns, around trees and property, yet still with enough to spare for shapeless heaps in the fields.

One other road gives access to the north, taking you as far as **Cala Morell** before it winds on to a dead end. Hardly worth a special visit for its upmarket villas and minuscule beach extended by levelled rock platforms, jokingly called sunbeds locally, it does have an interesting cluster of prehistoric caves in a gully

Wild flowe
in the
unspoilt
countrysid

just before a sharp bend going down to the bay. One has a massive central column, four surrounding chambers, an angled doorway and dents in the outside wall like giant fingerprints.

From here, the flat countryside begins to rise gently towards the small peaks in the centre of the island. To the south the boat-like outline of the **Naveta d'es Tudons**, dubbed the oldest building in Europe, is clearly visible from the main road. It can seem mundane when swamped by a crowd of tourists or children scampering on the roof, but caught in solitude in the early morning or evening light it becomes magnificent. More typically, two nearby *taulas*, the **Torre Trencada** and **Torre Llafuda**, the latter fortified by the Romans, are only found by trial, error and tact down tracks; both gain immeasurably from their quiet farm settings among wild olive trees.

Private exploration: The woods and farmland further east—including an area of legendary beauty called **La Vall** kept unspoiled by privacy—are largely inaccessible, cut only by roads to farms with the occasional plaintive notice, *No se va a ninguna playa*, (no beaches here). But you get a good feel of the farmland of the rolling northern valleys, and its *fincas* on the lane which leads to **Santa Agueda**, the ruined Arab fort reached by a steep paved Roman path.

To the south, you can walk up the **Barranco d'Algendar**, one of a series of hidden gorges, steep-sided and lush, with grandiose dimensions which seem astonishing fitted into such a small island. There is a breathtaking view from **Son Mercer de Baix**, a prehistoric settlement perched dizzyingly above the wild ravine of Son Fideu, hard to find but well worth the effort.

Two towns: Nestling in the hills below, surrounded by terraced *tancas*, **Ferreries** is the highest town or village in the island although only 450 feet above sea level. It grew up around a monastery founded after the Catalan conquest, but remained a poor village known mainly for its blacksmiths until this century, when it acquired a small furniture in-

la En
rqueta,
pular with
cals.

dustry. Now it lives easily and has expanded into a town with a grid of spacious streets and plenty of bars. The old village streets remain as a modest nucleus, but the church of **Sant Bartomeu** was rebuilt in the late 19th century with a gilt-encrusted retable curiously elaborate for the otherwise plain interior.

By contrast, **Mercadal**—the junction point of east and west—has the atmosphere and occasional farmyard smells of a town which still looks primarily to the land; here the galleried church has a carving of a saint hung with wooden models of a yoke, a plough, a hoe and a fence as offerings. There are bars and restaurants serving local food, useful shops selling earthenware cooking pots, hats, *albarcas* (comfortable country sandals with soles made from tyres) and a renowned confectioner selling irresistible macaroons called *amargos*. Many shoe shops will still have old patterns in evidence although their stock is not as local as it used to be. As recently as the late 19th century almost one half of the island's popula-

tion was involved in the shoe industry, but now only about 40 manufacturers still work. Mercadal's **Santa Eulàlia** church has been largely rebuilt, and the town's other main landmark, the windmill, is now the **Molí d'es Recó**, a restaurant with excellent Menorcan food.

Highest point: The windmill dominates the town and **Monte Toro** (1,171 ft, 357 metres) dominates everything. The **Santuario de Nuestra Señora El Toro**, now a convent, has been there since medieval times, although the overall effect created by aerials, satellite dishes, piped music, café and souvenir shops is largely secular, and visitors will be lucky to catch a glimpse of a nun. Linguists and traditionalists argue about the origin of the mount's name. The former maintain that it derives from the Arabic Al-Tor, meaning the main mountain; the latter believe it to be named after a wild bull which supposedly led monks to a cave where they found a statue of the Madonna and Child. Whatever the truth the latter is stronger for the imagination and ac-

Left, the Monte Toro madonna. Right, Menorquín jewellery maker.

cordingly the chapel's Madonna incorporates a bull.

In the courtyard is a memorial to Father Pedro Camps, born in Mercadal, who led a group of Menorquíns to Florida in 1768, after continuous persecution of Catholics by successive British governors. Descendants of that original group of emigrants still live in Florida.

On the northern coast unspoilt beaches around **Binimel-la** and the rugged **Cabo de Cabelleria** (good views from the lighthouse) are worth a detour. Closer to the mountain, and marked by a deep bay which penetrates into the island, is the bay of **Fornells**, which would have been another magnificent fishing village if only its water had been deep enough. Fornells was known in the past for its daring sailors, but now lives from the sea indirectly through a bream farm and tourism. There are watersports and boat trips to visit the caves of **Na Polida** and the lizards on the island.

For Spaniards Fornells is synonymous with lobster, which are said to be particularly good here (*calderetta*, lobster stew, is the speciality) and King Juan Carlos eats in the **Es Plá** restaurant on the waterfront when he's on the island (usually on day trips over from Mallorca). To the left of the small waterside square is yet another *zona militar*: here a garrison of one man whose main job is to check the papers of the international boats that come and go.

South of Monte Toro the wedge-shaped village of **San Cristóbal** was founded as an offshoot of Ferreries in the 18th century. It has been largely bypassed by tourism (cars head for the fine, but overcrowded, beach of San Aldeolato) and keeps its sleepy charm, with lovely examples of traditional rural architecture: a satisfyingly proportioned 18th-century church with a square bell tower, and small houses with half a dozen different styles of balcony, chimney, parapet and wooden shutters. On the surrounding slopes are webs of abandoned *tancas*, evidence of the recent drift away from working the land everywhere.

ɔrnells fish fit for a ng. ɔllowing ɪge, bow ɪndow in llacarlos.

THE ENGLISH INFLUENCE

Visitors to Menorca are left in no doubt of the enduring impression that the English colonialists left upon the island's past, present, and probably, its future. Remembering that the island, the most easterly of the Balearics, was dominated by the British for two-thirds of the 18th century, it is not surprising that a notable legacy of the period has been left upon the architecture, the customs and even the language of Menorca.

The British first arrived in 1708 as part of an English-Dutch expedition siding with the loyalists of the Archduke of Austria against the partisans of the French Bourbons of Philippe V. The battle lasted 11 days before the Archduke and his allies were victorious. Five years later the island came under British control under the terms of the Treaty of Utrecht.

The first governor, Colonel Richard Kane, set up his headquarters in San Felipe, a fortified castle at the entrance to Port Mahón. Moving notable Menorquíns into positions of public stature, he began his 21 year rule by centralising the bureaucracy and economic activity in the island's new capital of Mahón. After conducting Menorca's first census he made regulations to protect the agricultural sector and imported breeding stock to improve local herds. Legislative moves such as the ordering of the planting of new species of fruit trees and grain to improve the existing crops and the building of new roads earned Kane a gold star in Menorca's history books. He loved the islanders and they loved him; he gave them a present of a clock now on the town hall in Mahón, and they more recently gave his memory a present of his own first road across the island, the Camí d'en Kane. Kane died in 1736 at the age of 76 leaving behind a Mahón, and a Menorca, very much more English than when he arrived.

His sucessors, Brigadier Anstruther and General Wynward, unlike Kane, were sent to dominate the island. In moves to increase their own personal fortunes, Anstruther stockpiled goods received from England, selling them again once they had become in short supply. He censored mail and tried to control political opinion. His successor Wynward, in his turn, openly provoked confrontation between the British and the Menorquíns. They both returned to their homeland very wealthy men.

When the attempts at total Anglicisation of Menorca failed a new governor, Blackney, was sent to try and recover the near forgotten legacy left by Governor Kane. Unfortunately, his few short years at the job were witness to bad harvests, sickness and the conquest of the island by the French in 1756.

Lord Johnston and Lady Cecil began the second British domination of 1763-1781 by cutting down all of the wheat, levying taxes and trying to shut down the Catholic churches. When the subsequent governor, Mr Murray, arrived, the island was plagued by drought, hunger and epidemics. His open dislike for the Menorquíns left him with little popular support when the island was reconquered by the Spanish in 1782. After one more short, final British occupation, Menorca was returned once and for all to Spanish control in 1802 under the terms of the Treaty of Amiens.

The legacy left by the British domination of Menorca is both broad and deep. The largest single remnant must be that of the village of Villacarlos, which was built near Mahón's harbour-mouth fortress of San Felipe. Its geometrically designed streets expanding outwards from a central parade square were a clear departure from the then existing Spanish-Menorcan urban thinking in which the town radiates chaotically from around the Catholic church. The red and white colour scheme which adorns the city hall as well as many other buildings in Villacarlos and Menorca in general is also an often seen remainder of the British epoch.

During the 18th century, Palladian architecture was brought to the island, where it was often coupled with the then fashionable red and white colour scheme. *Fachadismo* (façadism), a method of adding a Palladian-inspired neo-classical façade to an existing house, became the last word in architectural fashion after its introduction. Today the colourful façades with their often dated geometrical frontons are common in both the villages and the countryside lending a dra-

matically distinctive Menorcan architectural image which has no counterpart in any of the other Balearic islands.

Without doubt the island's best known example of Palladian architecture is a large country house overlooking Puerto Mahón known as San Antonio or Golden Farm. Although guide books, and even the Menorquíns themselves, describe the house as being the "love nest" of Admiral Nelson and Lady Hamilton, it is only because they would like this to be true. Evidence exists that Nelson probably used the house as his lodgings during one of his stops in Menorca. But the tale that it was the scene of an amorous adventure between the legendary couple is based upon a few words carved into a desk which is kept in San Antonio's library. The inscription says, "Remember of me E", the suggestion being that E is Emma Hamilton. There is not one word about a Golden Farm entanglement in Lady Hamilton's correspondence, nor in any of the pertinent published biographies.

Apart from the stories of what Horatio and Emma did or did not do in the *finca* of San Antonio, the eye-catching multicoloured Palladian façades and the town of Villacarlos, the most ubiquitous remnant of the English presence must be that of the *guillotine* or sash window. Neither it nor its usual Menorcan adornment of white lace curtains, is seen elsewhere in the islands or on the Spanish mainland. The Menorquín *boinder* is also attributed to the British domination of the 18th century. The word is said to be derived from "bow window".

Inside the houses, Menorcan furnishings are solidly rooted in such well known traditional British designs as Queen Anne, Hoggard and Chippendale, originals of which can be seen in the grand mansions whose ancestry predates the period of the English influence.

Visible manifestations aside, the colonial influence permeates into the most subtle of the island's customs and traditions. The Menorquín dialect which derives from the Catalan language is sprinkled with Anglicisms at every level, from the most superficial to the most profound. Some, like *vermell com un Jan* (red like an Englishman) and *ball des cosil* (Scottish dances), are colloquialisms which have worked their way into the local dialect. Others are direct Menorquínisations of English words. For example *tornescru* and *bech* are the islander's versions of the words "turnscrew" and "back". The total lack of connection of these two words with their Spanish equivalents of *destornillador* and *respaldo* banishes any thought of their being derived from any other source than the period of the British domination.

According to British historian D W Donaldson, there are at least 50 commonly used words such as *beguer* or beggar (Spanish: *mendigo*), *bifi* or beef (Spanish: *carne*), *tibord* or tea board (Spanish: *bandeja*) and *chel* or shell (Spanish: *concha*) which fit into the two previously mentioned categories. A third group, and maybe the most interesting are the marks left on the language by Governor Kane himself. His favorite apples are still known today as *pommes de Kane* and according to legend, the locally grown *prunas de neverso* are named after his response to seeing a type of plum which up until that moment he had "never saw".

Still subtler than the impressions left upon the language are those which have entered the kitchen. In the Menorcan pantry *mantega inglesa* (English butter) is used in a variety of baked goods. The only direct remnant may be that of *plum queque* (pronounced ploom-kay-kay) which is nothing more than good old English plum cake.

Although the Menorquíns spent many difficult years under the domination of the English, they look back at the positive social gains made during the early decades under the guidance of Governor Kane with a sense of pride. In the 1980s they take for granted their bicultural heritage. In the past few years the majority of the Palladian-inspired houses have been declared historical monuments, Hanover Street in Mahón once again wears its original signpost and the English military hospital on the Isla del Rey is being refurbished as a cultural centre.

Today, for better or worse, the Anglicisation continues and it is now possible for a visitor to communicate totally in English and find "bangers and beans" in almost every snack bar. In many parts of the island it is now easier to buy a *Daily Mirror* than a local *Diario De Menorca*.

IBIZA, WHITE ISLAND

Once the European get-away for 1960s hippies, Ibiza has now become the gateway for the summer Euro-hip. Smaller than Menorca (coastal circumference of 130 miles (210 km), as opposed to Menorca's (177 miles or 286 km) it nevertheless receives more than double the number of visitors of its larger sister island. Most of these visitors are either British or German. Like the rest of the Balearics the island has been a haven at one time or another for a variety of colonial powers, who have named it variously Ibosim, Ebisos, Ebusus, Yebisah, Ivitza, Yabsa, Ybica, Eresos, Ivica and Eivissa.

Ibiza is an island of excess and attracts two very different types of sun and fun lovers. You'll see, on the one hand, the absolute worst of cheap package tourism rearing some very ugly heads around the bay of San Antonio and, on the other, the best of European nightlife to be found in clubland in and around the island's capital—Eivissa (Ibiza) town.

Having suffered at the hands of thieving pirates and invaders through the centuries, the Ibizencos (or Eivisencs) now welcome tourists with open bars and happy smiles. After all, in a long history of foreign dominance it's the first time they've had visitors who actually pay for the privilege of being there. The main reason for this island reaching such an elite status amongst the rare-groovers of America and Europe is the incredibly tolerant attitude of the locals, who are at most just tepid Catholics. There is very little that they haven't seen before and they are more than prepared to let anything go as long as it harms no one and doesn't interfere with their great summer pre-occupation of making money. So you'll see the wildest, most wonderful and colourful collection of people gathered from all round Europe making the most of Ibiza's laid back way of life. "Live, let live" and "Be Happy, Don't Worry" seem to be the island mottos.

Origins: Unlike Spain's other Mediterranean islands of Mallorca and Menorca, neither Ibiza nor Formentera have any megalithic monuments which would show evidence of pre-historic habitation. They were known as the Islas Pityussas, which derives from the Greek *nesari pituoussai,* meaning islands of pine trees.

As well as the ubiquitous ancient Greeks, other early tourists of Ibiza were the Phoenicians. They were followed by their distant cousins, the Carthaginians, from North Africa and, then who else of course but the Romans.

The Carthaginians called it the island of Bes, one of their ancient gods, from which the present day name developed. Bes was one of the more pleasant of the Punic deities, a kind of Bacchus of his day, responsible for making merry and happy marriages. A good thing they didn't name the island after some of their other, less friendly gods like Baal or Melkart who preferred the blood of human sacrifice rather than a flagon of wine and a few flowers.

The Carthaginians are also said to be responsible for the introduction of a very strange hound particular, and peculiar, to Ibiza. These long-eared, stretch-snouted, short-legged and dim-witted creatures exist totally oblivious to the maxim that they are supposed to be man's best friend. Inbred mutts though they be, these *podencos* are favoured by local hunters.

Burial ground: It could well have been the fact that there being no poisonous plant, insect nor animal on Ibiza, the Phoenicians brought their dead from the other side of the Mediterranean and buried them here in the rich non-toxic soil which would guarantee a happy afterlife. Because of such extensive Phoenician, or Punic, necropoli, there is an incredible wealth of artifacts and archaeology from that era. Indeed, there are two Punic museums, one within the walls of the old town, or **D'Alt Vila**, by the cathedral and the other just outside the town at the ancient burial ground of **Puig des Molins**.

Ibiza's ideal and strategic position half way between Africa and Europe also made the island a place for the living. Under the Carthaginians and the Romans, it became a great centre for trans-Mediterranean trading. As seafaring vessels in those days dared not wander too far from the coastline, it was an obvious stop-over port of call. The vast natural *salinas*, or salt flats, were heavily exploited not only for export of what was the most expensive white powder of its day, but also to help preserve much of the foodstuffs of the passing ships.

Roman relish: Just as Mahón in the neighbouring island of Menorca gave its name to locally invented *mayonnaise*, Ibiza was responsible for the more ancient delicacy of **garum**—if the Romans had eaten hamburgers, this would have been their relish—a sticky, gloopy ketchup made of fish gut. Otherwise there is very little left nowadays of Roman influence, except the roads, and they fan out from Eivissa town in a handful of straight and narrow rulers.

Ibiza, as with the rest of Spain, didn't

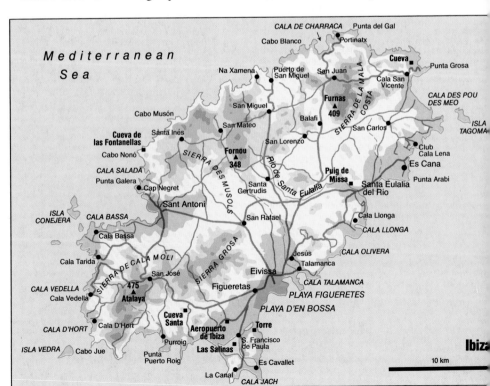

escape the Moorish invasion of the 8th century. Muslim rule lasted almost uninterrupted for 500 years. The Moors were a very tolerant lot. During their stay, synagogues, mosques and churches existed quite harmoniously side by side.

Ibizencos still have that Moorish gypsy air about them, like the Andalusian people of southern Spain. Their customs, traditional dress and music are all heavily influenced by Arab culture. Indeed, there still exists a small Moorish settlement near San Lorenzo, known as **Balafia**; the buildings are all flat-roofed, key-windowed and white-washed. Architects since have been copying this cubic style. Rooms are built to functional order in the shape of cubes; if more rooms are needed, more cubes are added. Even today, some of the smartest homes on the island have been built in this style and it is said to have influenced the biggest cube-maker of the 20th century, Le Corbusier.

After the reconquest of the island by the Spanish the Moors were sent pack-ing and the great Catholic church with its regal representatives began the lengthy, and at times, literally tortuous process of bringing the Balearics back into the fold.

Christian Conquerors: In 1235, King Jaime of mainland Aragón, entered the island and conquered it in the name of Christianity and since the day of Muslim surrender that year, Ibiza has remained both Catholic and Catalan.

Once Columbus had discovered the promised lands of America, Spain devoted most of its men and resources to protecting the plunder ships returning from the New World. Its Mediterranean lands and islands were left to defend themselves against attacks from exiled Muslims. The Ibizan corsairs came into their own at this time, out-pirating the pirates, patrolling the coastlines and getting rich as a result. In 1554, the King of Spain, wanting to help completely stamp out any Muslim presence, ordered the construction of the walls around Eivissa town.

Thereafter the island's fortunes slid

e walls of
Alt Vila.

THE HIPPY ERA

About 20 years ago, while Sergeant Pepper was teaching the band to play, many of the 1960s flower-power children were leaving the rat-race of major cities to search for real-life nirvana. To celebrate their new found freedom and to practise this fresh desire for love and peace, they moved out to the sunshine.

As the west coast of California became the shrine to every American mama and papa dressed in a kaftan, so Ibiza became Europe's summer home to every hippy who could get it just enough together to make the crossing from Barcelona to their Mediterranean paradise.

Spain in the 1960s was not internationally known for its progressiveness or liberalism. General Franco ruled with iron fists rather than open arms. But he lived in far-off Madrid and wasn't to know that the Ibizencos were very happy to have all this foreign money pouring into their bars and shops and businesses—even if it did come from beaded purses owned by long haired aliens of indeterminate sex.

Islands have often proved to be exceptions to most rules, and it is therefore logical that anyone seeking an alternative life-style would do well to look first at an island. These first visitors too found a happy holiday home in Ibiza. For most

of them, Spain was still very cheap and the Ibizan attitude offered an insular paradise in an inhospitable world. The Ibizencos are even more laid back than the other islanders of the Balearics, happier with hippies than with impetuous developers with plans to turn the island upside down.

Ibiza was "discovered" as a place that would do nicely by the members of the Marrakesh Express. In a world pursuit of peace, love and soft drugs, this bohemian band of hippy wanderers made for Goa in the winter months and passed through North Africa en route to the Mediterranean at the beginning of the summer. The island became an international ghetto to those most fond of tuning in, turning on and dropping out.

In turn, the rich and famous became attracted to this centre of summer "happening". Massimo Rivabene, who first started coming to Ibiza from Milan in 1969 and is still coming back, remembers Ursula Andress as his neighbour in a village near Sant Llorenç. He also remembers coming with his car which had to be lifted onto the boat from Barcelona in those pre-ferry days.

Eivissa then was a clean, unassuming white-washed harbour town, topped by a well-walled citadel which overlooked the fishing boats—just about the only vessels ever to dock there.

In the 1960s and 1970s, the swinging was done down by the port. Everyone stayed in the D'Alt Vila, went to the beach at Figueretas and made music, smoked joints and hung out along the Paseo Marítimo surrounding the harbour.

The island's first disco was Lola's, at the foot of the ramp into the D'Alt Vila by the Portal de las Tablas. It's still there, but is now home to a nightly drag act and a meeting place for the young and hip to decide which club they'll go to next. Then the idea was to sit around and get stoned and talk about the universe, now it's to buzz about on things more chemical and use up energy at the all-night clubs or on other earthly pursuits.

There are still hangovers from the halcyon hippy days. Some of the flower children still come back, though this time with the Volvo, designer labels and children of their own. But there are others who live here all year round. They have moved well away from the capital and can be found all living together communally near Sant Carlos. There are about a dozen families. No one's quite sure who's fathered whom, but the children have all turned out an interesting and colourful combination.

Hippies are melodious, odorous, sleepy, smiley people; as such they are a rarity these days, having been largely replaced by rather severe, intellectual idealist greens who have a great deal less fun but still wear all the gear.

Fortunately the true tradition still lives on at the Punta Arabí hippy market, near Es Caná. The all-year inhabitants prepare arts and crafts through the off-season to sell to the tourists in the summer months. These days they make more sand-pictures than peace pipes and people tend to come to stare more and buy less, but the spirit lives on. Where else could they live but Ibiza?

into decline as it became a pawn on the board of European politics. In 1715, during the Spanish War of Succession, the island ended up backing the eventual loser and so suffered the consequences by having its salt fields taken over by the victor. Their main source of income having been taken from them, the islanders became bankrupt and only just managed to limp through into the modern era.

Ibiza entered the 20th century as a poor, forgotten, almost abandoned piece of Spain, whose patrimony came about by history rather than design. When 1960s soul-searchers from America and Europe discovered these tolerant and welcoming "White Islands", the Ibizencos began to discover a new and exceedingly lucrative source of income which did not depend on the political whim and fancy of a Madrid government too far to care and too confused to interfere.

New arrivals: So the tourist boom began. The easy-going 1960s led into the packaged summer Seventies. Ibiza has enjoyed the money, living very much for today and not daring to think too much about tomorrow. Over 90 percent of the island's jobs are tourist related and the only other profitable venture on the whole island is the Salinas salt producing company.

Little is grown for the islanders' needs. Apart from the almond crops harvested for exportation, everything else comes in from the mainland. The young don't want to work the almost impossible land and instead are drawn to the bars, clubs and restaurants where they can make enough in the summer to be able to do very little in the winter.

Once a whitewashed gem in an emerald sea, **Eivissa** town is beginning to look a little tarnished at the edges—the streets not quite as quaint and charming, the beaches not always well looked after. The old pirate ethic to make for today and let tomorrow look after itself still lives on. But time, like the water drawn from the underground wells, could well be running out for Ibiza. Only the smartest hotels have a constant

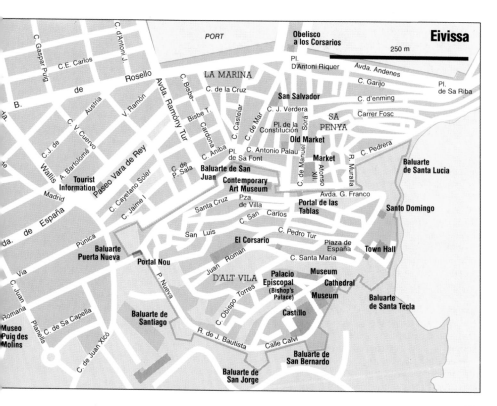

DOING THE PASEO

Siesta and fiesta apart, an integral part of Spanish life-style is strolling the squares or promenading the parks in the most essential of trivial pursuits: doing the *paseo*.

In other, more hurried, cultures, the shopping mall has become the focal centre for social activities, where young and old wander aimlessly, coveting the window displays. But in the days before people were born to shop, the purpose for the *paseo* was to meet, chatter, mix and mingle. You'd get to hear the real stories out on the *paseo*, the gossip that mattered. There was no need for newspapers or television, with their studious reports from faraway places, when Señora always had her finger on the pulse and her tongue ready to tell about what really mattered.

Doing the *paseo* is somewhere between a pastime and a profession, an essential couple of hours of lubrication that keeps the wheels of the week turning, providing topics for conversation, speculation and scandal. If you were impressed by the flood of people on the sea-front of Barcelona on your crossing to the island, you will be doubly impressed by the quantity that fill Ibiza's narrow streets. In warmer climates, street meetings were, and indeed still are, popular for two very simple reasons. For one, houses tended to be cramped, strictly the domain of the family, built small and dark to keep the costs down and the heat out, and so being outside meant air to breathe as well as space to move. Even today in Ibiza only intended *fiancés* are admitted to the domestic family sanctum; everyone else is met in the streets, the bars, cafés and in the restaurants.

Six days shalt thou labour but on the seventh thou shalt strut thy stuff; the Ibizencos are avid participants in the *paseo*. Come Sunday afternoons by six of the clock everyone is out on the stroll, and the aptly named Paseo Vara de Rey square by the port becomes the centre of the universe as far as Eivissa is concerned. Look and be looked at; dress up, eye up, be eyed up.

Three, maybe four, generations move around

the square in a ritualistic routine of meetings and greetings. Widowed grannies dressed like polished black beetles push perambulators. Contented parents idle arm in arm next to them. Well scrubbed children do their utmost to mess up their Sunday best by playing "Havoc and Scream" the length of the Paseo. Even the birds chip in.

Included in the circuit, and part of the rites of *paseo*, is a stop at an ice-cream vendor for the kids, an aperitif or two on a street-side terrace and the purchase of a bag of *pipas* (sunflower seeds) to consume at the bar or on a bench. (There is a definite technique to cracking open the seeds in your mouth, extracting the seed with the tongue and spitting out the shell without dribbling.)

Before the loosening of social attitudes and the arrival of the discotheque, the square served another purpose than sociable strolling. This was the official cruise centre. When the opposite sexes had little opportunity of getting together, the Sunday *paseo* was the place to meet. Here you'd hope to catch the eye of someone you fancied even if you were under the watchful gaze of promenading parents.

In the gallant old days the gentlemen would try, to catch the ladies' eyes, softening them up with compliments, which of course the ladies would pretend not to hear. Mind you, any lady who spent a whole *paseo* without compliment would see to it that she looked different next week.

Now in his late forties, Ernesto Ramón can well remember the trials and torments of dating his intended wife, Purificación. The process of getting off with girls was a very lengthy business which generally led to betrothal rather than a quick snog behind the bike shed.

It involved more ritual than romp and more stance than romance, and family feuds from pirate days made it almost impossible to fall in love with a descendant of an ancient enemy. When it was thought time for a daughter to marry, the *festejo*, or courtship, commenced. The men interested would gather at her house and try to win her parents' approval. Once a suitor was chosen then the two families would meet and actually visit each other's houses.

If you've made it into an Ibizan sitting room, you've entered into the family's heart.

supply of fresh water in their bathrooms during the busiest summer season. The authorities discount the possibility of a desalination plant as being too costly. They think they'll be able to cope. The question is, will the tourists? And for just how long?

The Balearic islands, like many other parts of Spain, are going through a resurgence of local identity. During the Franco years, only Castillian Spanish as practised in Madrid was allowed to be heard on the streets. Nowadays, in an effort to purge those pungent memories, every region in Spain is clamouring for autonomy and regional awareness. The visitor will come across this on the highways and by-ways as most of the road signs have been altered, by illegal paint pots usually, into local dialect. Ibizenco is a version of Catalan, the language based around the area of Catalonia. The first signs of confusion are outside the airport. If you're heading for the capital, indications to "Eivissa" will put you in the right direction.

Eivissa: There are essentially four parts to the main town of the island. The old walled city, D'Alt Vila, on high; the Sa Penya, or old fishing quarter; the Marina along the waterfront and the new town spreading out for some distance from the Paseo Vara de Rey.

The **D'Alt Vila** makes use of the natural defences afforded by high cliffs on which it is built, the other three sides being well protected by a wall of massive and seemingly unassailable proportions. And yet this citadel was supposedly stormed by Jaime I in 1235, recovering the island from Arab control, although tradition has it that Jaime's troops were allowed to enter secretly in the middle of the night by the ruling sheikh's brother, in revenge for the sheikh having stolen his wife.

Since its admission into the European Market, Spain has declared Ibiza's old town as a National Monument and a Euro-funded renovation project is underway to restore D'Alt Vila to its former imposing splendour.

There are two principal gates into the D'Alt Vila—the **Portal de las Tablas** (named so because of the huge slabs that used to serve as the drawbridge) and the **Portal Nou** (new). Traffic nowadays circulates by entering by the former and leaving by the latter. Within the walls there is the old castle, cathedral, town hall, contemporary art museum, a Punic relics museum and an open-air bar (*chiringuito*) serving cruisers, movers and late-night losers en route around the clubs through the night; it's also popular with the hard-working trash collectors that work through the wee small hours. The views from here over the bay are quite magnificent, as they should be from a position almost 300 ft (91 metres) above the sea.

The **Cathedral of Santa Maria de las Nieves** is built on well-hallowed ground on the site of a mosque, a Roman temple and, more than likely, a Carthaginian shrine.

Within the walls there is also a maze of impossibly tiny streets which sneak in and out of each other making it the most ideal place for hide and seek. Here too is **El Corsario**, once a pirate family mansion, now a reasonably smart hotel.

ad proach to issa.

Eivissa's many gay visitors frequent the Anfora disco here and the bars along the Sa Carrosa, just inside the walls. On the outside too, there are other busy gay bars above the Sa Penya quarter.

Tucked away under the D'Alt Vila at the end of the harbour, **Sa Penya** was once the fishermen's quarter and is still the poorest and shabbiest part of town. The small, cramped houses here have most families sitting about outside chatting, knitting or shelling peas till well beyond midnight. Then they retire indoors to snore the night away with doors and windows fully open to benefit from any odd breeze. Only five yards down the street along the harbour you'll see Wealth out shopping.

Night moves: Everything happens at night in the **La Marina** district. The shops are here, most of the bars and nearly all of the popular restaurants. In fact it is easy to forget that it is night as you walk through the brightly lit streets, (more like alleys), weaving amongst stalls, bar stools and restaurant tables. There is a definite recognised circuit to

paseo, or promenade.

Beginning at the edge of the harbour outside the popular, though unfriendly, **Montesol bar**, walk along the harbour's edge, the **Paseo Marítimo**, until you reach **The End**. This is not where the harbour stops but is actually one of Europe's smartest clothes shops. Here you can buy the latest Gaultier and the best from Boy—you can even get your autumn fashions here before going home. From here your stroll along the port will take you past some very good eating places and some very loud bars.

Before new moorings were built around the harbour to the west side many a fancy yacht, often bearing a Saudi Arabian flag, docked here. Once you reach the end (this time not the shop) of the Paseo Marítimo, turn along **Calle Mayor** and take in all the stalls which are open every evening till at least midnight. Here you can pick up some of the brightest designs in Europe, as jewellers and accessory artists come to clean out the tourist wallets.

Acquired taste: Another more typical

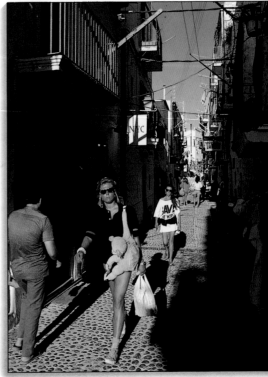

Left, the narrow streets of Sa Penya. Fashion shopping (right).

and less expensive souvenir of the island is a bottle of *hierbas*. This is a delicious aromatic mixture of herbs stewed in alcohol, and it varies from recipe to recipe. The Hotel Hacienda in the north of the island produces a bottle favouring more the flavour of lemon, mint and tarragon. Others are more heavily biased and based upon anise, and some are based on the carob bean.

Looking like black flattened bananas, carob are usually fed to the pigs, but the high syrup content makes them akin to the maple and a local favourite to distil with alcohol. Some bottles are sold with fresh sprigs of herb submerged in the liqueur. Whichever you choose, a *hierbas* is a good way to remember Ibiza.

Bar talk: Around midnight, outside the **Zoo** bar, the public relations teams of the major clubs begin their evening's work. Most clubs, like **Ku**, **Amnesia** and **Pachá**, have party nights two or three times a week and they send out very colourful and highly competitive press gangs to convince the lesser dressed mortals that their night would

not be complete without a visit to their venue. They usually stick you with little badges displaying their club's logo just so you won't forget, and sometimes hand out free entrance passes.

At the end of the evening *paseo*, find your favourite bar and hang out for a couple of hours before the really serious business of all-night dancing.

Beyond the Paseo Vara de Rey is the new town—a badly designed sprawl thrown together in recent years to house the overspill from the D'Alt Vila. It is to new apartments here that the locals moved with the money earned from tourism. The new covered *mercado* (market) is here too, as are the major bus stops from whence you can reach almost every corner of the island. One good thing about this area is that the ordinary family restaurants tend to be exceptionally good value compared to the main touristic circuit.

Close at hand: The nearest beaches are to be found at **Figueretas**, a mile-long stretch of holiday homes and hotels, which also boasts some smart places to

stay, including **Los Molinos** with its own pool and beach access. The bay goes beyond to **Playa d'en Bossa** which is, if not quite The Last Resort, very near to it. The package holiday was delivered here and it is doubtful that the postman will ever come back to take it away again.

The nearest and clearest beaches are at **Es Cavallet** and **Las Salinas**. Both are along the road signposted La Canal, off the airport road and at the end of the salt-flats. Las Salinas beach has the sea-fun stuff—windsurf boards, monoskis, kayaks—some good food huts and even some beach boutiques. Although the beach is sandy and quite clean, there are about 10,000 cigarette butts to be found every square foot and raffia-type seaweed does collect at the water's edge.

Beyond one of the island's many still-standing ancient watch-towers, Es Cavallet is probably the most popular nude beach on Ibiza. The families linger around the *chiringuito* bar at the beginning of the long sandy stretch. Other facilities here include rudimentary ball courts, a massage table (complete with masseur) and even at times a hair-dresser. Further along, and catered for too, is a very predominantly gay beach. Local buses to La Canal from Eivissa save a long walk to either beach.

Inland, along the Eivissa-Sant Josep road is the **Cueva Santa**, a small cave open to the public. A little further along this road you'll see signposts for **Casa Juana**, which is one of the island's better restaurants.

Sant Antoni: The island's second town, nine miles (15 km) distant from Eivissa, may as well be planets away. It was called Portus Magnus by the Romans because of its very sizeable natural harbour and is nowadays referred to as Portmany by the island authorities. Sant Antoni is built around one side of a large bay from whence you can see the sun set beyond a dozen small islands dotted off the shore. The whole place could be very romantic if it were not for the fact that this has become one of the favourite destinations for many of Europe's cheapest inclusive package holiday-

Sant Antoni package holiday paradise.

makers and it has ended up looking like a very grubby all-night drive-in supermarket.

The harbour front is heaving with clubs, pubs, boat trips and discos. There are souvenir shops stuffed with straw-hatted donkeys, bars which serve pints of beer, shandies and knickerbocker glories and restaurants which specialise in those very Ibizan dishes of baked beans, bacon and chips. Chic it ain't but fun for sure. The whole place is geared for people, young people, out to have a good time. And if your idea of having a good time is getting sunburnt, getting drunk and getting laid, then this is the place for you.

The **Parish Church** of Sant Antoni stands out in this bedlam like an oasis of tranquillity. Built in the 14th century on the ruins of a mosque it is a white-washed architectural mixture of fortress and Persian palace.

Just outside Sant Antoni, at Sa Vorera, is **Pike**'s, a fairly stylish and classy hotel which has been home to some of the island's more outrageous pop celebrity parties and also has a very good restaurant.

The coast by sea: There only being a very tiny beach in Sant Antoni, most beach bathers take a boat trip beyond the bay. Here there are more than enough beaches to make every day a different destination during a fortnight's stay. At **Cala Bassa**, across the bay, there is a lot of tourist development, but if you head further south, beyond the family time-share holiday lets and resorts of **Cala Vedella** and **Cala d'Hort**, you'll come across a little bit of South Pacific; the offshore islet, **Isla Vedrá**, featured as Bali Hai in the 1950s film of the same name.

Popular local legend also has it that Hannibal (he of the Alps and elephants) was born here. Given that the rock is un-inhabitable and that history has him coming from Carthage yet another local legend seems to be found ideologically unsound.

From Sant Antoni there are boat trips around the island to Eivissa or to Portinatx. Both trips giving you views you'd

the end of
ard day
the
ach.

LAS SALINAS

Ibiza has it all: sun, sea, sand and salt, particularly salt. There are nearly 1,000 acres of productive salt flats between Eivissa Airport and the deep blue sea, flats which have played a conspicuous role in the island's history.

Prior to the tourists, the past invaders of this Balearic island came because of the great abundance of the highly valuable commodity of natural sea farmed sodium chloride. Freezer ships and cool containers not being popular with those ancient Carthaginians, salt was used for preservation purposes and was especially necessary for sailors on long journeys. Salt beef, salt fish, salt with everything.

Ibiza's fortunes, and indeed falls, were based on its *salinas*, or saltpans. Everybody journeying the Mediterranean from North Africa to mainland Europe used and abused Ibiza's strategic position and stocked up with salt on their way through. From the sales of salt the fortification of Eivissa town was made possible and the walls around the D'Alt Vila were built in 1554 from the industry's proceeds. Captured pirates were put to work in the salt flats, and rather than waste money on prisons, criminals were put to work there too.

At the time of the wall building all of the islanders owned a share of the *salinas* and survived quite profitably on trading the salt for foreign grain. However, in 1715, following the Spanish War of Succession, the *salinas* were appropriated by the state as punishment to Ibiza for supporting the defeated faction.

The Ibizencos were still able to receive an annual rent and free salt until the middle of last century, when the *salinas* were sold to a private company and the islanders lost all rights, including their free salt.

The present owner of the rights and the saltpans themselves is Salinera Española SA. The company has improved and mechanised the methods of panning and collecting so much that nowadays the work of 600 is done by 20.

This is the only industry on the island not connected with tourism, apart from Ibiza Sound Recording Studio, which makes a profit. Of the one million tonnes of salt produced annually in Spain, Ibiza's *salinas* contribute 60,000, at $45 a tonne. Spain itself consumes 400,000 tonnes and the rest is exported—a great deal of it to Scandinavia and the Faroe Islands for salting fish. Some of it also finds its way onto dining tables.

Salt tankers can dock out at sea off La Canal, where a mechanised conveyor carries the awaiting cargo direct to the hold. But what if it rains? Antonio Torres Garcia, director of Ibiza's Salinera, says that no appreciable amount is lost—a crystallised crust is formed and anyway whatever is washed away into the sea can always be recuperated at a later date! There's plenty more salt available out there.

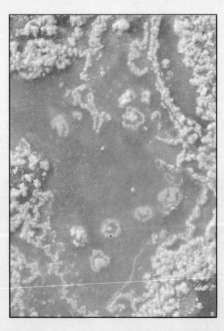

The process, Señor Torres explains, is simple, slow but very effective. Centuries of practice have seen to that. Two electric pumps allow two and a half thousand cubic metres of sea water into the below sea-level flats, but apart from that the industry is entirely "natural" and there is no need to alter its techniques: It takes about three months for the water to evaporate and the salt to precipitate, and after this time there remains a 10 centimetre layer of fine white salt ready for collection, often in a great sheet not unlike a sheet of ice.

Ibizan salt is of high quality because there are no poisonous plants nor creatures on the island and the ground itself is non toxic. Furthermore the precipitation flats themselves are also very clean with sound, solid hard clay floors so that no earth impurities are collected with the salt.

The *salinas* have made Ibiza a popular stopping point for migratory birds. From an ecological point of view, these salt fields are a very important reserve. Herons, storks and even flamingoes rest over here en route to the winter resorts of North Africa; trapped with the water is enough food to sustain them while resting.

Although visitors to the island can easily see the *salinas* and the mounds of collected salt awaiting the arrival of another cargo ship, the Salinera Española has no plans to turn the area into a tourist attraction with daily tours. However, the company is quite happy to sell salt to you, but only by the ton.

never be able to see otherwise. There are also trips from here to the Wednesday hippy market at Es Caná and also to the mainland and Formentera.

The coast by land: The road north of Sant Antoni to **Sant Miquel** via **Santa Agnes** is one of the most spectacular drives on the island. If you take some of the dirt track roads to the coast from here you'll come across enchanting, and quite deserted small, sandy coves or *calas*, like **Punta Galera** and **Cala Salada.** Just before reaching Santa Ines on this road, to the left and atop the Cap Nono, near a signpost called **Ses Fontanellas**, is a cave covered in supposed (but often questioned) Bronze Age paintings.

The island earth is rust coloured because of iron oxide mixed with the clay. The few crops are reared for export. In the early spring Ibiza practically turns white not because of snow, nor because of the salt blowing about, but because all the almond trees are in blossom.

North and east: Passing through, (and even stopping for a drink at), the small and endearing village of **Jesus**, the road runs alongside some heavy hotel coastal developments before slinking into the island's third town of **Santa Eulàlia del Riu** and the only one in the whole of the Balearics to be graced with a river.

Actually, this is rather a sad trickle of a stream than any *río grande*, and it dries up to a mud puddle in the height of summer. There is even a Roman viaduct barely visible from the bridge over the river. The town is topped with a white-washed church built, as is the town, in the name of the saint. Next to it, and hardly ever open, is a local museum containing paintings of a Catalan artist called Barrau, and surrounding it are typical small square Ibizan houses.

There is a busy fresh-produce market and some lively shopping to be done along its main streets. Some of the island's better restaurants are to be found here and, if you like large helpings and sweet sauces, one of the most popular is **El Naranjo.** For exercise, Santa Eulàlia has Ibiza's only golf course (near Cala Llonga), but having only nine holes,

don't expect to lose pounds.

Santa Eulàlia was once the home of writer Elliot Paul, who describes life in the village in the 1930s in his book *Life and Death of a Spanish Town*. In the book he describes how the driver of the once-daily bus was charged with tasks like buying medicines, cashing cheques, and taking the local fish catch to market. The local postmaster could neither read nor write and relied on his two daughters, who besides deciphering the addresses of infrequent letters read out snippets of news from the Ibiza newspaper that the bus brought back.

East of Santa Eulàlia is the beach resort of **Es Caná**, and a little further around the bay is **Punta Arabí**, the site of a hippy market every Wednesday, where the once kaftan-clad clan sell all manner of fairly useless, though some would say attractive, craft souvenirs. You can take boat journeys here from Eivissa and Sant Antoni on market days. On Thursdays, in the village of San Miquel to the north, there is another arts and craft market as well as occa-sional folk singing and folk dancing.

North of Es Caná and beyond more secluded coastal resorts, the road passes through **Sant Carlos**, where the hippies of yesteryear have settled down, and on to **Cala Sant Vicenç**. Unless you are lodged here, it is hardly worth the trek. Better beaches and more enthralling scenery can be found without having to suffer the urbanity and charmlessness of this holiday high street. From here there are views of the offshore isle of **Tagomago**, Ibiza's island wilderness with an unusual Pacific island name, which is uninhabited and visited mainly by scuba divers and fishermen. Like Cabrera, off Mallorca, attempts are being made to preserve Tagomago's untouched state.

Helium and Hacienda: The route between the two charming villages of Sant Joan and Sant Miquel is one of the prettiest. A hippy haunt called **Helium** can be found along this road, easily spotted by a very inventive collection of tin can sculptures in the garden. The most varied and dramatic scenery is to be found if you continue from Sant Miquel via Sant Mateu and Santa Agnes to Sant Antoni. Passing through so many saintly villages could well seem like a pilgrimage but the blessing will come with the journey's end.

Before reaching the **Port of Sant Miquel** a road twists and staggers steeply to the left and arrives at the island's most beautiful and best hotel, the **Hacienda**. Built high astride a cliff, over a secluded cove, it has one of the most attractive settings and its restaurant also has the island's finest chef. The Port itself is not so much a fishing harbour as another resort development. On the cliffs to the right is a bar affording a wonderful view underneath which are some visitable and quite awesome caves, where stalactites meet stalagmites in milkshake hues.

The bay of **Portinatx** still shows some of the charm of the island before the hotels were built. There isn't a great deal to do here and even trying to sunbathe can be a bit of a battle; you first have to find enough space to spread out a beach towel.

Left, long-legged attractions Punta Arabí Right, *campesino*

188

FORMENTERA

eceding
ges: rocky
tcrop at
Mola;
ssip in
nt
ancesc.
ft, a
ditional
ead oven.

Formentera, a ragged sliver of rock in the Mediterranean 2.5 miles (four kms) south of Ibiza, contains little of the obvious scenic or cultural interest found in the other Balearics. As the 4,000 islanders themselves put it, *te molt poca cosa que veure*, there is little to see: a handful of ruined watch-towers, a few windmills and three fortress churches. But the uncluttered simplicity, sometimes even raw harshness, of the landscape and the absence of distracting human grandeur have given the island other rare qualities: a sense of timelessness and of space despite its small size. And, when the light softens in the early morning and evening, an almost abstract beauty of colour and form. It comes as no surprise to learn that the islanders have the longest life expectancy in Spain.

How long Formentera will retain these qualities is hard to know. Some-

times called a miniature Ibiza of yesteryear, there are still areas of quiet farmland and as yet little glitziness, but it takes little to swamp such a small area. In summer the population doubles and the island teems with hired bikes, cars and safari jeeps. Tourism has brought addictive economic dependence and the lure of large-scale development may become increasingly difficult to resist.

Port link: One important protection remains to preserve the isolation: there is no airport. The island's main link with the outside world remains a small port, **La Sabina**, named after the Phoenician juniper trees which grow all over the island. Its straggling, modern appearance, an unpromising first impression when you come off the boat, belies its considerable historical importance. Limestone, dried fish, fruit and sea-salt have all been exported from here to Ibiza, although until recent times heavy seas and storms could cut winter communications for weeks at a time.

These days the increasing numbers of ferries and boats—the most characterful being *Joven Dolores*, a rolling tub in service for some 30 years—carry mainly tourists. The harbour is the focus of local life twice a year. In January the Three Kings bring in the children's Christmas presents by boat and in July the fishing boats gather here and sail out as a fleet to be blessed on the feast of Our Lady of the Sea, Formentera's principal annual fiesta.

Smells and salt: From La Sabina a road runs south past the **Estang d'es Peix**, a lake with sandy shores said to be well stocked with trapped sea-fish, and another loops east, skirting the larger **Estang Pudent**—literally Smelly Lake, an honest enough name at low tide thanks to its mass of weed. The surrounding country is flat and somewhat featureless except for hillocky dunes and the abandoned salt-beds, bleakly beautiful walled sheets of pink and yellow water or sparkling beaten earth, a solitary salt heap and an old railway track with small freight trucks nearby. A question mark hangs over their future. The owners are planning sale for development, but a local cam-

Formentera

5 km

Torre de Ses Portes
BIZA
ISLA ESPARDELL
ISLA ESPALMADOR
PLAYA D'ES PUJOLS
unta Pedrera   La Sabina
Estang del Peix   Estang Pudent   Es Pujols   Punta Prima
San Francisco Javier   San Fernando
LA HONA   Playa Mitjorn   Punta de la Creu
Cueva d'es Fum   Ferrer
Es Caló   Monastir   135
Guillem   107   PLAYA DE MITJORN   Mola   192   El Pilar
Punta Aguila   Maryland
Estufador
Torre
Cabo Berberia

Mediterranean Sea

paign is pushing for a national park to protect the area and the birds of passage—over 250 species—who come through here in winter.

Quiet metropolis: The road south leads past the only petrol station on the island to **Sant Francesc Xavier**, sometimes called the capital of the island but in reality a swollen village. If you sit in a café on the miniature plaza, opposite the windowless 18th-century fortress church and the shabby but gracious library, you can catch something of the feel of life here before electricity, the telephone and tourism arrived in one fell swoop in the late fifties.

The church at Sant Francesc, modern inside except for the lovely font, was built as a shelter from piracy, which plagued the island until the arrival of steamboats and the telegraph; the library used to be the town hall.

In the side streets there is everything from a chapel dating back to the 14th-century Catalan conquest by the Archbishop of Tarragona—which confirmed the island's link to Ibiza as one of the Pityussae rather than to Palma as one of the Baleares—to a health food shop. The shops include fishmongers and a co-operative where farmhouse sheep and goat's cheeses are sold in spring and early summer.

Tracks and trees: South and west, down networks of dirt tracks called the *carreteras del campo*, are lovely unspoilt patches of farmland criss-crossed by dry stone walls, now occasionally replaced by breeze-blocks, a sign of more hurried times. The fields, bald and brown in summer after the April harvest, are dotted by prickly pears, giant fig trees, (their branches supported by a ring of smaller trees) and carob trees, now the most important crop for export. The modesty of the geometrical farms which are fronted by unexpectedly gracious flowery porches and with wells, circular threshing grounds and domed ovens nearby, spell out the centuries of poverty and simplicity of life which gave rise to the famed longevity of the small number of islanders.

The road east loops round to **Es**

The sea-blessing fiesta in La Sabina.

Pujols, a fully fledged resort, small by some standards but not for Formentera, and rapidly spawning discos, beer gardens and apartments. Ugly club-hotel bungalows engulf the watch-tower on Punta Prima, the rocky eastern headland. Only the fine view of Ibiza, with the island of Vedrá rearing up like a sphinx and the fishermen's ramshackle boat houses, suggest the unspoiled bay where the island's first beach hotel was built thirty years ago.

Stone ring: Ironically the oldest known human monument on the island, a *dolmen* dating from 1600 B.C., stands unsignposted and rarely visited, just down the road at **Ca Na Costa**, a promontory into the Estang Pudent. The ring of upright stone slabs—discovered in 1976 with human remains, ceramics, jewellery and axes typical of a sophisticated Bronze-Age culture—is the best of 40 sites on the island, and it suggests that Formentera had a more fertile landscape which was destroyed by deforestation before the Phoenicians, Greeks, Romans and Moors all found the rocky

environment suitable only as a strategic military outpost.

The third main settlement on the island, **Sant Ferráu**, is traditionally the centre of the island's vineyards and, more recently, of its alternative culture. It is said that the hippies first gravitated here not so much for **Fonda Pepe**, its now legendary bar, but because they would be out of easy reach of the *guardia civil*, who at the time operated only by bicycle, and the first drug arrests were eventually made by police in hired taxis. Fonda Pepe still survives as a living museum of post-sixties youth culture in the high season, yet at the same time it is very Spanish, with loud music and local barflies of all ages.

Unexpected, but slotting happily into local life in Sant Ferráu, are an excellent privately run library and a workshop making guitars and other musical instruments. Nearby, the **Cuevas d'en Xeroni**, the only caves on the island open to the public, were found by a farmer making a well. Decorated by fibrous roots from the kitchen garden, they have disco lights and a bar.

Herbal tipple: The main road runs east down the spine of the narrow central isthmus, past a ruined Roman fortress (up an unmarked track near the 10 km milestone). The northern side is rocky, primitive landscape, sloping down from steep red cliffs at **Cala Encaste**, where you can swim off slippery boulders, to **Es Caló**, a fishing hamlet open to the road. According to local tradition this was the birthplace of *hierbas*, the local and variable herbal brew, first made here in an illegal distillery in the early 19th century.

To the south curves the **Playa de Mitjorn**, a sweep of narrow sandy beach, clogged with seaweed in places and backed by a number of tourist developments, notably the Hotel Formentera, a chunky white blot with Anglo-German timetables for organised sport, and Club Maryland, a holiday village in the same mould. Beyond here are some good small coves and rocky bays reached by footpath. Otherwise, the quiet stretch of sand near Torre d'es Catalá in the east is a good bet for undisturbed sea bathing.

Best beaches: Popular since the sixties but able to absorb the crowds and undeveloped except for small beach cafes, are the beaches on the finger of land north of the salt-beds, reached by sandy track or boat. **Llevant**, an open shoreline, has ocean-like breakers on windy days; on the other side **Illetes**, sometimes nicknamed Tahiti for its atoll-like offshore islands and milky-blue waters, is sheltered and has windsurfs for hire.

Just off the point, separated by a narrow strait that can be forged at low tide, is **Espalmador**, a privately owned small island with an idyllic lagoon (a favourite of the Spanish Royal Family) and an unofficial mud-bath from which the adventurous emerge daubed in sulphurous grey clay. The beach is better before or after the midday invasion of speedboats and daytrippers from Ibiza.

True privacy is hard to find but **Punta Pedrera**, an empty moonscape and the site of an old Arabi quarry on the northern tip of the western coast, has rocky secluded platforms, caves and crystal clear water, but hardly conforms to everybody's idea of beach bliss. Land was bought here for a millionaire's playground with a private heliport, but the plans have floundered in the face of local opposition.

Further down the same coast **Cala Saona**, a small bay with fine sand and a deep beach, has more classic Mediterranean charms: layered rusty cliffs, pine trees and a colony of French summer residents—you will often find a game of *boules* in the evening. The beach is one of the most popular with Formenterans at weekends.

Island ends: The most peaceful parts of the island are inevitably those without beaches: the peninsulas at either end, like the snout and tail of the dolphin of Formentera.

Most people speed over **La Mola**, the tail of the dolphin, a geographically distinct limestone plateau, pausing only for a quick look at the lighthouse and unexpected monument to Jules Verne, who set part of a novel here. **El Pilar**, a sleepy village with a whitewashed 18th-century church, tiny walled cemetery,

two defunct windmills and a choice of bars is known for its traditional fiestas, complete with old courtship dances, singing and poetry.

The coastline, honeycombed with caves, including the **Cova d'es Fum**, where a party of Viking raiders made off with Arab treasure having smoked-out the defenders, can only be seen by boat. But you can walk up from **Es Caló** to the ruins of the 14th-century monastery at **Es Monestir** or go south through farmland towards **S'Estufador**, a rocky break in the cliffs with a handful of boat sheds and small slipway where you can swim with safety.

The snout of the dolphin, the **Cabo Berberíce**, has the most atmospheric cliff walks, splashed with pink when the *frígola*, or thyme, is in blossom. If you walk between the two best-preserved 18th-century watch-towers, the **Torre de la Gavina**, and the **Torre d'es Garroveret**, both still standing in splendid solitude, it is impossible not to feel the centuries of defensive isolation underlying the tourist playground.

198

For the vast majority of the millions of tourists who visit the Balearics every year the things that matter are sun, sand, sea and sangria. This is as it should be: the whole purpose of a holiday is to get away from it all, and having left your own problems you don't particularly want to become embroiled with anyone else's.

In any case it is hard to believe, in a land of almost perpetual sunshine and evident prosperity, that the locals have much to worry about. But, beneath the glassy surface, the residents are at turns troubled, preoccupied and entertained by issues of local importance, few of which ever get into the pages of the English language publication. Often, the closest the visitor who does not read Spanish is going to get to the news is via a particularly garrulous hotel receptionist or a local whose tongue has been loosened by the profits of his car-hire business in a local bar.

Bar talk: Not the easiest of places for conversation—competing with televisions, game machines and coffee makers—the bars are not the forum for intellectual exchanges. It is often said that Mallorquín men are interested in only three things: women, football and gambling. Football certainly provides plenty to talk about; Real Mallorca, the island's leading side, has led a yo-yo existence of relegation and promotion between the Spanish divisions One and Two for more than two decades. There are more than 200 football clubs in the Balearics and there is strong support for the local sides at all levels.

Few communities display a similar attachment to bull-fighting. The Coliseo Balear in Palma once held its place with the great bull-rings of mainland Spain but it has declined in the past 40 years. Some say it is bad management, and "cowardly bulls and cowardly *toreros*" has been a press judgement for many years; others blame the depopulation of the countryside where support for bull-fighting was strongest.

Gambling is a pervasive presence: from

the remote, but entrancing, possibilities of the national lottery to the daily drawings of the ONCE (Society for the Blind) numbers, and to the face-to-face immediacy of the bar card game.

Drugs, jobs and more: So, when the unholy trinity of women, football and gambling has been disposed of, what more is there to talk about over a *cerveza* or laced coffee?

Inflation, of course, in Palma's hypermarkets one sometimes has the impression that the prices are moving up while the goods

sit on the shelves. Cars, of course, and where to park them; the Balearics have the highest ratio of cars per head of population in Spain. Drugs, of course; perhaps perceived as a plague brought by foreigners but also reluctantly recognised as a problem that is creeping down to the young of every village. Crime, of course; the loss of what was virtually total personal security (except for political dissidents) during Franco's time is regretted—without there being any significant wish for the return of those times.

Jobs, of course. Employment is related to tourism, but it goes wider. Mallorca has no heavy industry and most activity is in construction, infrastructure, and tourist services. A visit to the Polígono de son Castelló, a new industrial estate on the outskirts of Palma, although not recommended in the guide books, can be highly instructive. The range of service industries and suppliers is remarkable and all of them are busy.

Nonetheless, Mallorca's more traditional forms of employment are in decline. Shoe manufacturing, once a thriving industry, is in a depression from which it may not recover. One of the centres of the craft, a small town 15 miles (25 km) from Palma, had 30 factories 10 years ago but now has only three. Higher wages, heavy social security contributions and what many employers regard as

ods—and therefore fewer workers.

So the drift from the small towns and villages to Palma and the tourist centres accelerates. The farmhouses and cottages thus vacated are in time bought by well-to-do Palma residents as their second homes or by foreigners.

Scandalmongering: Are there, then, no scandals, no corruption, no political favouritism, for the locals to talk about? Of course. Considering the exponential growth of the Balearic economy over the past 40 years—a period which also included the giant, and by no means certain, leap from dictatorship to democracy—it would be surprising if some cracks had not shown on the surface of

inflexible employee-biased contract conditions have all combined to price Mallorcan shoes out of their once extensive and profitable export markets.

Agriculture has its problems, too. Traditionally based on almonds and olives, neither is now profitable in international markets. Mallorca's seven million almond trees and countless ancient olives do not produce high-quality fruit and are labour-intensive to harvest. Early potatoes, capers, wines and milk products achieve some small export success. But, by and large, those parts of Mallorca's agriculture which are most successful are those which use modern meth-

Balearic society.

These 40 years have turned so many centuries-old values upside down. Traditionally, for example, the youngest son of a family of landowners always received the agriculturally poor land near the coast as his inheritance; suddenly this land is worth immeasurably more for hotels and apartments than any of his older brothers' holdings. Shocks of this kind are difficult for a society to absorb without damage to its indigenous structures.

Mallorquíns are no less interested in making money than any one else. There have been times during the past quarter of a century when the pouring of concrete has seemed like the flow of lava from a constantly erupting volcano of greed and opportunism. If it were possible to tune in at one time to conversations in the thousands of bars in the Balearics, the dominant topic (after women, football and gambling, naturally) would be construction. Who is getting away with what, and how; who is getting his private road surfaced at public expense; how that permission for a new *urbanización* was obtained; why developers were allowed into an area designated as being of special natural beauty. And so on.

Faced with a mass of restrictions and permissions to be observed and obtained before

the role of the holiday industry. In 1977, at a symposium on tourism in Spain held in Palma, the representative of the Ministry of Information and Tourism in Madrid addressed the meeting with these words: "Thanks to tourism, all of Spain was saved. Before, we could do nothing. There was no money. Tourism is a miracle."

At the time, and subsequently, these often-quoted words have caused offence; to imply that the grandeur and richness—cultural and economic—of the Spanish and Balearic past counted for nothing, and that the edifice of modern Spain is built only on package tourism, is crass. Yet there is an important kernel of economic truth in what was said. The

building, many Mallorquíns go ahead regardless and worry about the consequences later. Quite often there aren't any, as an overworked bureaucracy and legal system tries to keep pace with ever-quickening developments. Sometimes fines are imposed, but not always collected, and—very occasionally—illegal buildings are bulldozed without compensation. The job of head of planning in a local authority cannot be an easy one.

Tourism's miracle: Somewhere in all of these topics, either central or peripheral, is

Left, some lives are unaffected by tourism's "miracle". Above, exchanging local gossip.

statistics speak for themselves: in 1950 there were fewer than 100,000 visitors to the Balearics; by 1960 the total was 400,000, 1965 saw over one million, 1971 three million, 1982 four million and in 1987 there were more than five-and-a-half million.

So it is not suprising that the issue which dominates discussion in the islands' political arenas, in press, radio and television, at business lunches and private parties, and—indirectly and implicitly—in every village bar and shop, is first, last and everywhere in-between, tourism—in all its extraordinary, immoderate, vulgar, gratifying, refreshing and sybaritic manifestations. Tourism—

how to maintain it and how to contain it. How to manage sensitively and progressively the ever-accelerating transition from an agriculture-based society to one of the most phenomally successful service industries in the world—a societal revolution of remarkable dimensions carried out by the Mallorquíns themselves in a mere quarter of a century. How to avoid the awful inevitability of the equation *construccion=destruccion.*

An over-riding question is how the islands can keep and increase their share of the Northern European tourist market against competition from Greece and Turkey and other resort locations elsewhere.

But, if the answer is, say, by making

Mallorca cheaper, how would that square with the evident dissatisfaction of local traders with the minimal spending power of most cheap package holiday-makers? Or with the increasingly persuasive lobby arguing that future prosperity lies in the direction of up-market tourism—which would require new and better hotels, more marinas with luxurious waterside villages, more golf courses, and better roads. And, if there were to be such an incremental infrastructural development, what of the pressures this would inevitably place on that precious tourism commodity, "unspoilt Mallorca"?

GOB talk: Here, another powerful voice

enters the debate, the environmentalists, gathered mainly in an organisation called Grupo Ornithologico Balear (GOB). Hardly a week goes by when the media are not reporting GOB's views on some proposed new tourist or industrial project. These Mallorquín "greens" have had some striking successes, given that the movement was a late starter among its European counterparts.

A major victory was the campaign to protect the majestic island of Dragonera, just off the southwest tip of Mallorca, from a development plan which, although it beggared belief in its insensitivity and inappropriateness, had progressed close to irrevocable permission. Dragonera was saved by an imaginative and determined campaign; the island now belongs to the Consell Insular. The local authorities have shown an ever-increasing readiness to act to save the remaining natural resources of the Balearics.

One of the hottest issues of recent years has been a law imposed by the local minister for tourism *restricting* new construction on the coastline, which was suddenly and arbitrarily put into effect when the authorities discovered that accommodation for no fewer than 27,000 tourists beds, mostly in new apartments, had been built between 1985 and 1988. This law, which is difficult to interpret and administer, has led to cries of "unfair" from some of those affected.

Ask a politician or businessman what the big issues are for the Balearics, other than tourism, and he may well reply "1992". This year seems to have an almost mythical significance for all Spaniards. A World Fair, commemorating Christopher Columbus's voyage from Spain to discover the New World in 1492, will be held in Seville, the Olympic Games will take place in Barcelona, and the European Community's unified internal market will come into force.

The Balearics will enjoy some reflected glory from the first two events; what the third will bring these islands is difficult to judge. But, if energy, resourcefulness, determination, imagination—and a certain ruthlessness—are needed to survive in the new EEC, these qualities will not be found lacking in the islands.

Left, one over-burdened runway at Palma Airport. Right, the preoccupations of making a living.

THE PULSE OF POLLENCA

Analysing a "typical" Mallorcan town is no easy task, largely because it is almost impossible to find one which is typical. Like any town anywhere Pollença bears only a superficial resemblance to anywhere else. Like most Mallorcan towns it has the same broad, tree-lined roads and narrow, pavement-less side streets, where the houses give out directly onto the road and the open doorways are draped with beaded curtains. It has the great crumbling church and the central plaza, where everyone meets at least once a day, and the weekly market for traders and farmers from the *campo*. Since all towns have this, Pollença may be said to be typical of all Mallorcan towns, but once you get to know it and stray beneath the surface a little, it becomes a place apart, a place to return to and enjoy.

Vital statistics: Pollença lies at the northern end of the island, off the main Inca road, 4.5 miles (7 km) from the great bay of Pollença and its sister town of Puerto de Pollença, which is just called "Puerto" locally, under the eastern side of Puig Tomir, a great grey mass of mountain that seems to overhang the town to the west. Agatha Christie was sufficiently impressed by Pollença to set one of her books here.

The current population stands at 12,448 inhabitants, and the town's livelihood, which was once purely agricultural, is now largely dominated by tourism, which employs many of the local people. Tourism has brought considerable prosperity but has had little or no impact on the day-to-day lives of the ordinary folk. They may be better off, but they don't show it, and like all island folk, they are clannish and prefer to keep to themselves and live within their close family circle—though Mallorcan families can be very large.

One curious thing about them is that they don't travel much. One summer I met a friend in Pollença, piling luggage into his car, and asked where he was going. "On holiday," he said. Where to? "To Cala Sant

Vicenç." Cala Sant Vicenç is about three miles (five km) away, but to a Pollençan that is almost abroad. They prefer to keep close to home and rarely venture into Palma or Puerto, which are too big, too modern, or too full of tourists.

The heart: For the people of Pollença, life centres around their plaza, the Plaza Major, or to be precise, the little terrace outside the Café Español, from where you can look out across the square and the rooftops to the sharp, tree-covered peak of Puig Maria, the

steep-sided hill that matches the Calvario hill that rises here in the centre of the town and can be climbed from beside the church up an endless flight of steps. In the Café Español the locals chat to their friends, watching the children, sipping cups of coffee or the occasional glass of beer, and wait for the day to drift by.

In this activity they are joined by summer residents, many of them old friends, and occasional passing tourists, but except on Sunday, which is market day in Pollença, few casual tourists ever penetrate this far into the town, and even regular visitors can easily get lost in the inter-linked network of minor streets, most of them one-way and all of them alike. It is surprisingly difficult to find one's way in, and then to get out. Besides, these casual visitors will speak English or German, French or Spanish. In Pollença everyone speaks Spanish but they prefer to speak Mallorquín.

The roots: Pollença is an old town, and like most Mallorcan towns has its own distinctive history. It retains a Roman bridge, the Puente Romana, as a reminder that the roots go back almost to antiquity, though some foreigners say, quietly, that the Puente Romana is simply Romanesque and was probably built by the Moors. The Moors who came after the Romans were driven out by

The town was built inland, away from Puerto and the sea, as a precaution against pirate raids, but the short distance from the coast often proved an inadequate deterrent. Turkish and Barbary corsairs raided the town at will during the 16th and 17th centuries, most noticeably in 1551, when a great raid led by the famous corsair, Dragut, was successfully driven off by the local hero, Joan Mas Farruagut.

This event is celebrated in Pollença every August at the *Fiesta de la Patrona*, when *los Moros y los Cristianos*, the Moors and the Christians, engage in mock-battle through the streets of the town for the best part of 24 hours, an event marked by bands, proces-

the Spaniards in 1229, after which little Pollença was ceded to the Order of the Knights Templar, who held the town until 1312, when their Order was dissolved and the town passed to the rival Order, the Knights Hospitaler of the Order of St John of Jerusalem, who held the town until 1802. King Carlos IV was then the Grand Master of the Order, and he took all the Order's Spanish possessions under royal control.

Much of central Pollença is still medieval, although a good number of buildings date from the classical period of the 17th century, and there are new houses and villas on the outskirts.

sions, fancy dress, fireworks and endless explosions from fire-crackers. Those who do not join in usually try to leave town during *los Moros y los Cristianos* and the dogs which usually lie panting in every scrap of shade are conspicuous by their absence. This fiesta, unique though it may be, is one of a series of fiestas particular to individual towns on the island.

The streets: Everything begins in the Plaza Major. In one corner the Club Pollença is the centre of social life during the winter months, dominated by the vast, dusty Baroque cathedral. Churches of many shapes, size and eras are common to all Mallorcan towns, and Pollença has many religious buildings. Some were erected by the Jesuits, who held land here at the end of the 17th century, and others by the Dominicans, who built the convent in 1578.

Some of the finest secular buildings in the town are the old houses along the Calle Jesús, many of which have fine carved corbels and Gothic-style pointed windows. The old Casa de la Vila, which is now the Town Hall, dates from the 18th century, and the Claustro, the cloisters of the Convent, are now employed every year to stage the Pollença Music Festival, which began in 1962 and is now a highly successful international event, with Doná Sofia, the Queen of Spain,

as its patron since 1976. This festival gives Pollença an importance which its inhabitants seem almost unaware of.

As with many Mallorcan towns Pollença is the centre for a thriving artistic community, local and international, and many artists, musicians, and writers have homes here, while the town supports several art galleries and produces ceramics, furniture and fine textiles in many small side-street workshops. Here too though, much of the initiative came from outside the ranks of the old

Left, Club Pollença, the social centre. Above, resting on the Calvario steps.

Pollençan community, for Mallorquíns are a conservative lot, not quick to take up new work or hobbies.

The locals have taken with gusto to some of the more recent accretions, like the tennis courts, the football pitches and the basketball arena, just outside the town, but the new golf course off the old Inca road is almost entirely occupied by foreign residents and visitors.

The Convent of Santo Domingo hosts the municipal museum. As with any other town there are other smaller features worth noticing, like the famous Gallo fountain, crowned by a cockerel, at the foot of the 19th-century stairway which climbs to the Calvario. This stairway has 365 wide steps and a fairly exhausting climb gives great views of the other great attraction, the convent chapel on the top of Puig Maria, just outside the town. Puig Maria can be ascended by car, but the road eventually peters out and then follows a hard ascent up an old mule trail, but the church on the top is charming and in the town, after the obligatory stop for a refreshing beer at the Café Español, there are visits to the 15th-century churches of Roser Vell and Sant Jordi (St George), or a longer excursion to the hermitage in the Ternelles valley, an hour's walk from the town centre. There's variety aplenty.

Local pace: At a guess though, most visitors or summer residents will put off such excursions until tomorrow, or maybe until the day after that, or perhaps next year... or sometime... Instead, there is the drift into town about four o'clock to get the papers and scan them over a cup of coffee, chat to friends who come strolling by, and stop, and sit down. Slowly, afternoon turns into evening and another long, hot day has drifted by.

Of course for the younger folk in the age of affluence life is more eventful than that and more exciting than it used to be. They have scooters and motorbikes to roar about on, creating a din that reverberates down the narrow streets at all hours of the day and night. Less inhibited, or perhaps less shy than the older people, they mix more easily with the newcomers and look forward to the annual arrival of the summer visitors. Even so, everyone admits that while the summer is livelier, and that's when the money rolls in, Pollença is much nicer in winter, when the summer people have gone.

IN SEARCH OF A SPECIALITY

The Balearics are something of a blank on the Spanish gastronomic map, known for little but tourist barbecues with paella and plonk. After a morning spent wandering around the markets or shops—past stalls and windows packed with wonderful fruit and vegetables, spankingly fresh rock and deep-sea fish, farmhouse cheeses and sausages, honey and herb liqueurs, breads and pies and cakes of every shape and size—it's hard to understand why, but, come lunchtime, when you are hungrily sniffing the aromas wafting out of private kitchens, the problem of where to sample it yourself becomes apparent.

Whether in downtown Palma or a village in Formentera, looking for a smart city restaurant or a cheap bar, it is mighty difficult to find good local cooking. Even the menus that do boast *cocina mallorquína*—or *menorquína* or *ibizenca*—usually offer a choice of no more than three or four dishes, perhaps a soup or stew, a paella or other rice dish, local fish or roast suckling pig , and a bowl of garlicky *allioli* with bread, which together give a sample of local flavours.

Home style: In part this is due to the character of Balearic cooking. It boasts a splendid peasant repertoire combining local flavours from the farmhouses and fishing villages with intriguing Moorish and other influences, but there is no native restaurant traditions. People eat their own style of cooking at home. Poverty, rural isolation and imposed colonial tastes simply never allowed local restaurants to develop and, even today, now that the old coast patterns of life have been swept aside, most people still prefer home to professional cooking. Significantly, everybody goes home for lunch, the leisurely main meal of the day, and in the towns you find far less casual socialising in bars or restaurants than on the mainland.

But there is another, depressing reason for menus without local flavour: the onslaught of tourism, so heavy here that its demand for chips, pizza, steaks and international glamour still dominates despite the spectacular

Preceding pages: Palma greengrocer. Left, *arroz brut* for the farm workers. Right, international specialities.

revival of regional cooking elsewhere in Spain. So, nonsensically, while Palma's restaurants may be as cosmopolitan as those of Madrid, with everything from French to Thai menus and plenty of choice from regional Spain too—Galicia and the Basque country for example—there is not one single recommended restaurant in the city specialising in local food.

Of course, this is not to say that you won't eat distinctively and well here, but it does mean you do have to know what to look for

and where you can expect to find it. For straight *haute cuisine*, throughout the islands Palma offers the biggest choice. The most notable restaurant in the city, if you are having just one evening out, is Xoriguer on Calle Fábrica, where a Basque chef cooks excellent *nueva cocina* with an emphasis on local ingredients, while at the top seafood restaurants there is a pretty impressive spread of shellfish and fish. High summer is best avoided for this kind of serious eating since the range of local produce shrinks and it is hard to find an appetite in the humid heat. You are more likely to enjoy a gastronomic trip in late spring, when the huge range of fruit and vegetables—including the Balearic new potatoes—are in their prime: in May you can also visit the Mostra de Cuina Mallorquína, a week-long festival with local wines and restaurant versions of the various regional dishes.

Market specials: At the other end of the scale, you can eat very cheaply and well by searching out speciality products in the shops and markets. Here the islands excel. The most famous local product, *sobrasada*, a finely minced sausage of pure pork salted and tinted red by *pimentón* pepper, mild or spicy, soft or hard according to age, certainly should be tasted. Traditionally made from lean cuts of black pigs fattened for flavour on beans, barley, figs and prickly pears during the *matanza*, the time of family pig killing and sausage making, *sobrasada* needs to be carefully bought to avoid factory imitations.

The second main object of culinary pride is the *ensaimada*, a puffy spiral of sugar-dusted bread as small as a croisssant or as large as a lifebelt that is carried around repectfully in elegant hatboxes. According to locals, the secret of its feathery richness, which is enviously but unsuccessfully imitated all over mainland Spain, rests in the combination of very pure pork fat—*saim* in Arabic—slightly salty hard water and a humid climate. Connoisseurs like their *ensaimadas* as flat as a wheel and freshly baked, for dunking into coffee or chocolate, or filled like a cream bun, for example with pumpkin jam, confectioner's custard or a soft almond paste, to carry home and eat like a cake. To an outsider, the fatty blandness of the dough is something of an acquired taste, but some people love it and fly home clutching a stack of *ensaimada* hatboxes, bought at the airport.

For most visitors, however, the pleasure of food here is more general. Take the quality and choice of local cheeses and sausages as an example. There are at least half a dozen cooked pork products other than *sobrasada* to be tried: *longaniza*, a thin loop of a sausage excellent for barbecues; *salsitxa*, akin to mortadella; *butifarrón*, herby blood sausage; *camaiot,* with very coarsely chopped meat; *cuixot*, a type of brawn, and the small amount of *jamón* made in dryer mountain areas. Equally, from autumn to spring you will find various local cheeses, often made from sheep or goat's milk, alongside farm-house Mahón, one of the finest hard Spanish cheeses. A selection of any of these to serve with good bread—either unsalted, rough white *hogazas* or the closer brown *pan moreno*—and fruity tomatoes dressed with local olive oil makes an excellent picnic.

Specials on the side: There are plenty of more unusual accompaniments too. In the markets, you will find fig cakes, sultanas, and wonderful almonds; strings of sun-dried tomatoes for rubbing over bread dribbled with olive oil to make *pa amb oli*, a favourite rustic Mallorcan breakfast; Menorcan capers and pickled *hinojo de mar*, or sea fennel; salted sardines and marinated anchovies. Olives are not reliably good, but the green

Mallorcan ones, small and slightly bitter, are delicious when marinated with wild fennel. Fresh fruit, of course, is always excellent, especially oranges and lemons; in the good ice-cream shops they're used to make fresh fruit *granizados*, sorbets swished around to break up the ice crystals.

Easier take-away food is available at the baker's. The Arab and Jewish influence is especially obvious in the *cocas*, *cocarrois* and *empanadas*—flatbreads, fluted pasties and pies with endlessly varied toppings and fillings. *Cocas* can be a blazing red sheet of roasted peppers, or elsewhere a bed for *sobrasada* sprinkled with sugar; spinach or cauliflower pasties are often studded with pine kernels and sultanas; lamb pies, at their best when home-made for Easter but sold in the shops throughout the year, may have pastry sweetened with orange juice or fillings spiced with cinnamon and cloves. Sweet things like *flaó*, a cheese pastry from Ibiza, *coca de patatas*, an airy bun based on potato from Valldemossa, or *galletas*, olive oil biscuits from Alaior, are often originally fiesta treats.

Unreliable wine: By comparison with all of this, wine for washing down your meals can be disappointingly characterless. Commercial quantities of wine are produced only by the Mallorcan vineyards, which were fa-

mous in Roman times for sweet Malvasia and again in the last century for blended reds based on native grape varieties, but have never fully recovered since they were wiped out by phylloxera in the 1890s. The few quality wines, produced in very limited quantities, really need to be bought direct from the *bodegas* and co-operatives in Binisalem, Felanitx and Porreres, the three main growing areas. Of these, José Ferrer's traditional red Reservas, Jaime Mesquida's more modern *tinto* made with Cabernet Sauvi-

Left, preparing *sobrasada*. Above, the finished article.

gnon grapes and the white Herederos de Ribas are worth looking out for.

Where to go: When you do feel like eating out in a restaurant, it is best to stick to a locally recommended place off the main tourist track. This may turn out to be anything from an old-fashioned country *fonda* to a smart seafood *marisquería* or one of the monasteries which takes in guests, more rarely one of the handful of restaurants which offers only regional cooking. Wherever you are, the best choices will be either seasonal *platos típicos*, unpretentious, often satisfyingly messy traditional dishes, or good local produce simply cooked.

Cooking styles vary considerably, reflecting both the fragmented history of the islands and their varied landscape, according to Caty Juan, an artist and expert on the island's cuisine. Menorca, for example, has all kinds of amusing British traces—*grevi, pudings, piquels* and the local gin swigged neat or with soda—as well as *mayonnaise*, or *salsa mahonesa*, said to have been discovered in Mahón by General Richelieu's chef during the French occupation and now served everywhere in large bowlfuls with bread before a meal. By contrast, Mallorca, a huge fruit and vegetable garden in Moorish times, shows the *mudéjar* influence remarkably clearly; almonds are pounded to thicken stews and sauces for meat or fish or to make refreshing almond milk, ice-cream and rich flourless cakes.

Staple diet: But local diversity reflects the local landscape. Many of Mallorca's best dishes are based on pork and vegetables: they are used in springtime in *sopas mallorquínas*, steaming bowlfuls of broth poured over vegetables and sops of thinly sliced dry bread; in summery *tumbet*, a robust sunny dish of fried peppers, tomatoes, potatoes and aubergines; and in *arroz brut*, a winter rice dish with game and sausages.

Menorca is known for its spiny lobsters, wonderful *calderetes* or fish soups, excellent dairy produce and a mass of different aubergine dishes. The most interesting local specialities of Ibiza and Formentera, like the salted dried skate, are almost impossible to find, but there are good fish stews or herby lamb, and the small local distilleries still produce fine *hierbas*, the aromatic anise liqueur which leaves hazily happy memories of any meal.

NIGHTLIFE

Nightlife in the archipelago, and particularly on Ibiza, has a quality that distinguishes it from other Spanish resort areas. But visitors should not expect to find it everywhere. Formentera is so small that it can only support two discotheques in the package-tourist beach of Es Pujols. Although Menorca's two main cities of Mahón and Ciutadella have a variety of bars and discos they are nothing special; even the prosperous disco-chain Pachá could not be persuaded to open a discotheque near Mahón until 1988, at last providing a place on the island open into the early morning. There is one unique discotheque to be found on the island, however; it is situated in Cala'n Porter and is set in a series of natural caves (Cueva d'en Xoroi) overlooking the sea.

Most of the unique venues on Mallorca are inspired by the fashions and trends set on the third-largest island.

Ibiza: Nightlife in the island's two main towns begins in bars and cafés around the port. The waterfront bars have always been popular gathering spots before a long evening; in Sant Antoni people sit on the terrace of the Café del Mar, sip drinks and watch the sunset, and in Eivissa a series of bars built into what were once fishermen's houses draws the crowds at dusk. People who have lived in Eivissa since the sixties recall how the women make an event of dressing-up in the budding "ad lib" style just to have drinks in port bars like El Mono Desnudo or Tanga. However, the ambience of chic sophistication created by the international clientele of these bars has long since moved across the port to the area around the Marina Botafoch yacht harbour.

The port bars are ideal places for different nationalities to mingle. Spaniards have a word for the game of picking someone up: *ligar*. The music blaring from competing bars is so loud that verbal communication gives way to body language. A discreet or blatant stare may strike up a relationship for the night or for the rest of the holiday.

Preceding pages: a gypsy fete. Left, Bellver Castle hovers above Palma. Right, drinking after dark.

Calle Mayor and the Calle Virgen have more bars and restaurants all set in the ancient houses of Eivissa's port district. The gay zone is just inside the walls of D'Alt Vila, where a massive rampart overlooks a number of gay bars with accompanying terraces. At the foot of this area is Ibiza's first disco, Lola's, built into the ground floor of an old house. A stone's throw away in the direction of the rampway leading to the main gate is a place called the Tube, whose punk clientele make it one of Eivissa's most col-

ourful bars, gay or otherwise.

Eivissa's only theatre, the Pereira, was closed for years waiting for an enterprising person to make it into some kind of nightclub. The task was taken up by the Dutch pop-music composer, Eric-Jan Harmsen, whose wife is an actress. She wanted a theatre; he got her one. So far the club is in what was once the theatre's bar and lobby area, but plans are underway to employ the forum of the theatre for ballroom-dinner-shows where music, dance, and food will be the fare. For the time being, however, the Pereira is a café-music bar open from eight a.m. to six a.m. with a restaurant that is open 20 hours a day. Eric-Jan's jazz performances at the piano are part of the nightly entertainment. Thanks to his extensive contacts in the music world, he is able to book well-known jazz artists.

Across the port is an area named after the yacht harbour, Marina Botafoch. Eivissa's Casino and the discos Pachá and Angel's have long been established here, and have been recently joined by a number of smart bars aiming to attract the monied and the beautiful. These include Keeper, Madrigal, and Mary Sol II. Other than sleek, *à la mode* decór, these bars offer the same music available everywhere else.

One place, however, that breaks the mould

other holiday resort towns.

Each Pachá is autonomous and reflects the character of the town it is situated in. Pachá was a pioneer in creating theme fiestas. Nowadays, in a fiercely competitive market, no disco can survive without these parties which serve to attract, to entertain, as well as to maintain the image of a given establishment. Pachá quickly became famous for its White Fiestas in which everyone is required to dress in that colour or risk being white-washed, an unpleasant experience.

Another characteristic fiesta is Flower Power, which, by means of music, decoration, and dress is meant to evoke the ambience of Ibiza 15 years ago when hippies were

in this part of the port is called Phyllis, after its American owner, who for 13 years had a restaurant in the old part of Eivissa. A speciality of the house continues to be barbecued spare-ribs, and it must be the only place on the island that offers Mexican food. Phyllis has brought some of her gypsy friends across the port, and on Saturday nights they sing and dance flamenco, a welcome relief from pop music blasting from every other corner.

Of easy access from Eivissa are Pachá and Angel's. Pachá is one of the oldest establishments on the island and is predated only by Lola's. It is one of a chain of 20 discos located in Madrid, Barcelona, and various

still an important segment of the social scene on the island. In the peak of summer, Pachá will hold as many as 3,000 people who are served by 15 bars. Drinks in the club average 1,000 pesetas each.

Angel's discotheque began as Charly Max in the late seventies and for a time made Pachá tremble for its disco primacy. But it lost the struggle for the élite crowd, closed for a year, and opened again with its present name. It then went after the mass tourist crowd by making deals with agencies which offer a night in Angel's as part of their tourist package to Ibiza. A bus brings the guests at 11 p.m. and takes them back to their hotels at

3 a.m. Angel's sound and laser light systems are reputedly the best on the island.

This night spot pioneered the "Mr" series of fiestas, which are now a regular offering in Ibizan discotheques. These fiestas bear such names as Mr Casanova, Mr Muscles, Mr Angel, and Mr Macho. These are balanced by the Miss Topless, Miss Erotic, Miss Body, and Miss Angel fiestas. Also attractive is the moderate 1,000 peseta entrance fee with drink. Second drinks are 500 and 600 pesetas each.

Amnesia, opened in 1977 on the road from Eivissa to Sant Antoni, is built around a centuries-old farmhouse, and for Northern European visitors it is a mellow realisation of

small disco-club in the country with gardens and a swimming pool, to a disco for the masses with umpteen bars and multiple dance floors. People are now discouraged from jumping nude into what little is left of the pool. Entrance is an expensive 2,500 to 3,000 pesetas with drink, depending on the night. If you are lucky you many come across a Ku agent handing out free passes in the port bars; it is not easy to fill a 3,000 capacity disco every night. Ku's 130,000 sq ft (40,000 sq metres) of space include boutiques and one of the best and most expensive restaurants on the island which specialises in Basque cuisine.

The manager of Ku, Brasilio, is a self-

their dreams. Instead of "Mr" or "Miss" Amnesia contests, this discotheque thrives on its Spanish setting, with white-washed architecture, palm trees and gardens. This place, along with Pachá, continues to be a favourite haunt of Ibiza's regular summer residents and their foreign friends.

Disco goddess: If Amnesia represents the spirit of Ibizan nightlife, the mega-discotheque Ku, named after a Caribbean love goddess, is its very heart-throb. In its 12 years of existence, Ku has evolved from a

Left, theme fiesta promotion in Ibiza. Above, a party on the beach.

styled ex-hippy with a doctorate in economics. His is the creative mind behind Ku's 50 theme fiestas which are exotically colourful, phantasmagoric, and uninhibitedly exhibitionist. If Pachá pioneered the theme fiesta, Brasilio has raised it to an art form. He has a whole tailoring department that produces the costumes needed for each fiesta.

For Brazilian Night, dancers and musicians are flown in from Brazil. It is no accident that many of the fiestas here are reminiscent of the Bacchanalian abandon of Carnival in Rio. Ku also provides a stage for rock groups and artists of international renown. One of the most spectacular events ever to take place here was a video-recorded performance of the song "Barcelona" by Freddy Mercury and the Queen of the Spanish opera world, Monserrat Caballé.

Amid the high-rise buildings of Sant Antoni there are a number of interesting clubs. In terms of disco-architecture especially outstanding is Es Paradis, located off the Avenida Dr Fleming. It was designed by owner José Aguirre who decorated his first discotheque at the age of 16. Es Paradis features classical columns and nude statues. The dance floor can be flooded with water or foam, and body painting is a special attraction of the house. This venue's biggest bash is the annual Water Fiesta which starts at 11

house-sized disco has a long line of people waiting to get in even at seven in the morning. The disco beat goes on here until noon.

Mallorca: There are as many centres of nightlife on Mallorca as there are beach resorts. The largest such area, the Playa de Palma, is on the eastern side of the Bay of Palma. On the western side are the elegant harbour of Portals Nous and the burgeoning resorts of Palma Nova and Magalluf. On the other side of the island there is considerable nocturnal activity in and around the coastal town of Alcudia.

In Palma itself the hub of night life in the 1970s used to be the Plaza Gomila, but the crowds have largely dispersed to the periph-

a.m. and continues all day and night. People are urged to attend scantily clad in order to take part in various water sports.

Another Sant Antoni disco worth mentioning is the New Manhattan situated on Calle Soledad, which often has a colourful sprinkling of punks. Especially impressive is a mud pit where wrestling matches between nearly nude amazons take place.

The momentum of the frenzy and hedonism of an Ibizan night is such that when the big establishments close at anywhere from five to seven a.m., many people want to continue. Space, located in En Bossa beach opens its doors at six a.m.. This huge, ware-

eral areas of Palma's bay. The bars and discos that remain in Gomila cater to teenagers, disoriented tourists, and sailors from the US Sixth Fleet.

All that is left of Gomila's former lustre is Tito's, which for 30 years was the centrepiece of the district. Starting out as a nightclub, it would feature stars like Marlene Dietrich, Tom Jones, or Charles Aznavour; for the last three years Tito's has been owned by an English company which runs it as a mega-discotheque, and its 1,500 peseta entrance fee makes it the most expensive on the island. The huge windows overlooking the port with Palma's Gothic cathedral in the distance form a spectacular backdrop to the exotic theme fiestas held here. A glass-encased elevator provides access from the Paseo Marítimo below.

On the Paseo between Tito's and Club Marítimo is a fashionable discotheque called Luna. The Crown Prince of Spain and his sisters, the Infantas, come here with their friends in the summer during the Royal Family's annual holiday. The core of this club's clientele are the young sons and daughters of families with residences or summer houses on the island. Although selection at the door is tight, most of the clients are regulars and are not charged.

At the entrance of Luna, the Mallorcan

disco which plays the most Spanish music, is a tower that was once part of the port's defensive system. The open-air entrance area is meant to evoke Ibizan venues with palm trees and a small, shallow pool. The interior of the club is a cave that has been carved out of live rock above.

With a name like BCM Disco Empire only a pharaonic façade is appropriate. This nightspot located in the resort town of Magalluf is housed in a building of 92,000 cu ft (28,000 cu metres). Rather than put the

Left, Tito's in Palma. Above, a floorshow, with port behind.

entrance on ground level the architects have placed stairways to the upper level. This touch helps instill the proper awe and respect into the clientele. The entrance fee of 1,000 pesetas includes a drink.

There are three sections to BCMs: upstairs the restaurant has windows looking out over the main discotheque area, then there is the dance-floor area itself, and downstairs the night club. Director Javier Ginart calls the BCM Disco Empire a nocturnal complex where a 16-year old can come with his parents and grandparents and they will all be entertained. Downstairs the fare is live, big-band music and cabaret shows. The lounge booths are posh, the lights are low, and the sound-level lower than upstairs.

BCM Disco Empire opens at nine in the evening. At one a.m. there is a light show using the five laser lights whose eight basic colours combine to produce 32 different hues. Four nights a week the disco also has theme fiestas, consisting of the standard "Mr" or "Miss" contests. The recruiting process for these events is carried out by a team which combs the beaches for bodies.

Across the island in the Puerto de Alcudia is a discotheque whose decor takes its inspiration from the region's Roman past; Menta itself was built to evoke a Roman temple. Its pool, ensconced in a garden, can be seen through large windows facing the dance floor. The most popular theme fiesta here is, naturally enough, the annual Roman orgy held in May, when people are not only permitted but encouraged to skinny dip in the pool. Menta's Spanish fiesta includes a horseshow in the parking lot, wine tasting, and Spanish dance. At Menta's helm is Duby, who worked here for two years as a disc jockey before being promoted to manager. He cannot resist his former occupation and regularly takes a hand at spinning discs.

In the old sector of Palma on Calle San Juan, not too far from the port, is the best place for a pre-nightlife drink. Abaco is built in a 17th-century mansion. The bar has been furnished with antiques and access is allowed to the kitchen and drawing room upstairs. The patio-garden has tables, luxurious plants and caged birds. Omnipresent candles and classical music in the background are the finishing touches. Exotic drinks are sold at high prices, but then what is being sold is the atmosphere.

BIRDWATCH

In recent years, the Balearic Islands, and Mallorca in particular, have become firmly established as one of Europe's finest bird-watching locations.

Not only do the Balearics enjoy a prime position in the Mediterranean where many migrating birds land each spring and autumn, but there is also a great diversity of habitats in relatively close proximity, which attract further varieties. Mallorca is particularly well blessed in this regard: there are marshes and reedbeds, freshwater lagoons and salt-pans, scrubland, fields, orchards and woods, rocky sea cliffs and, most impressive of all, wild mountains with soaring peaks and plunging gorges.

Although the best birdwatching areas are well away from the crowded tourist centres, the birdwatcher staying in one of the larger holiday complexes need not despair for many interesting species are widely distributed throughout the islands. One of the most pleasing features of the Balearics is the ease with which interesting birds can be encountered in the fields, orchards and woods close to one's hotel or apartment.

Residents: One of the most striking is the hoopoe, unmistakable with its crest which can be raised to resemble a Red Indian chief's head-dress. Yet, for such a handsome bird it can be surprisingly difficult to spot when it is foraging on bare ground where its sandy-pink plumage blends with the colour of the earth.

Also common throughout the islands is the little Sardinian warbler. The male, a dapper grey and white bird with a distinctive black cap and red eye, delivers his rattling song and scolds passers-by from the tops of bushes and tangled vegetation.

Other birds which are found in many areas are stonechat, corn bunting, serin, greenfinch, goldfinch and linnet, all of which frequently choose exposed perches on posts, wires and tree tops to sing and to call. The tiny fan-tailed warbler, however, usually delivers its repetitive, single-note song in

mid-air, fluttering upwards in a bouncing song-flight before dropping down again into a clump of weeds and grasses. Blackcaps are more difficult to observe, as they tend to skulk inside bushes and thickets.

Wherever there are pine trees it is well worth looking for crossbills and firecrests, whereas thekla larks and red-legged partridges usually frequent rough, uncultivated farmland, stony fields and dry scrubland. Here the keen-eyed observer may find rock sparrow, Marmora's warbler and the myste-

rious, secretive stone curlew. The Dartford warbler also occurs in Menorca, although it is less common in Mallorca; the opposite is the case with the cirl bunting.

From boulder-strewn hillsides, rocky coves and craggy cliffs comes the lovely, fluty song of the blue rock thrush. The midnight-blue cock bird is a most handsome creature. Sharing the same rugged locations, crag martins can be seen zipping around the cliff-faces, chunky, action-packed little birds. Kestrels and ravens are here too, familiar sights in the skies above Menorca and Ibiza as well as in the hillier parts of Mallorca.

Preceding pages: local painting by Betty White. Left, hoopoe, with lunch. Above, a male Sardinian warbler.

From cliff-top vantage-points it is possible to sight Cory's shearwater and the Balearic race of the Manx shearwater passing by off-shore and there is always a chance of finding Audouin's gull, one of the rarest gulls in the world, which can often be spotted in the harbours of Palma, Mahón and Eivissa (Ibiza Town).

Spring migrants: Although there are plenty of birds to be seen at all times of the year, the most popular are April and May when there is a huge influx of migrants from Africa, some merely passing through, others intending to stay and breed during the summer months. They are all joined by birdwatchers from Britain, Germany, Holland and Scandi-

navia who flock to Mallorca to witness the migration. The most favoured sites become quite crowded as binoculars, telescopes and cameras jostle for the most exclusive views of the rarest birds.

One such site is Cases Velles, an area of fields, orchards and woods nestling in a wide valley, halfway along Mallorca's deserted Formentor peninsula. A combination of topographical and climatic factors conspire to funnel migrating birds into this sheltered hollow. Wryneck, pied and spotted flycatcher, stonechat, whinchat, wheatear, black-eared wheatear, redstart and black redstart can often be found feeding among the trees and bushes.

Roller, melodious, subalpine and spectacled warbler, rock thrush, ortolan and golden oriole are also recorded regularly. Many of these species pass through the Boquer Valley near Port Pollença, another excellent location to search for migrants.

Among the springtime arrivals are European bee-eaters. Combining an easy, gliding flight with quick twists and swerves, these rainbow birds indulge in the most dazzling aerobatics, sometimes launching forth from roadside wires or power-lines on the outskirts of towns. Bee-eater nest-colonies are extremely vulnerable to disturbance. The sandy cliffs where they excavate their nest chambers all too easily fall victim to industrial activity or are destroyed to make way for building development.

Summer visitors: An attractive summer visitor is the woodchat shrike, often seen stationed, sentinel-like, on fences and wires. With its bold brown, black and white markings it is one of the prettiest of the shrikes, or "butcher birds" as they are known because of their habit of impaling their prey on thorns. In summer, turtle doves and spotted flycatchers are common breeding birds, blue-headed wagtails favour damp, grassy patches, while short-toed larks and tawny pipits are normally restricted to the drier, dustier parts of the islands. Nightingales, on the other hand, seem to be everywhere: their song bursts from every copse and thicket.

At night, the Scops owl can be located by its persistent call, reminiscent of a sonar "bleep". Like the resident barn owl, the Scops owl often hunts close to farms and other human habitation and can be heard beeping occasionally in the gardens of some holiday hotels.

On summer days hordes of swifts, swallows and martins swoop and skim over farmland and town rooftops. Close scrutiny may reveal the uncommon red-rumped swallow, on its way across the Mediterranean, the pallid swift and its much larger relative the Alpine swift.

Birds of prey: If there is one thing that distinguishes Mallorca as a birdwatching destination from its smaller neighbours, it is the high sierra that stretches along the northwestern coast. For this wild kingdom is the domain of numerous birds of prey, among them some of Europe's rarest.

The Balearic colonies of the Eleanora's falcon, a dashing and acrobatic hunter which breeds on sea-cliffs and off-shore islets, represent an important proportion of the world population of this endangered species. Among the more accessible colonies are those on the cliffs near the Boquer Valley and around the Formentor lighthouse. Soon after their arrival in April, Eleanora's falcons gather to hunt beetles over marshes and, sometimes, over Port Pollença and Alcudia on the coast.

The peregrine also breeds in this part of Mallorca although it is frequently seen over the smaller islands as well. This powerful aerial predator can sometimes be watched

tion (estimated at no more than 50 individuals) clings on in Mallorca's mountains. With a wingspan of nearly 10 feet (3 metres), these massive birds are a magnificent sight as they drift on broad, sail-like wings across the valleys or soar above the highest summits.

The much smaller Egyptian vulture is an occasional visitor to Mallorca but is comparatively common in Menorca.

The red kite, similarly, is more abundant in Menorca than Mallorca. It, too, has suffered needless persecution by hunters and farmers even though it is a harmless scavenger, not a killer. The red kite is an elegant bird in flight as it glides effortlessly on long, crooked, drooping wings, delicately finger-

cruising high above the waves and making breathtaking dives in pursuit of the rock doves and pigeons which nest in the cliffs high above the sea.

The mighty black vulture is another seriously endangered species, now found in only a few European locations. The Mallorcan population has had to contend not only with persecution by poisoning and shooting but also a dwindling food supply as better animal husbandry has reduced the amount of carrion. Despite this, a fragile breeding popula-

ing the hot air currents and tilting its rufous, forked tail from side to side like a sensitive rudder.

Eagles: The booted eagle, which occurs in Menorca and Ibiza as well as Mallorca, is not uncommon, though like many of the birds of prey, declining steadily. Not averse to dropping down into farmyards in search of easy pickings, the booted eagle is unpopular with some farmers.

By contrast, Bonelli's eagle is extremely scarce and only infrequently seen by the fortunate observer deep in the mountains.

Other raptors (birds of prey) occur in the mountain passes, usually on spring or au-

Left, a bird-rich habitat. Above, a black-winged stilt searching for food.

tumn passage, include black kite, honey buzzard, Montagu's harrier, hobby and lesser kestrel. The latter also breeds in Menorca and, less commonly, in Mallorca.

Birds of prey can be spotted in any part of the mountain range but some places are more likely to reward the keen raptor enthusiast. On the Pollença-Sóller mountain road there are several good observation points in the vicinity of Puig Major, Tomir, the two reservoirs, Embalse de Cúber and Embalse de Gorg Blau, and in the valley near the Lluc monastery. The Boquer Valley is also a favoured haunt of birds of prey and the clifftop ruins of the Castell del Rei at the seaward end of the Ternelles Valley can provide

exciting close-up views against a backdrop of dramatic coastal scenery.

Wetland birds: Not all raptors are inhabitants of the high peaks. Ospreys, although sometimes sighted diving for fish in the mountain reservoirs, more regularly fish in the lowland rivers, marshes and lakes of Mallorca and Menorca. On occasions they can be watched plunging into the shallows along the holiday beaches, particularly near Alcudia and Port Pollença. Likewise, marsh harriers, as their name suggests, are more or less confined to a watery habitat and can be seen in Mallorca and Menorca lazily quartering reed beds and marshes.

The main wetland sites are the Albufera Marsh on the north coast of Mallorca, Salines de Llevant in the south of the island and the Albufera Lake in Menorca. Others include the saltpans near the airport in Ibiza and Albufereta just outside Mallorca's Port Pollença on the road to Alcudia.

In the best of these locations, year-round residents include spotted crake, little ringed and Kentish plover, Savi's, Cetti's and moustached warbler. In spring, an extraordinary assortment arrives, some to breed, others to rest and feed on their journey north. Among their number are purple heron, little and cattle egret, squacco and night heron, little bittern, black-winged stilt, avocet. Temminck's and little stint, marsh, green, wood and curlew sandpiper, collared pratincole, little gull, gull-billed, black, whitewinged black and whiskered tern, reed, great reed and aquatic warbler. In winter, too, these watery areas are important, supporting numerous waders and wildfowl.

Threat of tourism: The wetland sites are the richest wildlife habitats in the Balearics yet they are also the most threatened as more and more hotels, apartments and *urbanizaciones* spring up. Happily, the Albufera Marsh has been protected since 1985 and seems set to survive as one of Europe's most important wetlands, thought the ever-burgeoning tourist developments are creeping closer and closer. Menorca's Albufera Lake has also been given reserve status. Other valuable wetland sites are still at risk, however, while some, such as the little Toucan marsh at Alcudia, have already been wrecked.

It is not only the wetlands that are threatened. Each year, more attractive coastline disappears and woods, orchard groves and fields that once teemed with birds, butterflies and flowers, like those behind Port Pollença near the Boquer Farm, are destroyed or disfigured.

Not all holiday-makers who visit the Balearics do so merely to soak up sunshine and sangria among tasteless modern buildings. There are many who come to enjoy the islands' quiet charm, the natural beauty of their varied landscapes and their rich flora and fauna. The Balearics still have much to offer such visitors, but for how much longer?

Left, the Albufera marsh, a protected reserve. Right, a European bee-eater.

OLD HOUSES, NEW HOUSES

Some authors divide the "typical" Mallorcan house into three categories: rural, village and city, and although the three may be discussed separately, there is an interdependence and interchange of style and structure which crosses the rural-urban divide to the point that it is almost impossible to talk about one without talking about them all.

Rural houses on the island normally grew from a central structure, the kitchen fireplace. The design was always functional and the dwelling invariably expanded in such a way that a central *patio*, or *clastra* became the pivotal element. In the *fincas*, as the country houses are called, this interior courtyard became the heart of the dwelling. It not only served as a meeting place but also had the important strategic function of protection of the inhabitants.

Spanish patios: The *patio* evolved into two types, open and closed. The more common closed design (the *fincas* of Massanella in Mancor del Vall and Galatzó in Calviá are two examples), is that where the house grew in the form of a box encircling an open space. It was entered through an arched doorway and vestibule large enough to allow the passage of animals and farm vehicles. The open *clastra*, such as that of the *finca* of Comassema in Orient, is the result of an incomplete enclosing of the central space as the house developed in the form of a U. Walling in the fourth side was a fairly common addition to this type of patio, as in *fincas* such as Ca' n'Eixartell in Pollença. But be they open or closed the elements which are ever present are a well (normally a cistern) with an adjacent watering trough, stone benches, various wall-mounted rings to which the horses were tied, a horse mount and the entrances to the various dependent buildings.

If the house was of some importance it was divided into three parts: the house of the owners (*casa de los señores*), the house of the farm manager (*casa de los amos*) and other buildings and spaces of the *finca*. The appearance of the country house depended

much upon the interrelated aspects of geography and agricultural exploitation, to which were added a touch of the owner's wishes. Visually the productive mountain *fincas* with their stone walls had a richer appearance than their inland counterparts which were usually built of sandstone blocks.

In the north the agricultural base of the farm was the olive. Consequently mountain estates required large spaces for the oil press (*tafona*) and for the storage and curing of the olives themselves. In the central plain where

the economy was based upon grain, the building was certain to have a mill, or, in the case of wine production, a wine press. Although neither of the latter required as much space as the enormous press and fulcrum of the olive press, they needed enough space for the mules to circle endlessly around a central grinding mill or a wine press.

Finally, the houses situated on the less economically productive littoral of the island which were active in hunting, fishing and the exploitation of the forests were dependent upon an additional element—a defense tower. Although the lofty structure became a common element in *fincas* throughout the island there are examples, such as Son Forteza Vell in Manacor, in which the tower totally dominates the house.

Family rooms: The living quarters of the country houses were divided into two independent sections. In large estates the *casa de los señores* was always located on an upper floor, a feature they share with their city equivalents. The rooms are reached by way of a monumental staircase. Entering the house is done through a grand salon with extremely high ancestral paintings and richly-curtained windows and doors. This impressive room was used only for the receiving of guests and parties. A smaller adjoining salon was used as a living room.

dral-like structure which can be seen for miles around.

Apart from the *casa de los señores* and the rooms and spaces associated with the farm itself the other half of the house is the *casa de los amos*, in which lived the farm manager (*el amo*), his wife (*la madona*) and his family. The kitchen was used as kitchen, living room and meeting place. Normally the fire was always lit and acted as a hub, around which centred the life of the *finca*. The fireplace was covered by an enormous *campana* (smoke hood) which opened directly to the roof and was surrounded by benches covered with animal skins and cushions. On the surrounding walls was a proliferation of cook-

The other important element which pertained to the *señores* was the chapel or *capilla*. The grandeur with which many were decorated indicated that their social significance was often as important as their religious necessity. If the chapel was connected directly to the house, as in the case of Raixa in Bunyola, it invariably had two entrances—one inside for the family and another to the exterior for visitors and the farm workers who came daily to take mass. At times the capilla took on a size and stature which was out of proportion to the house. The *finca* of Sa Torre near Llucmajor, for example, is thus named for its nearby cathe-

ing pots, clay water jars, wooden cutlery racks and other kitchen utensils.

As well as the *amo* and his farm staff, there was a separate staff of servants to attend to the masters. As the aristocrats gained in richness they established houses in the neighbouring towns. On visits to these villages, the *señores* carried on their business and social outings usually accompanied by their upstairs staff.

In town: Within the confines of the urban centres dwellings were erected more as a response to space than to necessity. Unlike the expansive "add-on" architecture that denoted the country *finca*, village houses were designed and built to fit into the limitations imposed by the surrounding houses. But because of common geography and the availability of materials the urban dwelling shared many common elements with its rural counterparts. Stone floors, vaulted vestibules, interior cisterns, semi-circular arched doorways and open-beamed ceilings are all common in both country and village architecture. The stone floors, often seen today with the sheen of hundreds of years of wear, were extensions of the stable which was often the economic base of the village house. As well as the stabling of small animals, it was used for grain and other assorted produce storage in the same way as was the

lages such as Valldemossa, the urban design followed the contours of the land.

Throughout the 1600s many of the country landowners moved to the city, their *amos* maintaining the productivity of the farm. During the following century, some of the *fincas* became Summer retreats.

The architectural styles of city dwellings were far more complex than those in the villages or in the countryside. Architecture became "cultured". Architects were hired to build or rebuild in the latest styles from Europe. Baroque and neo-classical embellishment was added to the lines of the Gothic city structure brought by the Catalans in the 13th century. During the 16th and 17th cen-

clastra of the rural *finca*.

The façades of the village houses were simple with little else than small windows and one arched or rectangular doorway. In the centre of Mallorca, in villages such as Petrá or Santanyí, they were almost always made of *mares* blocks of stone. The long straight sandstone coloured streets only lost their monochromatic appearance in the 19th century with the introduction of larger shuttered windows and the painting of the façades in varying colours. In mountain vil-

turies houses grew through acquisitions to become palaces with grand entrance *patios* and interiors fit for the aristocracy that lived within. Elegant Palmanian houses such as Can Vivot, Can Oleza and Can Morell (Palau Sollerich) were redecorated in French and Italian Baroque, and later French Rococo, establishing models for future renovations and development throughout the city. And eventually the new architecture was taken to the countryside as the wealthiest landowners adopted the new styles.

At the end of the 19th and the beginning of the 20th centuries "traditional" architecture in all its complexities fell by the wayside.

Left, many *fincas* are unchanged. Above, entrance hall in a Palma house.

Grand houses with neo-Gothic stairways and impressive *patios* were divided into small apartments.

The shock of the new: It is difficult to pinpoint when "modern" architecture started in Mallorca, since traditional styles have persisted in so many areas. Probably the main wave of new architecture arrived with some office blocks built in the late 1950s, though even some of these were faintly neo-classical. But by far the most pervasive influence came with the tourist hotels of the 1960s.

As much as possible, these were replicas of modern hotels in America or England, with perhaps a token archway or two by the entrance foyer to remind visitors where they travel to these areas and view a mini Miami beach, where visitors surrounded by breeze-block and plaster talked of "comfort" and "facilities".

These villagers, perhaps travelling by donkey cart or bus—only the wealthy could afford cars, even in the 1960s—were living in a style that many visiting foreigners only came to appreciate in the late 1970s: renovating old *fincas* and village houses and installing new kitchens and bathrooms to provide the necessary comforts and facilities.

The aim of any true *finca* reformation is to retain as much of the original character as possible, yet those same visitors would, 15 years earlier, have viewed the way the villag-

were. All other evidence of Spain or Spanish architecture was absent—perhaps intentionally, since most early package tourists were not particularly adventurous. Spartan cleanliness and comfort were the prime considerations, and Spanish warmth and architectural ambience was at least a decade away from being appreciated by most foreign visitors to Mallorca.

Parts of the coastline suffered badly from this architectural onslaught, though it was restricted to a handful of resorts occupying only a few miles. It must have seemed strange to the villagers of that time, who were still building in traditional stone, to ers lived with disdain—certainly not imagining that the cycle of architectural trends would find them trading places in the future.

Period revival: Good stone-masons for renovations are not hard to find, since the main era of building in stone is so recent, and is now going through a small revival. One example of how recently stone building in the classical style was still practised is Jaime III, Palma's main shopping avenue. Most visitors would guess its age at between 1890 and 1910; in fact, it was built in the 1950s. Building in similar style continued in the main throughout the next decade—with many areas, particularly inland villages, continuing traditional building styles well into the 1970s.

At this point there was an overlap, because traditional, rustic styling had come back into vogue with visiting foreigners. However, the demands for coastal resort living were almost the same: sea views, one or two bedrooms, with lounge and kitchen areas compact, yet ideal for one or two months' occupancy a year, and with generous terrace areas for catching the sun.

Pedro Otzoup was probably the first to answer this demand with his villages at Cala Fornells, a rustic Mediterranean-style village which meanders lazily down a hillside, with paths, archways, gardens and court-

lage, open terrace space had been sacrificed. The architect, François Sperry, who also created Port Grimaud, made no excuses for his almost single-minded adherence to his original plans, even though his consulting Mallorquín architects suggested a more traditional Spanish design.

Local flavour: The same group of architects had more say in the design of Puerto Portals, a collection of shops, boutiques and restaurants on the edge of a 650-berth luxury marina. Here, traditional archways and the mixing of ochre and white lend a more traditional Mallorcan flavour, though the influence for this particular style came originally from Italy and was introduced only partially

yards linking the complex. The style is eclectic, blending elements of Mallorca, Andalucia, Ibiza and Provence—with practically no two apartments the same. The style has since been copied, though seldom bettered.

At The Anchorage, a complete waterfront village in Illetas, a similar blending of styles has been adopted, though perhaps with more accent on the Provençal and with more mixing of colours. To some, the colour contrasts give a vaguely Caribbean flavour; but in achieving the effect of a four-storey vil-

into Mallorcan architecture in the 1700s. More common were natural stone facings, and in general ochre and white were employed only if the stone required rendering. However, apart from natural stonework and an often imposed exterior colour scheme, it is certainly more authentically Mallorcan than white—and a lot easier to maintain.

Even though many choice resorts have been plundered by developers with more taste for money than for style and environment, the situation is no longer deteriorating. Developments are generally more imaginative than five or 10 years ago; the maximum height in many areas is now down to four

Left, many urbanisations lack Spanish character. Above, a residence of some style.

floors; and the new coastal development laws restrict building within 330 ft (100 metres) of the coastline, although many planning permissions were gained before new legislation was passed.

What has probably most aided modern architecture and development is changing public demand. The requirement for small holiday flats with one or two bedrooms has dwindled and larger apartments and villas are now more popular. Generous terrace space, ideally partly open, is also a prime requirement. This means that developers have to stagger each floor, often using the natural fall of the hillside to do so.

More apartments are incorporating gar-

dens and increased green space, and local hope is that the magic 100 metres between the coast and the first cement will be utilised in the same manner. This would provide a more attractive coastal tree line when viewed from the water and also break up the harsh lines of concrete.

City planning appears haphazard, perhaps because of the volume of paperwork involved in gaining planning permissions and the slowness of the Spanish bureaucracy. Still, when a bad development goes ahead, there are complaints that permission was granted too hastily, and some listed buildings have been taken down to make way for

new structures. Thankfully, this is extremely rare and more due to bureaucratic oversight than policy planning; in general, listed buildings are heavily protected and, where possible, faithfully restored.

In many cases, local council grants are available for renovating protected buildings. As a result, some dazzling examples have appeared in Palma's city centre, mostly now in use as art galleries or exhibition halls.

Public opinion tends to guide events more than it used to do. Natural areas such as Dragonera island and Es Trenc have been saved from development by effective lobbying, and the recently completed "sea park" in front of Palma's cathedral was heavily criticised for its imbalance between concrete and green spaces. City planners have been taking more note of public opinion and pressure groups; invariably plans for large projects are published and held open for public examination. Worthwhile projects are therefore more likely to be refined rather than shelved completely.

Certainly, the next 10 years looks brighter than the last, since projects are now considered more on their merits of benefitting the island in general than a handful of developers. On the drawing board are numerous golf courses, shopping malls, convention centres, luxury marinas and sea promenades. Most projects are decidedly more adventurous, so that "areas" should be planned more cohesively, replacing much of the piecemeal development of the past. Another good sign is that most of the hotels and apartments built during the worst period of Spanish architecture and construction (the 1960s) are now coming close to the end of their life cycle. They will either have to be renovated or knocked down to make way for new structures—which, since trends and demands are swinging heavily away from high-rise block styling, makes the second option by far the most likely.

Within 10 to 20 years, the skyline of Spain's more notorious resorts could be reduced from eight to 10 storeys to four floors, with much more traditional Spanish styling and ambience. Pretty much as it was, in fact, before the first holiday invasions of the early 1960s.

Left, re-turning to the traditional. Right, the Anchorage, at Bendinat.

ISLAND DECO
Architecture after Gaudí

For whatever reason one goes sightseeing in the old part of Palma, it is difficult to imagine not ending the day without having paused in front of at least two well-known façades in the city—that of Can Forteza Rey and the Forn del Teatre. But as out of place as these two examples seem to be amongst the convoluted streets lined with senorial houses they are just the tip of the iceberg of the strange but fascinating world of modernism in Mallorca.

At the end of the 19th century, large Catalonian cities, choking with the smoke of industrialisation, were searching for a response to the inhuman face of progress. Fertile ground for the seeds of modernism, parts of Barcelona and other Catalan cities were transformed by the emergence of this artistic movement, epitomised by Gaudí's cathedral in Barcelona.

But this very social-economic context of industry and heavy labour which opened turn-of-the-century Catalonia to the influences of what was known in the rest of Europe as *art nouveau* didn't exist in the Balearics. Instead it was the failure of agriculture which eventually brought modernism to the islands.

First taste: In the 1860s, the mountain village of Sóller was devastated by an orange blight. Economically destitute, the villagers were forced to emigrate to the far corners of Europe in search of work. According to Salvador Bernet (*Ecclecticismo y Modernismo en Sóller*, 1889-1920), their years spent in places as far away as France, Belgium and Switzerland, "woke up the sensitivities of the newly rich Sóllerenses toward a world of culture and refinement." When they returned to the island they contracted well-known Catalan architects to bring the latest fashion in Europe—art nouveau—to Mallorca, often, Bernet continues "for reasons of snobbishness and ostentation". Thus arrived in Mallorca what has come to be known throughout Spain as *modernismo* and

at times as *la época de mal gusto*, or the epoch of bad taste.

According to historians and art experts, when a style or design begins to be imitated or copied it ceases to exist. Thus even though by 1902 art nouveau was architecturally dead though not quite buried throughout the rest of Europe, it wasn't until almost that time that the first modernist building was begun in Palma with the construction of the Gran Hotel by the Catalan architect Lluis Doménech Montaner.

Gaudí in Palma: Simultaneously, at the beginning of the century Bishop Campíns envisioned Palma's 14th-century cathedral restored. His idea was a new shape "that liberated it from the additions and (architectural) corruptions that the tolerance of past times had accumulated". Seeing Gaudí's Sagrada Familia in Barcelona convinced him that the famous Catalan architect was suitable for the restoration. In 1902 Gaudí arrived in Mallorca to take charge of the work. He brought with him his student Joan Rubió and together they planned various new designs for the cathedral which were begun two years later.

For all of Gaudí's international fame his changes in the cathedral didn't escape local criticism. Miguel Seguí Aznar, author of various books on architectural trends in Mallorca at that time, says, "A restorer must not be a revolutionary, nor an inaugurator of styles, he must adapt to the established norms. (Gaudí) did not realise a restoration, he made reforms whose modernist style clashes completely with the sober aspect of the cathedral."

Another critic, Santiago Sebastían, said of Gaudí, "The Catalan architect is above all a creator—a creator out of his time—and his genius doesn't get along well with a scrupulous respect for that which is historic." Whatever the arguments, the final result is nevertheless eye catching.

Local following: The controversial Gaudí and his disciple Rubió were soon joined by two young locals, Gaspar Bennazar Moner and Francesc Roca Simó. Although these two Mallorquíns, both of whom had studied in Madrid, have long lists of works attributed to their names it is ironically not an architect at all who has left the most visual and memorable legacy of Mallorcan modernism. Lluis Forteza Rey was a silversmith, and the prime diversion of his life, Casa Forteza Rey, has become the eye-catching standard bearer of modernism in Mallorca.

Meanwhile Joan Rubió was fulfilling a long list of requests for his skills in Sóller, among which were the parochial church and the Banco de Sóller. Another impressive work which is attributed to him (without positive documentation) is that of Can Magraner (Can Prunera), which remains as one of the few complete existing examples of modernism in Mallorca. The house, built in

1911, not far from the Plaza de la Constitució, is designed with a stonework spiral staircase as its principal feature.

A curious footnote is that although the house was designed and constructed with all of the good taste that money could buy, the Mallorquín owners felt totally out of place living in their modernist surroundings. They constructed a typical Mallorcan kitchen below the house, and when they finally returned after the builders had gone they spent most of their lives in the basement.

At Lluc: The third major centre of modernism in Mallorca is within the precinct of the Monastery of Lluc. As well as the reform of

the interior of the church, Gaudí, and later Rubió, constructed, on the mountain behind the monastery, a series of five sculptures which were intended to represent the Mysteries of the Rosary.

As in Catalonia, Mallorcan modernism often included the lavish use of ceramic tiles. Can Barceló, with its La Roqueta ceramic tiles designed by the artist Llorens, set the stage for the removal of the style from its status as an elitist art movement. Wall tiles, unlike complete buildings, were cheap, easy to use as adornments, and available.

The acceptance of modernism into all levels of island life is signified by the prolific use of such decoration on house façades and garden posts in far suburbs such as Son Espanyolet and Es Molinar. El Terreno, which was established at the beginning of the century as a summering place for wealthy Palmanians, also had its share of the style, some such as Villa Schembri have survived until today.

Tomb style: Modernism was not only felt by the living, it also had its impact upon the dead. During the first two decades of the 20th century funeral corteges often ended their journeys at tombs signed by Bennazar and families laid ceramic flowers and metal wreaths upon imitation wooden crosses in many of the cemeteries of Mallorca's villages. The best example, the cemetery of Sóller, is a virtual museum of the epoch, as also are the interiors of many of that particular town's houses.

The official date of the beginning of modernism in Mallorca is no more than a number established by historians, and so also is the date given to mark the end of the movement. There are examples of modernism on the island dated as late as 1920, but 1914, the year that Gaudí, for unknown reasons abandoned the island leaving the reform of the cathedral unfinished, officially dates the end.

Famous architects such as Rubió and Bennazar and exciting architectural contributions to the city of Palma such as Casa Rey not withstanding, with Gaudí came modernism and when he left, so did it, leaving some notable landmarks.

Left, Villa Francisca in Bunyola. Right, eyecatching mosaic on Casa Forteza Rey.

258

NEW ART

The Balearics seem an unlikely centre for contemporary art. There is no long standing tradition here: neither a major art collection nor a school, nor even the kind of cultural milieu usually associated with young art. In this century, of course, many artists, including one outstanding figure, Joan Miró, have come here from elsewhere, often attracted by the beauty, peace and easy going life of the islands. But their vision and their art has generally been firmly formed by the time they come to the islands and their markets have been elsewhere.

Now, however, there is a spectacular local boom. There are perhaps a hundred professional artists working in the islands, another thousand who dabble seriously and legions of *domingueros,* Sunday painters of seascapes and olive trees. At the same time there is a high level of general interest and a very strong art market: the press carries articles on art nearly every day and in Palma alone there are over twenty galleries dealing in local artists' work.

National trend: In part, this reflects what is happening throughout Spain. On the one hand, strong financial backing from central government is helping Spanish art to emerge rapidly from isolation into the international mainstream: the last five years have seen the number of exhibitions multiply, ambitious plans drawn up for several new museums of modern art and increasing attention from critics. On a commercial level, provincial galleries have mushroomed and a new art fair, ARCO, held every February in Madrid, provides a strong national focus.

Alongside all this, there has been an explosion in the number of young painters or students of art. Both critics and artists have commented, with some bemusement, that painting seems almost to have taken the place of politics or rock music in Spanish teenagers' hearts. Others would say, more cynically, that their main inspiration has been the quickly earned fame and wealth of a group of young Spanish artists nicknamed

los jóvenes for their precocious success in the normally staid art world.

In the Balearics, there are two more local pieces to the jigsaw. One is the region's newfound wealth. The profits of tourism and the flourishing black economy, grafted on to an older habit of small-scale family collecting, have fuelled investment in art while the rest of Spain is still suffering badly from a lack of private collectors. As Joan Guaita, a respected Palma dealer points out, "There are a lot of rich people here now and there are

only so many cars and houses they can buy." After that they invest in art. It may reduce the mystery of collecting to speculation in a product. Nevertheless, the fact that artists can sell their work is a very important starting point.

Media hype: The second local piece to the jigsaw is Miguel Barceló, one of the first and most successful of *los jóvenes,* who was born and brought up in the Mallorcan town of Felanitx. Largely self-taught—he painted furiously through his childhood and adolescence then later walked out of art school in Barcelona—he first hit the limelight and media hype in the early eighties, aged 25, and

Preceding pages: young artists in a Pollença café. Left, **Fum de Cucina,** by Barcelo. Right, street art.

has since gone on to become a major international name, known for his prolific output and artistic maturity.

Barceló has said, quite bluntly, that both artistically and in terms of local support his work owes little to the islands. Something of a nomadic loner, he divides his time between cities abroad and a house in the Mallorcan countryside. In his work, too, he has followed a personal route from flat, coarse expressionism to a lyrical style exploring traditional perspective, space and the drama of light. But despite this detachment and the fact that none of his work is on show in the islands, his success has had a huge impact on the local community.

few of the galleries in the centre of Palma. Small and informal, with changing exhibitions and a stock of work by the artists they represent, they present the best way of seeing local work unless you find your way directly to the different artists' studios. At Altair, a ground-floor galley tucked away in Calle San Jaime, all the work is abstract; at Ferran Cano, in Calle de la Pau, where there are studios above the gallery. Ferran Cano is younger and more *avant-garde*, but at Sala Pelaires, (Calle Pelaires) there are mixed traditional and younger styles.

Among the work of the older artists—old in terms of the youth cult here—Ramón Canet's strong, free abstract expressionism

"So many kids looked at his quickly earned fame and wealth and thought they could get that too." explains Catalina Serra, the art critic of *Ultima Hora*, the largest local newspaper.

"On the one hand, it's had a very good effect because it has encouraged so many young people to paint; on the other hand, there's a certain spirit missing. We have a commercial rather than artistic movement here, competitive and lacking critical discussion. That is not a good thing."

Local galleries: The disparity of styles and quality resulting from the boom quickly becomes clear from a short walk around a

stands out; Joan Bennassar's massive figurative forms, often reminiscent of Picasso, and the naive, tragi-comic figures of Maria Carbonero are also popular locally. With the younger painters, there is a confused but energetic and interesting search for an original painting vocabulary, which has been taking them in different directions—towards surrealism, collage, frenetic abstraction or primitive, splashy work. Here Tofol Sastre's painterly abstracts, filled with light and a sense of nature, are among the most promising work. He is self-taught and, like many of the artists now coming through, still in his early twenties.

But, while it is very clear that there is no unifying school, certain shared charcteristics do emerge to an outsider. First and foremost, nearly all the work is painting, with very little sculpture. There is also a sensuousness, derived not so much from colour, as you might expect, but a shared fascination with materials and, particularly, heavy paint surfaces, sometimes almost sculpted in oils or mixed media. This undoubtedly reflects the influence of Antoni Tàpies, great informalist master, and, more generally, the influence of Barcelona, once the Spanish capital of the *avant-garde*, where most of the artists have studied or spent time.

Beyond this, too, there is sometimes a quite specific feel of the islands themselves. This may be very clear in figurative subjects drawn from everyday life; at other times it comes through in images or colours charged with local meaning, even though they may have been used in a determinedly cosmopolitan way. Calvo Serraller, art critic of *El Pais*, has seen in Barceló's work the psychology of an islander, curiously adventurous yet at the same time withdrawing from the outside world. In his landscapes and still-lifes, the two worlds meet in double-edged imagery: bowlfulls of soup that are turbulent and threatening seas, outsize vegetables or even bones uprooted from the background landscape.

Generation gap: Inevitably, in a fast moving decade and a market preoccupied with discovering and protecting its own, older generations and outsiders have benefitted less than local young artists from *el boom*. "Unless you are 21, it becomes harder and harder," comments Ellis Jacobson, an American-born artist who has lived in Palma for many years. "Now Spanish artists of 30 and up are having difficulties."

So, too, are some of those who come here from elsewhere to work in peace and quiet— a long tradition embracing Elmyr de Hory, the famous faker who was filmed on Ibiza by Orson Welles, and Manolo Mompó, the fine Spanish abstract painter.

Today, this group, including Steve Afif, Jim Bird, Ellis Jacobson and Ritch Miller, still look as much to markets elsewhere as local galleries although their work is some of the strongest on the island. Equally, major Spanish painters like Campano or Sicilia, who have houses and spend time here, or Mallorcan born Ferrán García Sevilla, a conceptualist described as "a sophisticated anarchist," have nothing to do with the Palma market.

Looking ahead: Where, then, does the future lie? In artisitic terms, the neo-expressionism and *transavanguardia* which have dominated the eighties have faded fast and, while it is not yet clear exactly what will follow, a return to abstract art has already begun. But the boom certainly shows no signs of ending. "It is almost as though the fury of painting and exhibiting and buying and the desire to paint are at a frothing stage," comments Ellis Jacobson. The galleries' sales confirm this. They say that they are finding increasing numbers of buyers abroad and that unfortunately local prices remain comparatively low.

"It is a time of change", comments Joan Guaita. "The market is solidifying. Collectors are becoming more discriminating all the time and the standard of work is rising every year. Also, artists of real stature, like Karel Appel, are beginning to move here. These are all signs that the best is yet to come."

Equally important are the moves afoot to push for more public space for modern art. Exhibitions in Palma, at the Llonja and Palau Sollerich, both splendid historic settings, have been imaginative and drawn good crowds in the past. But they have remained strictly limited through lack of funding and a political deadlock in regional arts policy, and the only permanent modern collection is that of Anglada Camarasa's highly coloured, post-impressionistic work, from the turn of the century, housed in a small museum in Pollença.

Now, however, private sponsorship is being accepted and, more important, momentum is gathering for a contemporary art foundation where both local people and tourists would be able to see the fruits of the current boom. Many people feel this would encourage a much needed critical awareness and help younger artists develop their work without leaving the islands. Certainly, it would be an important first step in moving from a precarious boom towards a firmly rooted home-grown tradition.

Left, a painting by Ibizan artist Jussara Heberle.

TRADITIONAL GARDENS ON MALLORCA

Although it is difficult to think of any newly built house, be it in Mallorca or elsewhere, without an adjoining garden, the history of the garden in the Balearics goes back so far that it almost predates the house itself. The earliest ornamental gardens on the island date back to before the Spanish reconquest by King Jaime I of Aragón in 1229. These 12th and 13th-century gardens left behind by the Moors, were a combination of flower garden, made up of typical native plants, and a vegetable garden and orchard called a *huerto*.

Early evidence: That the roots of many of the still existing gardens date back so far is attested to in both historical documents and legend. As early as 1864, historian Joaquin Bover wrote of an important country estate called Raixa, "When (Jaime I) divided the Arab *fincas* (farm estates) amongst his nobles after the conquest, Raixa was given to the Count of Ampurias as a reward for his loyal services…" Another of the well-known rural mansions, La Granja, is also documented as far back as Arab times under its Moorish name of Alpich, but perhaps the best remainder of the Moorish influence exist in the gardens at Sóller (on the Alfábia road near Bunyola).

Although the Christian conquerors moved harshly and swiftly to minimise the Moorish influence in Mallorca, the island's gardens kept their heritage far longer than anyone might have expected. Hispano-Arab style was still the predominant influence well into the 17th century. It wasn't until the turn of the 18th century that a series of socio-economic factors began to change the existence and the design of the gardens.

Status symbols: More and more of the landed aristocracy abandonded their *fincas*, leaving them under the control of farm managers, and moved to the city of Palma. The *possesió* (country mansion) became less a way of life and more a symbol of prestige and wealth. As a symbol it was often re-

Preceding pages: the *pergola* or covered walkway in Alfábia. Left, resting in the Hort del Rei, a garden in Palma.

formed in the latest European fashion of Baroque or neo-classical. Italian-inspired gardens were designed to compliment the house, and the changes so overshadowed the former gardens, they almost disappeared.

Every garden thus modernised had a geometrical plan. In the examples of two of the most famous—Raixa and Canet—the central focus is a stonework staircase. (Raixa is located just south of Bunyola and Canet is off the Valldemossa road near Esporles). In others, such as Son Berga Nou in Establiments, tree-lined entranceways were designed to visually link the garden to the house. In yet others balustraded walkways and elongated *pérgolas* or covered walkways were designed to act in similar ways.

Elegance and romance: The 18th-century Mallorcan gardens took on an elegance totally unknown in previous centuries. They were adorned with columns and sculptures set into an Italian-inspired insistence upon absolute symmetry. But while details of the 18th-century Italian stonework such as the grand cypress-lined stairway of Raixa and the marble temple in Son Marroig (on the north coast near Deià) attract the eye it is probably the modifications done in the following century which leave the visitor with the longest lasting impression.

With the 19th century came romanticism. The trend was away from symmetry and towards the use of the existing landforms, using nature as it stood. The use of cut stone was almost eliminated, replaced by more natural materials such as terracotta, stone and clay in the elaboration of grottos, rock gardens and waterfalls, best exemplified in the gardens at La Granja, near Esporles.

Because of the anarchy which existed before the introduction of the neo-classical in the 18th century, the romantic garden had much in common with its medieval predecessor, leading the owners of the *finca* to call the upper section their "medieval garden".

Watery eminence: The single most important factor in the mounting of a garden was that of water. Consequently the most impressive Mallorcan gardens, past and present, are those on the edges of the Sierra de Tramontana (the north coast mountain range). The importance of water is illustrated by Arthur Byne in his classic 1928 book *Mallorcan Houses and Gardens*. He describes how, in 1239, the abundance of water in the *finca* La

Granja attracted a group of monks who were awaiting the completion of their monastery, Santa Maria la Real. In a grand gesture the house and land were donated to the order by its then owner Count Nuño Sanz. The monks became so attached to its profusion of waterfalls and springs that when the Count later tried to recover it from them they fought to hold onto the property for 250 years until they eventually sold it to the Vida family.

Until the recent building of the two *embalses* (reservoirs) of Cúber and Gorg Blau, the *finca* of Raixa, with its 330 ft (100 metre) long main water-holding pool, had the largest surface area of water in Mallorca. Additions of the following century in the romantic style gave even more importance to the grand *estanque* or pool by surrounding it with tree-lined pathways all leading to a stairway and balcony jutting into the immense area of water. The resultant combination of *gusto italiano* and the ground conforming romantic additions has made the Raixa garden into one listed amongst the most notable gardens in all of Spain.

Byne also noted the importance of water as a decorative element. In his description of the nearby *finca* of Canet, he writes, "The beautiful terraced garden with its numerous reservoirs, makes (it) one of the most attractive locations on the island."

Alfábia is another romantic garden in which the use of water is paramount in its design. As well as its covered *aljub* (reservoir) and an unusual *pérgola* of spraying water, the lily ponds, like those in Canet, are surrounded by bamboo and palm trees which give sections of the garden a totally exotic air. Water was, and is, indispensable in the mounting of a garden—be it a Hispano-Arab inspired *huerto* or a neo-classical or romantic monument of exotic plants and rock waterfalls. The main difference between earlier and later types was that, in the monumental garden, Byne notes, "The water is available to serve the garden in ways decorative as well as in ways practical."

The history of the garden in Mallorca has passed its thousandth birthday and the majority of the gardens continue to be a mixture of the decorative and the productive.

Right, part of the lower garden of La Granja, where careful landscaping is retreating in front of nature.

TRAVEL TIPS

GETTING THERE
274 By Air
275 By Sea
275 By Rail
275 By Road

TRAVEL ESSENTIALS
276 Visas & Passports
276 Money Matters
277 Health
278 What to Wear
278 What to Bring
279 Animal Quarantine
279 Porter Services
279 Reservations
279 Extension of Stay
279 On Departure

GETTING ACQUAINTED
280 Government & Economy
282 Geography & Population
282 Time Zones
282 Climate
282 Culture & Customs
283 Weights & Measures
284 Electricity
284 Business Hours
284 Holidays
284 Religious Services

LANGUAGE
285 Useful Words

COMMUNICATIONS
286 Media
287 Postal Services
287 Telephone & Telex

EMERGENCIES
288 Security & Crime
289 Loss
289 Medical Services

GETTING AROUND
290 Maps
290 From the Airport
290 Domestic Travel
290 Water Transport
290 Private Transport
291 On Foot

WHERE TO STAY
291 Hotels

FOOD DIGEST
294 What to Eat
295 Where to Eat
300 Drinking Notes

THINGS TO DO
301 City
301 Country

CULTURE PLUS
302 Museums
302 Art Galleries
303 Concerts
303 Ballets
303 Opera
304 Theatres
304 Cinema
304 Architecture

NIGHTLIFE
304 Pubs & Bars
308 Gambling

SHOPPING
308 What to Buy
308 Shopping Areas
309 Shopping Hours
309 Export
310 Complaints

SPORTS
310 Participant
311 Spectator

SPECIAL INFORMATION
311 Doing Business
312 Children
312 Gays
312 Disabled
312 Students
313 Pilgrimages

FURTHER READING
313 General

USEFUL ADDRESSES
314 Tourist Information
315 Consulates

GETTING THERE

BY AIR

The islands of Mallorca, Menorca and Ibiza have modern airports, and are served regularly by both scheduled and charter flights from a large choice of departure-points, mainly in Europe. A partial list of the carriers serving the Balearics shows the diversity of routes: Iberia, Aviaco, SAS, Spanair, Lufthansa, Condor, LTU, Luxair, British Airways, Caledonian, CalAir, Britannia, Monarch, Swissair, Balair, Hapag-Lloyd, AeroLloyd, Air Berlin, Pan Am, Dan Air, Air Europe, Air France, Air Inter, Sabena, Martinair, Transavia, Conair, Finnair, etc.

Scheduled services operate from several Spanish mainland cities, and these are flown by both Iberia and Aviaco.

Visitors to the fourth largest Balearic island, Formentera, can make their connections in Ibiza, from where frequent ferries, including car-ferries, cross to the port of La Savina. Ferries also operate to Formentera from Denia and Alicante on the Spanish mainland.

The best value method of visiting the islands by air is with one of the many available all-inclusive package tours offered by tour-operators and travel agents from points all over Europe, and seasonally from the US, Canada, Iceland, etc. Major European tour-operators such as Thomson, TUI or Spies have appointed agents throughout the world, through whom it is possible to reserve a holiday and leave from the airport most suitable to you.

It is also possible to travel independently, choosing your own airline, hotel, and using taxis for your transfers. The price of independence can be high, without the benefit of the airline-seat and hotel-room discounts which the tour-operator can negotiate. The savings available in buying a ready-assembled holiday do not mean you will be part of a regimented group, with a tour-guide waving a little flag, leading a long line of tired sightseers. The only time you need be with others is during the flight and on the bus transferring you to and from your hotel.

Particularly in the summer high-season, expect bottlenecks and delays in the baggage halls of the three major airports. As the majority of arriving flights are one-stop charter rather than multi-stop scheduled services, the incidence of lost or mishandled baggage is lower than at many airports.

Hold-ups are also sometimes due to the sheer numbers of flights in the summer peak (July and August), all trying to arrive at the preferred times. Air Traffic Control centres in France and on the Spanish peninsula, over which most flights operate, controllers have to carefully space flights out in the interest of air safety. In the peak period problems are aggravated by obsolescent equipment and insufficient staff at these centres, compounded by the absence of forward-planning to cope with steep rises in visitor numbers. Spain's Minister of Transport has allocated funds for a new radar to handle traffic coming over Marseilles, which will reduce the volume which the Barcelona centre has to handle, and reduce high-season delays.

Apart from the tour-operator baggage-label showing your hotel name, it is a good idea to distinctively mark your luggage with strips of coloured Scotch tape; avoid putting fluffy woolly markers on the baggage handles; although pretty and highly visible, they are usually ripped off during loading or unloading. Upon claiming your baggage, check for damage, as any problem will need to be reported to the airline immediately; if not claims may not be accepted by the carrier. Lost baggage should also be reported before leaving the airport, so that when found it can be forwarded to your hotel, marked on your luggage labels. Most visitors on charter flights are met at the airport by a representative from the tour company or hotel, with transport. The system works well, and the representatives are friendly and useful sources of local information.

These representatives regularly visit the hotels under their charge, to brief clients on local do's and don'ts, shopping hints, interesting excursions and so on. Any problem which cannot be solved with the hotel management should be put before the representative, usually a local resident, trained in problem-solving.

The Customs officers at the islands' airports are thoroughgoing experts at judging arriving passengers, and for the most part will simply amiably wave whole planeloads through without examining their luggage. Unlike some other airports, there are no Green or Red channels. Anyone who needs to obtain clearance for commercial samples should tell an officer. Customs officers in Spain are helpful and unfailingly polite.

BY SEA

Services by sea to the Balearic Islands are provided by convenient ferry routes, primarily from Barcelona and Valencia, with summer operation from the French port of Sète and from Genoa and Algiers. In summer, there are also services to Alcudia, in Mallorca. Ferries operate from Alicante and Denia to Ibiza and Formentera. There are also regular inter-island ferries, and a fast hydrojet (two hours) runs between Palma and Ibiza.

All the ferries from Valencia and Barcelona carry automobiles, trucks, boat-trailers, etc. Passengers can reserve a cabin for the eight- to 10-hour trip, but the ordinary ticket gives entitlement to an airline-type seat in one of the lounges. There are usually restaurants and coffee-shops, and large bar-lounges, the latter usually noisy with continuous television reception.

The principal operator of these ferry services is a publicly-owned line called Trasmediterranea, popularly known as La Tras. As with other ferry lines, La Tras has appointed agents throughout the world, with reservations available locally through your own travel agent.

BY RAIL

Services by rail, including sleepers and car-carriers, operate from all over continental Europe, feeding into either Valencia or Barcelona for transfer onto the ferry to the Balearics. It is essential to make advance reservations. The highest frequency of ferry service is from Barcelona.

Spain's publicly-owned railway, RENFE, operates on narrower gauge tracks than the remainder of Europe, but a decision has been made to equip some major routes between large cities with a high-speed train service, TGV (Tren de Gran Velocidad) which will start with conversion to wider track, and eventually, better through-services between Spanish and other European cities.

RENFE has appointed agents throughout Europe and in many other parts of the world.

BY ROAD

Taking the family car to the Balearics can be the most economical way of travelling. Several of the European automobile clubs offer all-inclusive packages. For example, the West German DAC issues a brochure with a choice of destinations, in which the package consists of hotel rooms, ferry charges and route maps with choices of diversions, excursions and stopovers en route. Generally speaking, the economics of driving to the Balearics become more attractive with a longer stay, and particularly if accommodation can be obtained on a cheap rate. This method of travel ensures independence and mobility during your stay.

Although Spain's highways are often criticised, particularly by Spaniards themselves, the truth is that the crowding at holidays and long weekend is due mainly to an enormous increase in the numbers of private automobiles registered over the last few growth years; road-building has not been able to keep pace with demand. The Ministry of Public Works and regional and local governments do a praiseworthy job of widening and improving existing roads, building new highways and creating by-pass roads around cities. Most main and secondary roads in the Balearics are in good condition, and comparable to most of Europe.

Among Spanish provinces the Balearics has the highest number of registered road vehicles per capita, which indicates the good health of the local economy, but also reflects the existence of the many self-drive car hire outlets.

As in most of Spain, the main highways have a top speed-limit of 100 km (62 miles) per hour, and seat belts for front seats are required when out on the main roads—use of seat belts in town hasn't yet been accepted by the car-driving population. Children should only ride in the back seats.

TRAVEL ESSENTIALS

VISAS & PASSPORTS

Thanks to the importance of tourism Spain puts few barriers in front of prospective visitors. However, for political or security reasons, and sometimes only to apply reciprocity, citizens of some countries have to have a valid visa stamped in their passport. Check with your booking agent.

Spain has ended the requirement to fill out landing cards for the Balearics, and there is no Immigration or Customs declaration form, as in so many other destinations. Citizens of countries in the European Economic Community normally walk through the National Police (Immigration) controls by showing the front cover of their passport. Visitors who have a visa will normally have the passport stamped with the date of arrival. Applications for extensions of stay can be arranged, but cost time and money, and it is better to obtain a long-stay visa in the first place. A passport or similar travel document is required from all visitors.

MONEY MATTERS

Spain's currency is the peseta. The division of the peseta into decimos (tenths) has been abolished. Bills are in circulation in denominations of 10,000, 5,000, 2,000, 1,000, 500, 200 and 100 pesetas. In addition, coins are available (in decreasing order) in values of 500, 200, 100, 50, 25, 10, 5, 2 and 1 pesetas. Exchange rates against major foreign currencies show constant fluctuations, and so no equivalents are shown here. It is a good idea to carry your money in travellers' cheques issued by a known major issuing-house. Bringing lesser known travellers' cheques, Scottish or Irish pound notes will probably cause inconvenience and delay at the time of making change, but practically any industrialised nation's currency will be accepted somewhere.

Increasingly, Eurocheques are acceptable directly in shops and can certainly be changed in banks. Although the banks in the three airports are open for daytime operations, it is a good idea to arrive with about pts. 5,000 in 1,000 notes, sufficient for out-of-hours arrivals, buying the first drink, or paying the taxi driver. The use of credit cards is general throughout Spain, and increasingly these are acceptable for most transactions. Most major cards are known and acceptable, especially VISA/BankAmeriCard and American Express.

Certain types of bank-cards can also be used to draw cash in pesetas from out-of-hours machines at banks. Incidentally, VISA is the preferred card quoted as acceptable in newspaper advertisements for massages or other intimate services, usually offering home or hotel calls by male, female and in-between practitioners. In the Balearics, there is something for everyone...

Bank hours vary between cities and towns and the resort-areas, but the agreement between the banks' association and their employees' unions calls for the following trading times:-

Winter (mid-September to mid-June)
Mon. through Thurs.	0830—1630
Fri.	0830—1430
Sat.	0830—1300
Sun.	Closed

Summer (mid-June to mid-September)
Mon. through Fri.	0830—1430
Sat. and Sun.	Closed

Money-changers, travel agencies and some vehicle-hire outlets will also change money. Look for a board in the window showing major currency exchange rates. These tend to vary and it is worth shopping around, particularly if you intend to change a fairly large sum.

Some independent operators have a talent for following currency changes and will often give better rates by anticipating changes or by not charging excessive commission. An example is the corner business near Plaza Gomila in Palma, Mallorca, run by Jaime Galera. "Jimmy" Galera has been changing currency and cheques (including Veterans' Administration and other countries' Social Security cheques) for visitors and resident foreigners for so many years that he has a fine feel for currency movements, and will usually quote competitively. Most hotel concierges or cashiers will also change foreign currency, although in many cases this service is treated as a prerequisite of the job, and can be more expensive.

Since Spain joined the EEC banking regulations have been changed, and several foreign banks have been able to open their own offices. Leaders in the field have been Barclays, with branches in the Balearics (three so far in Mallorca) and over 50 more on the mainland. Others are First National City Bank, National Westminster (in association the Balearics' Banca March) and many more.

HEALTH

The most important health advice is not to attempt to get sun-tanned too quickly. Always use a sunscreen product and be especially careful with children, who don't know the danger, and who can dehydrate with often frightening speed. Drink quantities of non-alcoholic liquids, and if necessary take salt pills with you.

Some visitors assume the Balearics to be teeming with bugs specially designed to upset the digestive processes. This is not so. The average visitor will find *different* conditions, but a few sensible precautions and habits can be adapted to avoid problems. Eat and drink in moderation, and in the case of unusually sensitive digestions bring your own tried-and-true medications with you, although most products such as Rennies and Maalox are available in local chemists.

In cooking, vegetable oils are often used instead of animal fats. For example, olive oil instead of lard or butter in fried eggs. True Balearic cooking uses a large variety of herbs and spices, and includes the use of hard-to-digest items such as peppers. Garlic is widely and generously used.

To give yourself time to get acclimatised, order bland foods over the first few days, absorbing the local cooking in your own time.

Alcoholic drinks in the islands are much the same as anywhere else, but beware of two factors. The first is the size of the "shot" of liquor. It is quite normal to be given a two fluid ounce shot, and not unusual to be poured a three to four fl. oz. drink, a lot bigger and stronger in most other countries. Watch the barman pour your first drink, particularly in the case of mixed drinks such as gin and tonic where the size of the shot is difficult to ascertain once the drink is mixed.

The second caution is the practise of buying bulk liquor (known locally as *garrafa*, the Catalan word for demi-john) and re-filling brand-name bottles. Not all *garrafa* is bad for you, but there is no doubt that a lot of it will give you a headache, and in some cases it can affect your eyes and other functions. Don't be kidded by people who say this is only a trick practised in small or poor-area bars. Some of the most popular bars and discotheques do it, and charge at least as high as the price for the real brand you think you're getting.

Whisky drinkers are more likely to get the real thing, as whisky is difficult to imitate in taste. Each whisky (whether Scotch, Bourbon or Rye) has its own particular flavour, usually recognised by a regular single-brand drinker. If you don't want to risk getting served *garrafa* ask for a drink which can be opened before you, such as a bottle of beer.

Popular brands of liquor are also "shadowed" by look-alike bottles, and often similar names, containing quite palatable liquor. Among those copied are Bacardi, Gordons, Tia Maria, Gran Marnier, Cointreau, Smirnoff, Baileys, etc.

One final health note for anybody taking pills regularly; don't forget that if you have diarrhoea, your pill may not stay with you long enough to be effective. This is particularly worrying if the pill concerned is contraceptive, and could create a new dimension for the phrase "Made in Spain".

WHAT TO WEAR

Experience shows that the average visitor to the islands brings at least one suitcase, and usually a shoulder bag. It is not unusual to find at the end of the visit that as much as 60 percent of the items packed have not been used. Naturally it would be wise to bring warmer clothing in winter, but generally speaking, the average summer tourist spending between two and four weeks could quite adequately travel with one small case or normal size shoulder bag.

The best advice about what to wear in the Balearics depends on gender and temperature. Dress is generally very casual on the islands. Apart from high-society events, any wedding or funeral is quite normally attended by women in simple-to-dressy outfits, while the men will usually wear a suit, or trousers and a jacket, but without a necktie.

Jeans, T-shirts, and sandals are quite acceptable for trips into town, while shorts or bathing suits are better confined to the resort or beach areas. Depending on the place to be visited, dress up or down from these norms. Bear in mind that overseas trip are always a good opportunity to buy new shirts, shorts, shoes, hats, handbags, etc., so the more you bring the less you can take back with you.

Don't forget an eye-shade or dark glasses, and a hat to protect you during the first few days during summer's heat.

WHAT TO BRING

Spare eye-glasses, contact-lenses, dentures. Your personally prescribed medications, plus a spare prescription from your doctor for replacement medicines. A camera, whether still, movie or video.

Your preferred sunscreen product, although most brands are available locally. And, although you're getting away from it all, your doctor's or paediatrician's and your neighbour's telephone numbers. Give your neighbour a contact address or number for you in the islands, in case of an emergency at home. Check your health insurance coverage before leaving home.

ANIMAL QUARANTINE

There are no animal quarantine restrictions into or out of the Balearics.

There is sometimes a problem at the end of the season, particularly in Ibiza, caused by cats and dogs left behind by summer-long visitors, who have acquired or adopted a cat or dog as a pet, and then abandoned it on returning home. The local authorities then have the task of collecting and disposing of these animals, particularly the dogs, which tend to band together and attack sheep, often killing or maiming more than they eat. These packs, if they get out of hand, can also attack humans. Strange animals shouldn't be petted, fondled or fed, or you might find they have adopted you.

PORTER SERVICES

These are available at the three principal island airports, at a set charge per piece of baggage handled. Porter services at the sea ports are not readily available, but assistance can be requested from the Purser. If not travelling with a car, it is advisable to travel only with what you can carry yourself.

Although all five- and four-star hotels have baggage porters, it is not usual for lower-rated hotels or hostels to have a dedicated person for this job. Most establishments will usually find someone, whether a waiter, gardener or maintenance man, who will give guests a hand with baggage.

RESERVATIONS

Essential for air and ferry travel during summer, Easter, Christmas and New Year, and other busy periods. In Spain, religious, civic and national holidays tend to be elongated into long weekends, by taking the intervening working days off, a practise known as a *puente*—a bridge. Inter-island flights and ferries are also booked ahead, and often have a long wait-list, with the stand-

bys being augmented by youths on military service visiting home. Package tours to the other islands are available from most travel agents, and these can usually also be arranged through tour guides and your hotel's concierge.

EXTENSION OF STAY

If you want to stay longer at any one place during your visit, ask as early as possible for changes in bookings for hotels and transportation. In the months of July and August, it is practically impossible to arrange an extension of stay in the same hotel, and longer stayers will have to search out a smaller hotel or hostel, preferably in a city centre, where there is more likely to be space.

An alternative is to go to an English-run bar and ask whether any rental apartments are available. Many such apartments exist, although they are not registered with the tourist regulatory bodies, and don't pay taxes on the earnings from such rentals. They are usually owned by English-speaking non-residents, who ask other English-speaking residents or businesses to refer possible renters to them. It is a practice which the tax and tourist authorities are gradually bringing within the rules.

ON DEPARTURE

Most hotels require your room to be vacated at noon on the day of departure, in order for their housekeeping staff to prepare the room for the next incoming guest. Your departure might not be until that evening, but many hoteliers will provide a room for storage of your luggage, and some will set aside two rooms—one for men, one for women—so that guests wanting to stay in the hotel, possibly at poolside, can change into and out of their resort clothing, if they wish. Hoteliers who offer this service, apart from being considerate to clients at the end of their stay, are also encouraging checked-out clients to remain around the hotel, probably as cash-clients at the pool bar or other outlets.

GETTING ACQUAINTED

GOVERNMENT & ECONOMY

A democratic monarchy, Spain is governed by a Congress and a Senate. The head of State is the King, Juan Carlos I; his direct heir and successor to the Crown is Prince Felipe, Prince of Asturias. The Government, based in the capital, Madrid, is popularly elected, and is headed by the leader of the majority party or grouping, who is known as the President or Prime Minister. The remainder of the parties form up in opposition, and debates can often be seen on television, being no more, nor less boring than legislatures in other countries.

Key debates on matters of wide interest, such as Education or Pensions are worth watching, with spokesmen for every political group having their turn at the podium, and the relevant government Minister having to respond to every point made.

Spain's various regions—formerly provinces—enjoy a high degree of independence or autonomy; they are as follows:

1. The Junta (Assembly or Council) de Andalucia, Sevilla.
2. Diputación General de Aragón, Zaragoza.
3. Gobierno de la Comunidad Autonoma de las **Islas Baleares**, Palma de Mallorca.
4. Gobierno de Canarias, Santa Cruz de Tenerife.
5. Diputación Regional de Cantabria, Santander.
6. Junta de Comunidades de Castilla-La Mancha, Toledo.
7. Junta de Castilla y Leon, Valladolid.
8. Generalitat de Catalunya, Barcelona.
9. Junta de Extremadura, Merida-Badajoz.
10. Xunta de Galicia, Santiago de Compostela.
11. Comunidad de Madrid, Madrid.
12. Gobierno de Navarra, Pamplona.
13. Pais Vasco, Vitoria-Gasteiz.
14. Principado de Asturias, Oviedo.
15. Comunidad Autonoma de Murcia, Murcia.
16. Comunidad Autonoma de la Rioja, Logroño.
17. Generalidad Valenciana, Valencia.

From the spelling differences between the Galician *Xunta* and the *Junta* in Extremadura, and the *Generalidad* in Valencia and Catalunya's *Generalitat* it is clear that although almost all Spaniards speak Spanish (also known as Castillian), many also speak a regional language. These languages, the teaching of which was forbidden in schools during the 40 years of Franco's rule, have survived by being taught at home.

The restoration of democracy to Spain has meant a resurgence in the use of the various regional languages, which are now on schools' curricula and used by poets, songwriters, authors and, officially, in the regional parliaments. There are television and radio broadcasts in Catalan, Galician, Basque, and regional newspapers use all the different idioms daily.

Although the Spanish economy has traditionally been thought of as being based on agriculture, particularly products requiring long periods of daily sunshine such as olives, citrics and legumes, Spain's modern economy is increasingly diverse. Automobile manufacturing, as a sector, although foreign-owned, is sixth in size in the world, and fourth in Europe, with West Germany, France and Italy leading. Volkswagen, Seat, Ford, GM and other major auto-makers all have construction or assembly plants in Spain, and the industry is a large exporter.

The other large foreign-exchange earner is tourism. Spain, with a population of some 35 million, had about 50 million visitors in 1988, and increases are forecast over the subsequent years. The Balearic islands enjoy their share of this visitor traffic, with Mallorca taking the larger proportion.

Visitors to the Balearics:

•Formentera, with 5,000 population and a surface of 31 square miles (82 square kilometres), receives 15,000 visitors annually.

•Ibiza with a total of over 60,000 residents (about 5,000 are foreigners) and an area of

220 square miles (572 square kilometres), receives over 1 million annual visitors.

•Menorca, with 62,000 residents and 270 square miles (699 square kilometres), gets visited annually by some 600,000 people.

•Mallorca, with near to 600,000 residents and a surface of 1,405 square miles (3,640 square kilometres), receives over 5,600,000 annual visitors.

In total, the Balearics receive in excess of 7 million mainland Spanish and foreign visitors annually.

There are four Stock Exchanges operating in Spain (Madrid, Barcelona, Valencia and Bilbao), and trading has shown a very large increase since the mid-seventies, to the point where a joint government/business effort has been undertaken to re-structure these exchanges and their methods to accommodate the increase. The government operates a publicly-owned industrial corporation, the Instituto Nacional de la Industria (INI) which incorporates various other state-owned or para-statal bodies, some of which are in the process of being privatised. Among the larger such companies are shipping lines, airlines, steel foundries, aircraft and ship construction industries, fuel distributors, the telephone system and television channels.

The banking and insurance sectors are growing, and becoming more efficient and client-conscious since the borders were opened for the establishment of foreign companies in Spain. Foreign banks and insurance companies have started new Spanish companies, and also formed partnerships with existing Spanish operations. Spain's labour unions (*sindicatos*) are based on industries or skills, such as mining or carpentry, and are affiliated to one of the two major federations of trades unions. One is the mainly socialist UGT, and the other is the mainly communist CC.OO. The broad aim of both the government and unions is to reach agreement with each other and with the CEOE—the employers' federation—on a lasting "social pact" to reduce the wastage and economic costs of continuing confrontation in the negotiation of working-hours, earnings increases, conditions, pensions, etc. Only time, and patient negotiation will tell whether this ideal is within the reach of the present-day work-force.

Spain joined the European Economic Community in 1986, and is preparing at all levels for 1992, when the European Internal Market is due to be established. Also in 1992, Spain expects record visitor numbers, helped by the hosting in Barcelona of the Olympic Games, and the holding in Sevilla of EXPO 92, a major World Fair, celebrating the 500th anniversary of Christopher Columbus' Spanish-funded voyage to the Americas.

Since joining the EEC, Spain has achieved excellent economic growth, with major investors such as Hoechst, Nestlé, General Foods, General Electric, the Kuwait Investment Office and several Japanese industries participating in the expansion. Thousands of family-run businesses, high unemployment, poor telephone service, a torpid swollen bureaucracy and other negative remnants from former times still stand in the way of even better results for Spain's economy.

Fuelled by a reaction to high taxation, value-added tax, unemployment, onerous hiring-and-firing and employee-benefit conditions, plus the Catch-22 regulations and bureaucracy, there is an active underground economy. This substantial slice of the economic pie often out-produces the high-profile sectors, reacts faster to customer needs and is competitive at the point of sale. A positive approach to incorporate underground businesses into the regular economy by correction of the problems or by incentives seems to have taken second place to the hiring of more inspectors and bureaucrats to unearth them.

In the Balearics, as in the mainland Galician and Basque regions, smuggling is still a traditional and busy activity, and some of the islands' big fortunes had their start in the night-time importation of tobacco and medicines, although today's demand is more for pirated computer software, movie videos and "chocolate", "horse" and "snow" (drugs). Some of the uncounted caves on the islands' coasts are still used as distribution warehouses for this ancient trade, and the occasional successes by Customs are widely reported in the newspapers, TV and radio.

GEOGRAPHY & POPULATION

The Balearic archipelago, located between the mainland of Spain and the North African coast, consists of the principal islands of Mallorca, Menorca, Ibiza and Formentera, with surrounding and outlying smaller islands, very few of them populated.

The islands have a population of some 800,000 inhabitants, in a combined area of 1,936 square miles (5,000 square kilometres). Palma de Mallorca is 132 nautical miles from Barcelona, 172 from Algiers and 287 from Marseilles.

TIME ZONES

The Balearics, as part of Spain, adhere to the time-zones used by the continental EEC countries. Between the months of October and May, this is Greenwich Mean Time plus one hour, but in summer one more hour is added. Dates of time changes are announced well in advance each year. Clocks go forward in spring, and go back in autumn, giving rise to the useful mnemonic "Spring forward, Fall back".

At noon in the Balearics in autumn/winter (GMT+1) it is 06.00 in Coboconk, Ontario and in New York; 01.00 in Kurri Kurri, New South Wales and in Sydney; 08.00 in Colonel Pringles, Argentina and in Buenos Aires and 15.00 in Le Tampon, Reunion Island and Curepipe, Mauritius.

At the time of writing, the United Kingdom and Eire adhere to changeover dates which are different from the EEC dates and there are a few days of disjunction each year—for example, when the EEC put clocks back one hour in October to GMT+1, the British Isles and Europe enjoy the same local time for a short period until the British and Irish put their clocks back to straight GMT for winter.

CLIMATE

The Balearic Islands lie on the 39th and 40th North parallels, in the Balearic Sea, a part of the Mediterranean, and almost exactly on the Greenwich meridian. On the mainland of Spain, Barcelona and Valencia are the nearest principal cities, while on the northern coast of Africa, the nearest city is Algiers.

The three main islands enjoy more or less the same weather conditions, with local variations caused by phenomena such as Mallorca's mountain ranges.

The Balearics' average high temperature annually is 21.2°C (70°F), average low 13.8°C (57°F) and the sun shines annually to an average 59 percent. Rainfall in Mahón (Menorca) is 580 mm a year, while that in Palma (Mallorca) only reaches 480 mm.

CULTURE & CUSTOMS

The Balearic people are industrious, having their past rooted in agriculture, fishing and trading, conditioned by the cultures of the various invaders.

Successively, the Balearics have been wholly or partially run by the Phoenicians, Romans, Byzantines and Muslims. The last of these, the Moors from northern Africa, were driven out after over a half century of largely benevolent rule, by Christians from Catalunya led by James I in 1229. Throughout history, the Balearics have been attacked by raiders and pirates, some of whom sought to establish a base from which to attack passing shipping. They all had a hard reception from the Balearic defenders, who relied on the skill of their *honderos* or stone-slingers. The Romans also learned to respect these *honderos*, and eventually equipped their ships with leather armour against the accurate hail of stones.

Eventually, both the Romans and the Carthaginians incorporated Balearic slingers into their armies as missile troops, and relied on their skill in many subsequent engagements elsewhere in the known world.

Present-day visitors can see the benefits

left by the various colonisers, in architecture, farming and fishing techniques, in language and the arts. The name of each island has changed over the ages, with Menorca having been known as Minor, Mallorca as Major or Majurka, Ibiza as Ebusus, and Formentera as Ophiussa.

Modern Balearic people are similar to island cultures elsewhere. They are hardworking and tend to mind their own business, maintaining a fairly closed, private family life. Today's invaders, the world's tourists, find the atmosphere to be welcoming and receptive, with native islanders being very adaptable, willing to provide for the requirements of visitors.

Available are the typical foods and drinks usually found in other countries, such as German sausages and beers, English tea and toast, pizzas, croissants, crêpes, chow mein. Nobody needs to feel homesick, foodwise.

The songs, dances, and musical instruments also owe something to previous ruling cultures. Island folk musicians use wooden clappers—big castanets—fifes and drums, bagpipes, etc. They sing about work and life; and in the villages, during their fiestas, the words are often made up on the spot, with insults, lewd suggestions or even accusations of scandalous conduct not being excluded. Saints' days are as important in the islands as they are on the mainland, and this applies to individuals as well as to towns and to villages.

Spanish children are normally named after a saint, and on that saint's day, they celebrate their *santo*, so that on 29 June, St Peter's day, all the Pedros will treat their friends to drinks, and sometimes, at work, there will be a brief break, while Pedro lays out some savouries and cake, along with wine, so that he and his colleagues can mark the day of San Pedro. The fishermen in Palma celebrate St Peter's day with a seaborne procession around the city's harbour, in which one fortunate trawler-owner will have been selected to carry the effigy of St Peter, removed from the church of the same name, and mounted in the vessel's bows.

This boat, with St Peter aboard, will lead a picturesque procession of boats, all decorated, loaded with family and friends, around the harbour, in a symbolic blessing of the waters by their patron saint, while the following boats, Coastguards, Customs boats, private sailboats and other fishing boats rend the air with their whistles and sirens and fire off rockets. St Peter is then paraded around the fishing-folk's neighbourhood, in a preamble to a full night of celebration.

On 24 June, all the people named after St John, including King Juan Carlos, celebrate their saint's day. On this day, the town of Ciutadella in Menorca also has its huge annual fiesta, with traditionally-dressed horsemen pirouetting in the streets, and even riding into people's patios, or jousting with each other, in the streets.

At the festival of Martinmas, farm-owners will invite friends to take part in a *matanza*, the slaughtering of a pig, and its conversion into all the pork by-products. Participants contribute whatever talent they have, with some doing the butchering and cutting, others making sausages and so on.

Two of the traditional sausages in the islands are the *sobrasada* and the *butifarra*, with the first having a spicy red-pepper coloured filling, soft and spreadable on the local bread, while the *butifarróns* are black, blood sausages, also spicy, often with a strong flavour of anise. These are also made on the mainland, where they are called *morcilla*, and often have rice added to their filling. A plate of barbecued pork and lamp chops, along with a *sobrasada* and a *butifarrón*, some local bread and the local strong red wine are a meal not soon forgotten.

WEIGHTS & MEASURES

In common with the rest of Spain, the Balearics adhere to the metric system, so visitors can order purchases in metres and centimetres, or kilogrammes and grammes. The sizes of houses or apartments are referred to in square metres. Cloth is often sold by weight, as are most fruits and vegetables.

In referring to farm land, an ancient measurement based on the palm, which measures 0.38 square metres, is sometimes used. Measuring larger areas means using the *destre*, consisting of 454 *palms*, going up through the *hort*, which is 50 *destres*, then the *cuartón*, which is two *horts*, and finally to the *cuarterada*, which is four *cuartones*, and measures 7.103 square metres.

The measures for weight, also still used in country districts, is the *arroba*, which weighs 25 pounds. This scale starts at the lower end with the *cuarto*, which consists of four *adarmes* (literally, four whits), then going up through *onzas*, which are four *cuartos*, then to *libra* (pound), which is 12 *onzas* (ounces), to the *arroba*, 25 pounds, on up to the quintal, which is four arrobas, and finally to the *carga*, which is three *quintales*.

ELECTRICITY

Many places on the islands still have dual voltage, with both 125 volts and 220 volts being available, often in the same house or apartment. In an effort to eliminate the obsolescent 125 volt service the islands' utility company, GESA, has undertaken a long campaign to get users to switch to 220 volts, with price incentives for those making the conversion early.

For some time to come, however, it is sensible to check the voltage on lamps and electric appliances before use.

BUSINESS HOURS

The islands have traditionally observed the noon-time siesta, with businesses and shops generally open from 08.30/09.00 to 13.00/13.30, and from 16.00/16.30 to 19.00/19.30. As an exception, shops and businesses in Menorca tend to re-open after lunch at a later hour, around 17.00.

In certain sectors of business, these traditional hours are changing. For example the big department stores such as Galerias Preciados, and the out-of-town hypermarkets generally open all day, from 10.00 to 21.00, but close on Sundays. Other businesses, related to businesses in other countries and different time-zones, will also sometimes have differing hours.

In summer, generally from June through August, many government and professional offices are open only during the mornings.

HOLIDAYS

Due to the floating nature of some holidays, an annual *calendario laboral* is issued, and this lists the national holidays for the coming year. The aim is to ensure that there are 14 holidays per year. Local city, town and village festivals are added to these, on a local basis.

The basic Spain-wide holidays are:

January	1st and 6th.
March/April	Easter Thursday, Friday and Monday.
May	1st.
June	Corpus Cristi.
July	25th.
August	15th.
October	12th.
November	1st.
December	6th, 8th, 25th.

The local festivals for the towns and villages in the Balearics are listed in a booklet issued by the Govern Balear, available at tourist offices in each island. (See under *Useful Addresses* at the end of this section).

RELIGIOUS SERVICES

Catholic churches are located in all towns and in the neighbourhoods of larger cities. There are also temples and churches for other religious or spiritual beliefs.

MALLORCA

Anglican Church, Nuñez de Balboa, Palma, Tel. 237279

Baha'i Centre, Gabriel Llabres, 25, Palma, Tel. 274618

Baptist Mission, Aragón, 24, Palma, Tel. 462805 or 469369

Seventh Day Adventist, Despuig, 22, Palma, Tel. 233941

Mormon Church, Marques de la Cenia, 35, Palma, Tel. 450743

Dutch Ecumenical in Cala D'Or, Tel. 657209

Evangelical Church, Murillo, 8, Palma, Tel. 231810

Full Gospel Fellowship, Juan Alcover, 13,

Palma, Tel. 681330
Jehova's Witnesses, Belchite, 6, Palma,
Tel. 681219 (plus four other locations)
Swedish Lutheran, Avda. Joan Miró, 113B,
Tel. 231241
Jewish Synagogue, Monseñor Palmer, 3,
Palma, Tel. 238686
Reformed Baptist, Ortega y Gasset, 15,
Palma, Tel. 274224
Salvation Army at Hotel Barbados SOL,
Tel. 403715

IBIZA

English-speaking services by the Resident
Chaplain, Joe Yates-Round, Tel. 343383
Jewish Cultural Group. Call Yenta at Flora-
bunda, Santa Eulàlia.

MENORCA

English-speaking service is usually held at
the Church of Santa Margarita, in the Calle
Stuart, Villacarlos.
Times of services are to be found posted in
several places around the island, and certainly in the English Library, Calle Deyá, 2
Mahón.

LANGUAGE

Although Spanish (or Castillian) is the
national language, the Balearic people also
use a vernacular language, which in Mallorca is known as Mallorquin, in Menorca,
Menorquin, and in Ibiza, Ibiçenco. All three
local languages are similar in vocabulary
with component words having their origin in
Italian, Latin, French, Portuguese and Arabic. A visitor with knowledge of a Latin or
Romance-based language can manage to
understand much of what is being said.

In his book *Majorca Observed*, Robert
Graves referred to Mallorquin, stating it to
be as ancient a language as English, and
more pure than Catalan or Provençal, its
closest relatives. Road signs on main highways are in Spanish and Mallorquin. Some
locals feel that there is a danger that the
vernacular language is being swamped by
outside residents, and there is some evidence
to support this. As in parts of the world
where bi-lingualism exists (Wales, Canada,
etc.) street and highway signs are defaced.

Thus, for example, on the road between
Palma and the airport, one could see *Centre
Ciudad* (City Centre) in Spanish, re-sprayed
Centre Ciutat, or *Aeropuerto* changed to
Aeroport. Or sometimes just a sprayed gen-
eral demand, *En Catalá*.

Interesting left-overs from the time when
Britain's Royal Navy had its Mediterranean
base in Menorca are words and expressions
used by modern-day Menorquines in every
day conversation. Examples are:
A bow-window is called a *boinder*
A screwdriver is a *tornescru*
A bottle becomes *botil*
Marbles are *mervils*
A leg of pork (shank) is *un xenc*
A black eye is *un ull blec* (*ull* is eye in
Menorquin)
To rap on a door with your knuckles is to *toc
de necles*

COMMUNICATIONS

MEDIA

There are several excellent Spanish-language newspapers published in the islands. Some of these are the *Diario de Ibiza, Diario de Mallorca, Ultima Hora,* and *Diario Insular de Menorca.* In addition, all of the major mainland newspapers such as *El País, Vanguardia* and *Ya* are available at most kiosks. Most of these newsstands also have today's (or at worst, yesterday's) *Figaro, La Stampa,* the *Times, Daily Telegraph, Daily Express, Daily Mail* and *Sun,* along with *Die Telegraaf,* and other European papers, including the International edition of the *Herald Tribune.*

Spanish television gives good coverage of international news and sports, particularly events which involve Spanish participation. Thus, there is a good coverage of tennis, soccer, basketball, golf, grass and roller-skate hockey, handball, water-polo and others. To enjoy the many movies shown by Spanish television, it is possible to have receivers altered at moderate cost, to enable the reception of the original sound-track, whether in English or other language.

Radio stations are varied in both quality and content, and more than one of the Spanish stations broadcast continuous music. The English-speaking station in Palma is worth listening to, and offers a variety of local personalities, each of whom present their own individual type of show, with local news, music, interviews, quizzes and other items. Radio 103.2 FM, as it is called, also carries advertising and is a very good source of information about the island.

In Ibiza, two local stations carry about one hour a day of English broadcasting, one being on Radio Popular on FM 89.1.

In Menorca, there is also an English programme on the local station.

English-speakers in Mallorca have their own peculiar love-hate relationship with the *Majorca Daily Bulletin.* Otherwise known as the *Daily Bee,* the newspaper has something for everyone. Feature articles, many from the wire services, goofy photos ("crocodile breast-feeds abandoned puppy..."), and entertaining local columnists. World news sometimes appears with a delay of a day or so, as it often needs to be translated from Spanish parent-paper *Ultima Hora.* Nobody publicly admits to buying the *Daily Bee,* but everybody seems to have read it, and many people quote from it. There is a useful, if confusing, small-ad section, completely unclassified, so that to find the coffee percolator you want to buy, you'll have to wade through "boat for sale", "kitten needs home", and "learn Spanish in eight weeks". There is a useful listing for local and BBC radio, television and satellite programmes, and good sports coverage.

The best parts are the gossip columns, full informative local chat, either about apparently well-known total strangers, or about the columnist's own family and friends. The paper appears six times per week. Good value, and often very funny.

Another English paper is *The Reader,* which can be picked-up free of charge at several points on the island. Also a good read, it is a monthly and offers editorial comment, letters from readers, a good London Column, funnies from the world's press, advice to foreign residents, cartoons, recipes, coming events, some island satire, and the advertising which enables it to be read for free.

In Ibiza, there is a twice-monthly English paper, published by Sally Wilson. Very informative for both residents and visitors, it is well-produced and worth buying. In Menorca, there is an annually-published guide, *Menorca 89* (90 in 1990, etc) which is an useful holiday companion. Published by a locally-resident Briton, Noel Evisson, it has facts and figures and advertising. It is available free at convenient pick-up points on the island. Another English publication in Menorca is the newsy and informative *Roqueta,* published (and largely produced) by

Annette Bell. *Roqueta* comes out monthly during April-September, and there is one winter issue, in December. It is filled with useful information and articles about the island and its people. Many English speaking non-resident home-owners subscribe to the magazine.

POSTAL SERVICES

The Spanish postal system has deteriorated rapidly over the 1980s, and nobody with genuinely urgent mail would place it in the system's care. Service is not so much just slow; it is unreliable, with a letter or package sometimes being surprisingly delivered within two days, but with an equal chance that it could take three weeks, or just simply disappear.

Emergency steps have been taken, with the introduction of an Express mail service, with red-coloured mail boxes appearing alongside the regular yellow ones, but all this has done is to relegate anything put in the yellow boxes to a low priority. Fortunately, the gap has been partially-filled by the local motorcycle messenger services, the international express companies such as DHL, and the general availability on the market of that modern-day miracle, the telefax. Other competitors have appeared to cope with packages and urgent documents throughout Spain, and these include the railway system.

English-speaking residents in the islands regularly keep British postage stamps at home, and get their mail hand-carried by people travelling on the frequent services to the United Kingdom, where their delivery either within the UK or other destination is more reliable, and faster.

Postmen in Spain don't have to deliver packages regarded as being oversize. Packages and parcels are therefore sent to a central post office, and a collection slip sent to the addressee, who must then go down, show identification and collect the mail. One of the results of the modernisation of post offices is the installation of what looks like bullet-proof glass on the counters, making it hard to communicate with the person on the other side. Among the saving graces which the post office had, despite all its faults, was the possibility to talk in a relaxed way with the staff, who for the most part are helpful and good-humoured, but now are fenced off from the public.

Place your name and address on the reverse side of envelopes or parcels, preceded by the word *Remitente* (sender). The Spanish post office will not open undeliverable mail in order to obtain a return address.

TELEPHONE & TELEX

The telephone service works reasonably, with publicly available coin-phones being available throughout the islands. This guide will not go into details of the drawbacks experienced by telephone subscribers, such as the unreadable and irregularly mailed accounts and the arbitrary cutting-off of telephone service.

The visitor will find difficulty in reading the local telephone directory, a single book for all the islands, as a search for somebody's number may have to start with a knowledge of which town or *pueblo* he lives in. Thus, the person you seek may live in the municipality of Calviá, but his number may be listed under Portals Nous.

Although it is easy to dial anywhere in the world from a coin-box, it is difficult to complete a collect call, and impossible to have someone call you, as the coin-boxes do not advertise their number.

The main post offices usually have telex and fax services available to the public, but on business days there is often a queue, with messengers from different companies sending messages to various parts of the world.

Post offices will only accept incoming messages if the recipient is actually present.

Alternatives exist, and Palma has at least two business services offices, with English-speaking staff who will help you find numbers, place your telephone call, send your telex or fax, and hold any incoming messages. One of these services is Intelcom, Paseo Maritime, 21, 07014 Palma de Mallorca, telephone 458387, telex 69949 (anitae), fax 458386. The other is Network Business Communications, Avenida Joan Miró, 149, 07015 Palma de Mallorca, telephone 403903 or 403703, and fax 400216.

Both these organisations charge either a membership fee or a temporary resident fee, apart from the price of the metred phone or telex service. Intelcom also offers dedicated office space, with full secretarial services, and represent parcel express and insurance companies. At the time of writing, no such equivalent services was available in Ibiza or Menorca.

EMERGENCIES

SECURITY & CRIME

As in the case of any busy seaside or ski resort, there is much visitor-related crime in the islands. Many foreign criminals come to places such as the Balearics in order to commit crimes during the summer season. In addition, the islands have their own home-grown criminals who prey on local citizen and visitor alike.

A fairly recent factor, the steeply-rising numbers of people who have become dependent on stupefying drugs and who depend on crime to pay for their expensive daily requirements, has worsened the problem. The tourist is an easy mark.

Although advised not to wear jewellery, not to carry cash or valuables, to make use of the hotel safe and not leave valuables in the hotel room, most people prefer to follow their instincts rather than good advice. There is little point in resisting if three or more persons surround you, demanding your money and valuables. You cannot fight effectively (and they may be armed) and you can't run. Best not to get into a discussion, and simply hand over what you have.

Leave your hotel key at Reception when you go out, or you may lose it and find your room has been ransacked before you can get back to it. If you must carry a hand or shoulder bag, avoid walking near the kerb, as much of the bag-snatching in the islands is done by two people on a motorcycle, one driving and one snatching. The other preferred place to snatch and run is at busy intersections, when the average pedestrian is distracted by looking at the traffic or the traffic-lights.

One specialist, since forcibly returned to his native North African country, used to stalk women, either alone or in couples, run up behind and, with both feet, drop-kick one of the victims. While one was on the ground, in pain, and the other distracted in trying to aid her, our now-deported friend would grab both bags and run. Surprisingly, most bag-snatchers and hold-up artists don't generally keep credit cards, cheque-books or pass-ports, as these are incriminating evidence if they are caught. Generally, they'll scoop the cash out of the bag or wallet, and very quickly dump the bag in the nearest avail-able refuse bin.

The local emergency number to call the police (Policia Nacional) in Palma, Ibiza and in Mahón is 091. In Ciutadella (Menorca), the number is 381095 and in Manacor, Mallorca, 550044.

The Fire Service has local numbers every-where (consult the directory) except in Palma, where 080 is their emergency num-ber. Ambulances are operated by the Span-ish Red Cross as well as by private operators. For the Red Cross, call 200102 in Mallorca, 301214 in Ibiza, and 361180 or 365400 in Mahón (Menorca). All the emergency num-bers are easily found in the first few (green) pages of the telephone directory.

The keeping of the peace in the islands is in the hands of a variety of different bodies. The emergency numbers quoted above are for the national police, a country-wide force with their regional HQ in Palma. The police work in tandem with the Guardia Civil, whose principal task is to watch over smaller towns and the countryside generally. The Guardia Civil are billeted in dedicated hous-ing all over the country, living with their families in these *casa-cuarteles* (residential barracks).

In most towns and cities there is also the Policia Municipal, whose activities con-fusingly overlap those of the other two bodies. The municipal police generally concentrate on the flow and control of traf-fic, but due to their local character and knowledge of the vernacular, tend to get involved in family disagreements, tourists' problems, etc.

In the sea ports there is often a brigade of the Policia del Puerto, whose jurisdiction extends to the property of the local Junta del Puerto. In Palma, these people help police the main harbour-road, the Paseo Maritime, and parking fines along this stretch can be levied by them. There is also an individual known as a Vigilante Jurado (sworn-in watchman), who can be seen in banks and other commercial premises, and are often armed, a condition permitted by the fact that they are legally deputised.

LOSS

If your loss was in or near your hotel, report it first to the management. If the loss involves a claim against an insurance policy, go to the nearest police station and make a report, a copy of which you must return with your insurance claim. If your loss includes your return tickets and passports, refer it to your country's consul, included in the list of useful addresses at the end of this guide.

MEDICAL SERVICES

Spain has a Social Security service, with hospitals in all major towns. In addition, there are privately-run clinics in many places. Mallorca has a large Social Security hospital, on the edge of Palma. There are also large clinics in and around Palma, most associated with one or another private pa-tients' insurance plan. The Spanish Red Cross also operates a clinic in Palma, and in common with other clinics, runs its own ambulance service.

Dotted around the various resorts, there are also medical centres, some of them quite small, where routine and emergency treat-ment can be obtained, or where first-aid can be applied prior to transfer to a specialised hospital. In the Palma area there are medical practises run by foreign doctors, most of them being English-speaking.

For emergency ambulance service, call:

Palma	200102
Ibiza	301214
Mahón (Menorca)	361180
Ciutadella (Menorca)	381993

GETTING AROUND

MAPS

A good map is essential. Any bookstall will have a wide choice, but among the clearest are those produced by Firestone locally and by the Hildebrand Travel Maps from West Germany.

FROM THE AIRPORT

In Mallorca, Ibiza and Menorca, there are public bus services from the airports down into Palma, Ibiza town and Mahón, respectively. From these town centres, other public bus routes lead to towns inland.

The taxis at all three airports are clean, well maintained and usually have helpful drivers. Compared to other European locations, the prices are not expensive. Generally, these taxis will use a meter, and the prices of long runs are usually posted at the airport. Out of hours, there are surcharges. The driver is required to give you this information on request.

DOMESTIC TRAVEL

There are only two train routes on the islands, both on Mallorca. The first goes from Palma to Inca, and the second is a quaint period train running between Palma and Sóller, meandering through tunnels and mountains, offering some of the best views on the island. At Sóller the train connects with a tramcar, which goes on down to the Port of Sóller. This is one of the best day trips on the island.

All three main islands also have a good choice of scheduled bus services radiating out from the principal towns. Train and bus schedules are obtained free of charge at the downtown offices of the Oficina de Turismo, operated by the Balearic Government.

WATER TRANSPORT

It is possible to take water-borne excursions to various places of interest from many ports and resorts. Many of these excursions will head for a pre-determined cove, where a lunch, usually paella, will be served. There are normally bars available on these excursion boats.

In some of the resorts it is possible to rent small, low-powered motorboats, and of course most beaches have twin-boom Pedalos suitable for two. Windsurfers can be rented at most beaches. There is a well-developed boat-charter industry in the islands, with boats for rent from a sailboat for two, through to a major yacht, complete with deck crew.

Ferries connect all the islands and in summer there is a Hydrofoil service between Palma and Ibiza, usually twice daily.

PRIVATE TRANSPORT

The best transport for the islands is your own, if you can take it over with you. Although an international driving licence is useful, most countries' licences are acceptable by car rental agencies.

Both major international car hire firms as well as local businesses are represented on all four main islands. Also available are scooters, mopeds, motorcycles and bicycles. The smaller mopeds can be driven without a licence, but are only licenced to carry one rider, so if two want to share the same transport select a scooter or bigger motorcycle.

When driving in Spain, make clear signals of your intentions when turning, and remember that motorcyclists signal a right turn by holding up their left arm. Seat-belts should be worn, except in towns. Highway police levy fines on the spot for non-use of seat-belts, and occasionally operate radar traps for excessive speed. Always have your driver's licence with you when driving, along with your passport, or a photocopy.

On a two-lane divided highway, use the fast lane for passing only, signalling both before you pull out and when you return to the right-hand lane. Watch for speed restrictions. Traffic signs are international, with Stop signs actually having the word Stop on a red background. The triangular Give Way or Yield sign reads *Ceda el Paso*; give way to traffic on your left on roundabouts.

In the event of an accident in a rental car, follow the rental company's instructions, as they are your insurers. In your own car, note the other vehicle's licence number and get the driver's name and address, and note the name of his insurance company. If there are injuries, call the police and do not move the vehicles involved. If no one is hurt, you need not call the police.

In towns, many garage doors and other entrances have a *Vado Permanente* sign, accompanied by a police permit number, enabling the enforcement of the No Parking sign. Parking in front of one such sign can mean a fine, and a trip to the car pound to retrieve your towed-away car.

Palma has a ticket system for parking. These tickets, which come in 30, 60 and 90 minute values, should be punched and displayed in car windows. Tickets are available at tobacco shops.

ON FOOT

The best way to appreciate the finer points of the ancient downtown areas is walking, avoiding traffic nightmares or problems with parking. In addition there are published walking-tour guides of the local countryside. In summer, ensure you wear a hat and carry a water-bottle while country walking.

Hitchhiking in the islands is similar to elsewhere; it can be a long wait before someone stops to pick you up.

WHERE TO STAY

Spanish authorities categorise visitor accommodation thus:

H   Hotel
HR Residence hotel
HA Apartment hotel
RA Residential apartment
M   Motel
Hs   Hostel
P   Pension
HsR Residence hostal

These abbreviations appear on a sign at the door of each lodging business. The letter R indicates that the establishment does not provide restaurant service, although it may offer breakfast or even a cafeteria service.

Apartamentos Turisticos (AT), are graded by being awarded one, two or three "keys", which grading appears on the sign at the door. Hotels are graded by stars, from the budget priced one-star through to the high-priced five-star deluxe hotel. Hostels and Pensions are graded three, two or one stars.

An excellent book published by Spain's tourism ministry covers the total accommodation on offer; *Hoteles, Campings, Apartamentos—Baleares*. The Secretaria General de Turismo is at María de Molina 50, 28006, Madrid.

HOTELS

MALLORCA: PALMA

Son Vida Sheraton Hotel, Urbanizacion Son Vida, *****. Overlooking Palma and its Bay. Grand Luxe. One golf-course, another under construction, tennis, many other facilities. Tel. 451011.

Valparaiso Palace, Francisco Vidal, La

Bonanova, *****. Overlooking Palma, views of harbour and Bay, set in lush gardens. Indoor and outdoor pools, separate health clubs for men and women. Tel. 400411.

Melia Victoria, Joan Miró 21, Palma, *****. Reigning over the Palma harbour front, the Melia Victoria has its main entrance close to the nightlife around Plaza Gomila, and its lower, harbour exit leads directly to the centre of the night's activities on the Paseo Maritimo. Tel. 234342.

Bellver Sol, Paseo Maritimo 11, Palma, ****. Faces out over the harbour front, close to the centre of town. One of the more than 100 Sol hotels, the number one chain in Spain, now expanding internationally. Tel. 238008.

Palas Atenea Sol, Paseo Marítimo 29, Palma, ****. The Palas Atenea is highly commercial offering function rooms and conference facilities, and a good address for a travelling business person. Overlooks the harbour, close to downtown. Tel. 281400.

Racquet Club, Urbanizacion Son Vida. Formerly an excellent four-star rating, the Racquet Club is closed while a German group builds a new hotel in the area, associated with the second golf course being built in Son Vida. When ready, no doubt it will be one of Palma's principal hotels. In the meantime, information can be had by writing to Mr Peter Haider at the Son Vida Club de Golf, Son Vida, Palma.

Uto Palma, Joan Miró 303, Palma, ****. Located at the sea's edge in Cala Mayor, the Uto is an HA apartment hotel. A part of the Iberotels chain, it has pools, gymnasium and sauna, seaside terraces, and is near to all the Cala Mayor action. Ideal for families with children. Tel. 401211.

Nixe Palace Hotel, Joan Miró 269, Palma, ****. A seaside hotel, the Nixe Palace has a small beach, sun-terraces and other facilities. A good hotel for the business traveller who wants to be away (10 minutes) from downtown. Tel. 403811.

Costa Azul, Paseo Maritimo 7, Palma, ***. Although only a three star, the Costa Azul is listed as an old favourite with families and business travellers over the years. Right on the harbour front. Tel. 231940.

Saratoga, Paseo de Mallorca 6, Palma, ***. The Saratoga is convenient for the business traveller on a tight budget, close enough to be able to walk to most lawyers, banks, businesses and shops downtown. Tel. 727240.

Jaime III Sol, Paseo de Mallorca, Palma, ***. Close to all the downtown area. Tel. 725943.

OUTSIDE PALMA

Maricel, Ctra. de Andratx, Km 7, Ca's Catalá, ****. The Maricel is in a category all its own, being one of the original hotels along the coast road near Illetas, 15 minutes from Palma centre. Old world courtesy and charm from the employees, many of them long-service with the hotel. Seaside, pool, quiet. Tel. 402712.

Club Galatzó, Urb. Ses Rotes Velles, Calvía, ****. Off the beaten track, popular in the German market. Tel. 686270.

La Residencia, Son Moragues, Deià, ****. Individually designed and decorated rooms, quiet luxury in this hill town, home to artists and poets. Famous for excellent cuisine. Tel. 639011.

Hotel Formentor, Playa de Formentor, *****. Overlooking the beach, this peaceful traditional hotel is family-run and many of the staff have spent their entire career here. Surrounded by pine trees and gardens. Tel. 531300.

Hotel de Mar Sol, Paseo del Mar, Illetas, *****. Tel. 402511.

Bonanza Playa, Carretera de Illetas, ****. Built into a cliff at the sea's edge, the lobby area is at street level on the top floor, with rooms and extensive facilities below. Family run with year-after-year repeat clients. Tel. 401112.

Gran Hotel Albatros, Paseo de Illetas 13,

****. Family run, full facilities. Tel. 402211.

The Villamil, Ctra. de Andratx, Km 22, Paguera, ****. A member of the Trust House Forte chain. Overlooks the beach, and has gardens and sun-terraces to relax in. Tel. 686050.

Hotel Son Caliu, Urbanizacion Son Caliu, Palma Nova, ****. Attractive gardens, right on the beach. Many of the facilities are indoors, aimed at off-season clients. Tel. 680162.

Hotel Bendinat, Urb. Bendinat, ***. A family run hotel. Only some 30 rooms, ensuring individual attention for clients. Located on a small point, with good sea swimming right at the end of the garden. Tel. 675254.

The Sis Pins, Anglada Camarasa 229, Puerto de Pollença, ***. A family run hotel, the Sis Pins is across the road from the sea, and families return here every year. Tel. 531050.

MENORCA

Port Mahón Hotel, Paseo Marítimo, Mahon, ****. The Port Mahón overlooks the fjord-like port, once the Mediterranean base for Nelson's Royal Navy. Quiet, almost sedate, it makes a good base for a business or holiday visit. Tel. 362600.

Apartamentos Royal, Carmen 131, Mahón. A tourist apartment with a grade of two keys. Central and convenient to downtown. Pool, gardens and bar cafeteria. Tel. 369534.

The Hotel del Almirante, Crta. Villacarlos, near Mahón. Interesting and sympathetic conversion of British admiral Collingwood's residence, good views of Mahón harbour, hacienda-style accommodation around swimming pool. Tel. 362700.

The Almirante Farragut, Av. de los Delfines, Ciutadella, ***. A very large hotel, built on a promontory over the sea, with a small beach on one side. In summer, tour-operators from all over Europe keep the Farragut fully-booked. Tel. 382800.

IBIZA

Although there are city-centre hotels in Eivissa (Ibiza town), the level of activity and noise is high. As distances around the island are relatively short, it is best to stay outside and make trips into town for shopping or nightlife.

Anchorage Hotel, Puerto Deportivo Marina Botafoch, Paseo Marítimo, Ibiza, ****. Right in the newest marina in town, with views across the harbour of Eivissa and its citadel. A variety of shops and restaurants surround the hotel, which is five minutes from downtown. There is no pool, but Talamanca beach is an eight minute walk away. Tel. 311711.

Pike's, Ctra. Sa Vorera, Km 12, C'an Pep Toniet. Classified as a *pension* with two stars, Pike's is really difficult to grade, being nearly unique. Owned and run by Australian yachtsman Tony Pikes, the hotel has less than ten rooms, and provides a relaxing retreat for jet-setters and well-known actors and singers, etc. Set in a restored farmhouse, there is a pool and garden, and a good restaurant. No phone number is advertised, and children aren't welcome.

Les Jardins de Palerm, near Es Cubells. In the same genre as Pike's, Les Jardins is unclassifiable although listed as a *pension*. Self-described as "a little piece of Paradise", it is the ideal hideaway for lovers or honeymooners, and children aren't encouraged. Operated by jack-of-all-trades René Wilhelm, a Swiss former Formula III driver, decorator, fashion designer, boutique owner, etc. Excellent *nouvelle cuisine* restaurant, pool, gardens, in this 10-room retreat. Tel. 342293.

Hotel Club Village, Urb. Caló den Real, San José. Recently opened and as yet unclassified, this hotel perches over the sea, surrounded by pine forest, with a stairway down to the beach. A tennis-players' paradise, with four courts and professional coaching. Pool, sauna and whirlpool and a good restaurant make this a favourite new place, particularly in the German market. Tel. 344561.

Ca's Catalá, Calle del Sol, Santa Eulàlia. Classified as a Residence Hostal, the Ca's Catalá is owned and run by Kim and Jill Brown, he is Canadian and she British, and offers nicely-furnished single and double rooms, a pool and garden. Breakfast only is served, but non-residents drop in for this and also for midmorning coffee and pastries. A very nice, tucked-away in-town home from home. Tel. 331006.

FORMENTERA

Club La Mola, Playa de Mitjorn, ****. Tel. 320050.

Hotel Formentera Playa, Playa de Mitjorn, ***. Tel. 320000.

Hotel Roca Bella, Playa Es Pujols, *. Tel. 320185.

There are other hotels, apartments and hostels scattered around the coast near to or on beaches. The largest grouping of such places is around Cala Pujols, Es Caló and along Mitjorn beach.

FOOD DIGEST

As everywhere, restaurants in the Balearics come in all shapes, sizes, and standards, some with owner-chefs offering fresh and imaginative food, some a standard menu with a high content of frozen ingredients, some cheap, some expensive, some with good ambiance and poor food, some with both and some with neither.

In general, however, restaurants which stay open all year usually score better on service and food than seasonal and beach restaurants, which perforce offer less at a higher cost; they have to live for 12 months on 6-7 months' income.

Basically, the answer to the question "what to eat?" is "everything". If it is served by professionals, whether it is local, Oriental or French, it should be good. Wherever you are staying, there'll be a choice of restaurants nearby, and the distances to other towns are not great.

Although there is no menu visible at local bars, you can generally ask what they have to eat (they have to eat themselves) and you could be pleasantly surprised with a thick homemade stew or a fresh salad with grilled seafood.

There are all sorts of typical foods on the islands, from paella and *arroz brut*, through suckling pig and tender lamb, to *caldereta de langosta* and *tumbet*, or elvers in garlic-oil, or *calamares en su tinta* (squid in inky sauce—it sounds better in Spanish, and tastes great).

Four categories of price-level have been used:
C for cheap or low prices
R for reasonable prices
M for middle of the range prices
H for higher prices

BREAKFAST

Club de Mar Bar (C), Paseo Marítimo, Palma.
Where the yachties gather.

Colmar Bar (R), Paseo Marítimo 27, Palma.
Next to Palas Atenea Hotel, on the harbour.

Bar Bosch (C), Plaza Pio XII, Palma.
Opposite C & A department store.

Bar La Oficina, Paseo Mallorca 26, Palma.

In **Ibiza**, Eivissa and Sant Antoni, any bar along the harbour will serve breakfast, and in Santa Eulàlia, any bar around the downtown main crossroads.

For breakfast in **Menorca**, try bars on the Esplanada and other squares in Mahón, and in Ciutadella in the main Town Hall square.

SPANISH/SEAFOOD

Porto Pi (H), Joan Miró 174, Palma. Tel. 400087.
Near Club de Mar and Rififi seafood restaurant. Serves gourmet Basque and nouvelle cuisine.

Mesón Tio Pepe (M), Pont d'Inca, Palma. Tel. 680880.
Bodega atmosphere, enormous T-bones, selected suckling pig and a mixed-grill so big you'll have a problem finishing it. Avoid Sunday lunchtime.

Diplomatic (M), Palau Reial 5, Palma. Tel. 726482.
Dressy; busy lunchtime weekdays.

Es Parlament (M), Conquistador 11, Palma. Tel. 726062.
Dressy; busy lunchtime weekdays. Claims to make the best paella in town.

Honoris (H), Camino Viejo de Buñola, Palma. Tel. 203212.
Stylish ambiance, good cuisine. On the edge of town.

Alborada (M), Rosa 5, Palma. Tel. 725799.
Galician seafood and meats.

Bodega Bilbaina (R), Bonaire 19, Palma. Tel. 713510.
Basque cuisine.

Bodega Santurce (R), Concepción 34, Palma.
Basque food in this family-run hole in the wall. No reservations, no coffee, open only lunchtime, uncomfortable seating, but unbeatable value.

Loreley (M), Paseo Mallorca 32, Palma. Tel. 711542.
Basque cuisine. Good *salpicón* and *bacalau*.

La Noria del Paleto (M), Luis Fabregas 9, Palma. Tel. 281001. Murcian cooking; good beef, lamb.

Rincon de Asturias (R), Ramón Muntañer 36, Palma. Tel. 299062.
The cuisine of Cantabria, seafood and meats.

Reino de Leon (M), Ruben Dario 7, Palma. Tel. 723588.
The cooking of Castille, meats, sausages.

Cala Estancia (R), Punta Estancia 18-20, Ca'n Pastilla. Tel. 267035.
Near Palma, seafood.

Ca's Cotxer (M), Crtra. Arenal 31, Playa de Palma. Tel. 262049.
Mallorcan and seafood.

Punta de Son Gual (R), Crtra. Palma-Manacor Km 11. Tel. 490484.
Excellent shoulder or leg of lamb, other choices. Avoid Sunday lunchtimes.

Rancho Picadero (R), Flamenco 1, Ca'n Pastilla. Tel. 261002.

Indoor barbecue. Suckling pig, other choices.

Es Salé (C), Joan Miró, Palma. Near Plaza Gomila.
No reservations. Tony Moranta and family offer choice and variety at budget prices.

Bar Carlos (C), Joan Miró, Palma. Opposite Hotel Borenco.
Typical Mallorcan food by Rafa Bonet, smoky and crowded, evenings only, good value.

Cerveceria Dique (C), Paseo Marítimo 3, Palma. Tel. 452194.
Budget-priced meals, closed Sundays.

Restaurante Vistamar (H), Crtra. Valldemossa-Andratx Km 2. Tel. 612300.
A pleasant country restaurant in a converted farm.

El Pesebre (C), Joan Miró 38, Palma. Near Plaza Gomila.
Budget-priced lunch. Noisy if soccer game on TV.

Celler Montenegro (C), Calle Montenegro, Palma. Behind Plaza de la Reina, downtown Palma.
Good Mallorcan home cooking.

Zarzagan (H), Paseo Marítimo 13, Palma. Tel. 237447.

Caballito de Mar (M), Paseo Sagrera 5, Palma. Tel. 721074.
Fish cooked in sea-salt, expensive and takes time to cook, but must be tried once, with al-i-oli.

Casa Eduardo (M), Muelle Viejo, Palma. Tel. 721182.
Family-run, overlooks fish quay.

Rififi (H), Joan Miró 182, Palma. Tel. 402035.
Excellent seafood. Near Club de Mar.

Restaurant Miramar (M), Port of Andraitx. Tel. 671617.

Casa Gallega (M), Pueyo 2, Palma. Tel. 714366.

Try the *salpicón*, *pulpo a banda* or fresh salmon.

El Pilon (M), Cifre 1, Palma. Tel. 726034.
Central. Grilled snacks, tapas.

Club Nautico Cala Gamba (M), Paseo Cala Gamba, near C'an Pastilla. Tel. 261045.

Vecchio Giovanni (M), San Juan 3, Palma. Tel. 722879.
Excellent Spanish and Italian dishes.

IBIZA

Sausalito, Plaza Sa Riba, Eivissa.
Swordfish, lamb. French owner.

El Brasero, Barcelona 4, Eivissa.
Duck, salmon. German owned.

El Shogun, Pasadis 5, Eivissa.
Sushi, Sashimi, Sukiyaki.

Pike's, C'an Pep Toniet, Sant Antoni.
Salmon-stuffed hake, more.

Sa Capella. Ctra a C'an Germá, Sant Antoni.
Pork of all kinds.

Es Pi D'or, Cala Gració, Sant Antoni.
Salmon, fish soup, more.

Helmut's, Ctra a San José.
German home-cooking.

Celler C'an Pere, San Jaime, 63, Santa Eulàlia.
Seafood, pork, lamb.

Rincon de Pepe, San Vicente 53, Santa Eulàlia.
Tapas, snacks.

Mr Pickwick's, San Vicente 47, Santa Eulàlia.
Steak and kidney pie, more.

Daffer's, San Vicente, Santa Eulàlia.
International menu.

C'an Domingo de C'an Botja, San José.
Seafood in rich sauces.

Sa Soca, Ctra a Sant Antoni.
Ibicenco cooking.

KU, San Rafael.
The Basque restaurant at the top disco.

Lur Berri, San Rafael.
Hake, clam sauce, pastries.

MENORCA

Cap Roig (R), Near San Mezquida. No phone.
Great view, seafood.

Casa del Mar, (R), Anden de Poniente 112, Mahón. Tel. 350742.
Seafood.

La Tropical (C), Luna 36, Mahón. Tel. 360556.
Budget-priced Menorcan food.

Pilar (R), Cardona y Orfila 61, Mahón. Tel. 366817.
Local Menorcan cuisine, evenings only.

Rocamar (R), Cala Fonduco 32, Mahón. Tel. 365601.
Seafood, in the port.

Casa Manolo (R), Marina 117, in the port of Ciutadella. Tel. 381728.
Seafood.

Cas Quintu (R), Plaza Alfonso III 4, Ciutadella. Tel. 381002.
Menorcan and other dishes.

Ca'n Miquel (R), Rosario 77, Fornells. Tel. 375123.
In the port. Serves seafood.

Pan Y Vino (R), Torret.
Small, atmospheric restaurant popular with the resident population of expatriates.

FORMENTERA

Bergantin (M), Port de la Sabina. Tel. 321040.
International menu.

Capri (M), Es Pujols. Tel. 321118.
Seafood.

Es Muli de Sal (M), Illetas.
Regional food.

Sa Sequi (M), Ses Salines.
Seafood.

San Fernando (M), San Fernando. Tel. 320835.
Seafood.

Truy (M), Es Pujol.
International menu.

Taberna La Formentereña, Playa Mitjorn Km 9.
Dutch hostess Yvonne and crew offer their beach restaurant. Excellent *Espinacas Balear*, seafood, meats with irresistible sauces.

ITALIAN

MALLORCA

Don Peppone (R), Bayarte 14, Palma. Tel. 454242.
Home-made pasta.

Eboli (R), Joan Miró 17, Palma. Tel. 285938.
Owners Carlos and Coloma specialise in flambe dishes and steak tartar.

La Trattoria (R), Joan Miró 309, San Agustin, and Teniente Mulet 10, Palma. Tel. 237986.
Popular with locals. Take-away.

Mario's (R), Bellver 40, Palma. Tel. 281814.
Smiling Lili, owner-chef Mario and son offer Italian, but also spare-ribs, seafood, steaks.

Cittadini (R), Pintor 2, Cala Mayor, Palma. Tel. 403922.

La Fontana (M), Industria 6, Palma. Tel. 451666.
Near downtown shopping.

MENORCA

Pizzeria Siena (R), At Cala Torret.

Il Porto (R), In Mahón Harbour. Tel. 368222.

IBIZA

Nou Pinocho (R), Next to Calle Macabich, Ibiza town. Tel. 304665.

Pinocho (R), D'enmig 18, Santa Eulàlia. Tel. 310176.

Pinocho (R), Plaza España 1, Sant Antoni. Tel. 340327.

ENGLISH

MALLORCA

La Vileta (R), Camino Vecinal La Vileta 215, Palma. Tel. 281021.
Friendly pub atmosphere, traditional English Sunday lunches.

The English Rose (R), Puigpunyent, a 15 minutes' drive from Palma. Tel. 614180.
Pub and restaurant, mainly British clients.

Olivers (R), Corner Damete and Cotoner, Palma. Tel. 451042.
Owner-chef Ian and wife Karen offer English cooking from a varied menu.

Bertorelli's (H), Sa Porrassa, Crtra. Cala Figuera.
Select Anglo-French menu.

Es Comellá (M), Crtra. de Son Font, Calviá. Tel. 670180.
Friendly English pub atmosphere, with owner David mixing the drinks at the cosy bar.

Villa Montserrat (R), Joan Miró, San Agustin.
Varied menu, nice ambiance, eat outside in summer.

Hawaii Bar (C), Paseo Marítimo 27, Palma. Tel. 454569.
Typical English snacks, fish and chips Fridays.

MENORCA

Bar La Paloma (R), Ruiz y Pablo 17, Villacarlos. Tel. 368609.

Bar Delfin (R), Carrer Gran 22, Villacarlos. Tel. 369182.
HQ of local cricket team.

El Sereno, Farmhouse Carvery (R), San Clemente road, near airport.

The Copper Kettle (R), Plaza del Carmen 5, Mahón.

Sa Parereta (R), Near San Luis. Tel. 369025.

El Picadero (R), Crtra. Mahón a San Luis. Tel. 363268.

IBIZA

Pike's (H), Sant Antoni, Ca'n Pep Toniet.

Restaurante Miramar (R), San Juan 27, Santa Eulàlia. Tel. 331272.

Grumpy's Bistro (R), San Juan 3, Santa Eulàlia. Tel. 332175.
HQ of local cricket team.

FRENCH/INTERNATIONAL

MALLORCA

Ancora (M), Ca'n Barbará, Paseo Marítimo, Palma. Tel. 401161.
Nouvelle cuisine.

Bahia Mediterraneo (H), Paseo Marítimo 33, Palma. Tel. 457653.
Elegant ambiance. Seafood on menu.

Carrascal (M), Femenías 18, Palma. Tel. 450344.

Don Procopio (H), Femenías 18, Palma. Tel. 454261.
Rather formal.

Mediterraneo 1930 (H), Paseo Marítimo 33, Palma. Tel. 458877.
Elegant Thirties atmosphere. Some traffic noise.

Penelope (H), Plaza Progreso 19, Palma. Tel. 230269.

Cosy family-run restaurant.

La Casita (R), Joan Miró 68, Palma. Tel. 237557.
Specials every day. Small, one genial waiter.

Le Bistrot (M), Teodoro Llorente 6, Palma. Tel. 287175.
French menu. Busy lunchtime, near shopping.

Tirolia (R), Teniete Mulet 46, Palma. Tel. 280238.
Dutch host Peter will recommend his pizzas and steaks with rich sauces. Well-run, cosy.

Los Gauchos (R), San Magin 78, Palma. Tel. 280023.
Near Catalina produce market. Also some Mexican, Argentine dishes.

Blas (R), Salud 12, Palma. Tel. 458448.
Attractive menu. Reputation for duck creations.

Las Olas Steakhouse (R), Plaza Gomila, Palma.
Prime steaks, house sauces. Friendly owner-waiters.

ASIAN

MALLORCA

Shangri-La (M), Paseo Marítimo, Palma. Tel. 452575.
Chinese.

Gran Dragon (M), Two locations:
Ruiz de Alda 5, Palma. Tel. 280200.
Calanova, Palma Nova.
Chinese.

Mandarin (R), Joan Miró 17, Palma. Tel. 238138.
Chinese.

Tai-Pan (R), Plaza Mediterraneo, Plaza Gomila. Tel. 230053.
Chinese.

Maxim's (R), Apuntadores, Palma.
Chinese.

Panda (R), Teniente Mulet 32, Palma. Near Plaza Gomila.
Chinese.

China Express (R), At Gomila Park, Palma.
Chinese.

Canton (R), Joan Miró 243, Cala Mayo.
Near Marivent Palace.
Chinese.

Hong Kong (R), Plaza Gomila, Palma. Late eating.
Chinese.

Sheesh Mahal (H), Boulevard Blau, Paseo Maritimo 27, Palma. Tel. 236423.
Indian.

Rajmas Tandoori (M), Joan Miró 309, San Agustin. Tel. 405766.
Indian.

Shogun (H), Camilo José Cela 14, Palma. Tel. 235748.
Japanese.

The Crazy Dolphin (R), At the Roundabout, Portals Nous near Marineland.
Indonesian.

La Baraka (M), On the beach at Palma Nova. Tel. 680052.
Arabic.

Bon Lloc (R), Moral 7a, Palma.
Vegetarian.

Raixa (R), Zavellá 8, Palma. Tel. 711711.
Vegetarian.

AFTERNOON TEA

MALLORCA

J Dalmau, Paseo Mallorca 38, Palma.

Ca'n Frasquet, Orfila 4, Palma.

Forn del Santo Cristo, Pelaires 2, Palma.

MENORCA

The Mad Hatter, Mahón Harbour, near the Aquarium.

The Tea Pot, Stuart 4, Villacarlos.

IBIZA

Any of the harbour-front bars and ice-cream shops in Eivissa (Ibiza town), San Antonio, Santa Eulàlia and other beach resorts.

BEACH EATING

On all four Balearic islands, the advent of summer means the re-opening of the many and varied beach restaurants and bars, commonly called *chiringuitos*. These are located on any and most beaches where access is relatively easy (their supplies need to be delivered) and where people congregate.

Even some very small and remote coves have a *chiringuito*, dishing-up grilled sardines, squid, and other delicacies. Of course, most also serve chicken and chips, and hamburgers, children's favourite holiday food. Usually, a *chiringuito* operator, having obtained a permit from the local municipality to run the catering on the beach, will also probably have the concession for *tumbonas*, beach beds, and possibly pedal-boats as well.

DRINKING NOTES

A dedicated drinker will enjoy the islands, not only for the colossal number of bars, but for their variety. There are cocktail bars, piano bars, disco bars, bar-cafeterias, bar-restaurants, cabaret bars, casino bars, beach bars, *bodegas*, gay bars, roof-top bars, youth bars and even bars in the hospitals.

Drinking here is civilised. The waiter or barman will run a tab, not asking for payment with each drink. Exceptions are some beach bars, or bars where there is so much activity that control is difficult.

Lunchtime drinking, particularly in a *bodega* (cellar) can be very enjoyable, sipping a sherry or other aperitif before eating. During the meal remember that Balearic-grown wines are available in great variety, from a strong Binissalem red, great with strong, highly-spiced island food, to a sparkling white or rosé (*vino de aguja*) to accom-

pany a lighter meal. Mainland Spanish wines are also available.

Favourite liqueurs are the islands' anis-based *hierbas* or, from the mainland, an interesting combination of anis and juniper berries called Patcharán. Most visitor-oriented bars serve sangria, a cold punch containing red wine, liqueurs, clear lemonade, spices, slices or chunks of mixed fruit, and sugar to taste. A sangria recipe is like the perfect martini or the perfect paella; everyone you meet says they make the best.

Be sure of what you are drinking, however, as not all bottled liquors are what they seem to be from the bottle's label. See comments about this in the *Health* section, and also remember to avoid drinking too much hard liquor while exposed to the sun. For a list of various types of bar, turn to the section on *Nightlife*.

THINGS TO DO

CITY

The major cities in the islands are many hundreds of years old, with traces of their prehistoric and more recent past readily visible. A visit to Mallorca would be incomplete without a tour of the Almudaina Palace and a visit to Bellver Castle in Palma, or to the Roman ruins in Pollença.

In Palma, a worthwhile experience is to ride past the moored yachts on the Paseo Marítimo in a horse-drawn *galera*.

In Eivissa (Ibiza) climb up the hill to the D'alt Vila, the heart of the ancient city, to the Cathedral, City Hall and some of the great mansions of the old rich burgher families. Later, relax in Vara de Rey or on the harbour front, in one of the cafés, enjoying the excellent ice-cream and pastries, and the passing parade.

In Mahón, stroll through the town, viewing the unique architecture, heavily influenced by the British. Visit the covered city market, a former convent. In both Mahón and Ciutadella, walk along the deep fjord-like harbours, with their fishing boats, yachts and selection of restaurants.

COUNTRY

In Mallorca, well-planned bus tours of various points on the island are available, as an alternative to driving yourself. Among the sights and places to visit are the towns of Valldemosa, Banyalbufar, Deià, Sóller (by train) Pollença, Porto Cristo and the Caves of Drach, and the long sandy beach in the Bay of Alcudia.

Take one day to visit the Port of Andratx, and enjoy a seafood lunch or dinner in one of the harbourside restaurants. Or rise very early one morning and go to one of the farming towns on market day, Sineu on Wednesdays for example.

From Ibiza, take a day-tour of the adjoining island of Formentera, or one of the many beaches around the island, for example Cala Boix or Cala Pada near Santa Eulàlia. Nearby, on Wednesdays, is the Hippie Market at Punta Arabi. Another interesting activity in Ibiza is to visit various of the whitewashed churches such as that at San José, Sant Jordi, etc.

In Menorca, Neolithic ruins are everywhere, and the top of Monte Toro affords a magnificient view of the island's countryside. Menorca also has many attractive coves and beaches.

On all four Balearic islands there are well organised tours of the principal interesting sights and features, with a knowledgeable guide to point out sights and indicate where to go afoot on arrival. These travel packages, usually by bus, are bookable at most travel agencies, with the concierge in hotels, or with any tour representative. Whenever possible, the buses stop at the best viewing points.

The Govern Balear issues a leaflet detailing the various tours available, and this can be picked up at the Tourist Offices and at many hotel front desks.

CULTURE PLUS

MUSEUMS

MALLORCA

Principal locations are:
The Archives of the Kingdom, Ramón Llull, 3, Palma.
Arab Bath-house, Serra, 3, Palma.
Bellver Castle, Municipal History Museum.
La Lonja, Paseo Sagrera, Palma. Exhibits change frequently.
Cathedral Museum, Palau Reial, 29, Palma.
Mallorca Church Museum, Mirador, 7, Palma.
Mallorca Museum, Portella, 5, Palma.
Almudaina Palace, Palau Reial, Palma.
Palau Solleric, San Cayetano, 10, Palma.
Pueblo Español, Capitán Mesquida Veny, 39, Palma.
In addition, outlying towns on the island have museums and exhibitions on various subjects, such as Algaida's Glass-blowing Factory and Museum, Alcudia's Municipal Archaeological Museum, Artá's Prehistoric village and Regional Museum, Binissalem's Wax Museum at the Faro de Mallorca, Deià's Archaeological Museum, created by Dr William Waldren. The Son Marroig Collection at Deià displays the Archduke Ferdinand's collection of art and objets d'art; the Lluc Monastery Collection is at Escorca; the Junipero Serra Museum at Petra, and the Charterhouse in Valldemossa was made famous by Chopin and George Sand. A complete list of these and other museums is published by the Govern Balear.

IBIZA

Principal locations are the Archaeological Museum, situated in the highest part of D'alt Vila in Eivissa (Ibiza town), with displays relating to the Punic remains excavated on the island; the monument of the Chapel and Catacombs of Santa Inés, located at Sant Antoni; Carthaginian Temple, dedicated to the Goddess Tanit, in San Juan. Many of the churches on the island are in themselves museums, and worth a visit.

MENORCA

In the Ateneo de Mahón there is a museum which has a collection of 17th- and 18th-century ceramics, and an exhibit of over 100,000 varieties of undersea plants. The museum is at Conde de Cifuentes, 25, Mahón. Also in Mahón the Archaeological Museum is located in the rebuilt Cloisters of the church of San Francisco. As in the other islands, the various churches are worth a visit, for a better appreciation of the island's history.

FORMENTERA

At the eastern end of the island's big lagoon, Estany Pudent, is the Megalithic Monument at Ca Na Costa, dating back to 2000 BC; at Ses Clotadas, near Es Caló, is the Roman camp of Ca'n Blai. There are defense look-out towers in five locations, and the churches at San Fernando, San Francisco Javier, and the chapel of Sa Tanca Vella are worth seeing.

ART GALLERIES

In Palma, Mallorca:
Agora, Pedro Dezcallar y Net 4. Tel. 712530.
Altair, San Jaime 15a. Tel. 711004.
Art Fama, Centro Comercial Los Geranios. Tel. 721307.
L'auba, Baron de Pinopar 4.
Bearn, Concepción 6. Tel. 722837.
Byblos, Av. Argentina 16. Tel. 238082.
Danus, Danus 3.
Ferran Cano, Paz 3.
Jaime III, Av. Jaime III.
Joan Oliver Maneu, San Martin 1. Tel. 721342.
Lluc Fluxa, Ribera 4. Tel. 719090.

Nou Art, Concepción 5. Tel. 717261.
4 Gats, San Sebastian 2-3. Tel. 726493.

In Pollença, Mallorca:
Actual Art, Philip Newman 5, Pollença. Tel. 533313.
Bennassar, Plaza Mayor 6, Pollença.
Norai, Pollença. Tel. 531679.
Mestre Paco, C'an Berenguer, Crtra. Pollença-Port.

In Sineu, Mallorca;
S'Estació—Centro de Arte de Sineu.

In Menorca;
The Picture House, Crtra. Mahón-Ciutadella Km 2.
Sa Tanca, San Luis.
S'Alambic, in Mahón port.
Mono Boutique, in Mahón port.
Blanc i Verd, Romal 16, Alayor.
Penya de S'indio, Mercadal. Tel. 375277.
Antigona, 9 de Julio 5, Ciutadella. Tel. 384063.

In Ibiza;
Es Molí, Santa Gertrudis. (In this town there are several galleries, some seasonal.)
S'Hort, in San Miguel.
Galeria Sargantana, in San José.
Galeria Bérri, San Agustin.

In Eivissa, Ibiza;
Sa Nostra Gallery, Aragón 11.
Skyros, José Verdera 8.
Carl Vander Voort, Plaza de D'alt Vila.
Alternativa, Crtra. Ibiza-San José Km 5.6.

CONCERTS

MALLORCA

A varied programme of concerts results from initiatives taken by government, business and private bodies. The choice includes all forms and types of music, with the majority of the activity being in the winter, when there are visiting soloists, jazz festivals, chamber and pop groups, etc. The Pollença Summer festival is a major international musical event.

The major summer concert is the once-yearly staging in the natural amphitheatre of the Torrent de Pareis of a performance by the Capella Mallorquina. A magnificient setting in which to enjoy a leading mixed choir. The Torrent concert is usually held on the third Sunday in July.

Concerts of various types are held in the Teatro Principal, the Auditorium's main hall or the smaller Sala Mozart, and other venues. Open-air concerts are also held in various town and village plazas, football grounds and bullrings. Announcements of upcoming concerts are printed in local papers, including the *Majorca Daily Bulletin.*

IBIZA

Ibiza receives visits from travelling groups and orchestras, but is more famous for holding spectacular pop concerts in various parts of the island, notably in the world-famous KU discotheque.

MENORCA

Has its own programme of concerts, sponsored and commercial, announced in press and on posters.

BALLETS

Various Spanish and international ballets visit the islands, principally Mallorca, where the usual venue is the Auditorium on the harbour-front in Palma.

OPERA

Opera companies visit the islands, mainly Mallorca. Spanish light-opera—*zarzuela*—companies frequently appear at Palma's Teatro Principal.

THEATRES

Spanish plays (mainly comedies) are staged frequently at Palma's Teatro Principal or at the Auditorium, and some of these also visit Menorca and Ibiza. In winter, foreign residents, mainly British, produce plays for their own community. Among the most active are the two theatre groups in Santa Eulàlia, Ibiza.

CINEMA

Despite the growing popularity of home movies on video, there are still queues at the many cinema theatres to see first-run movies, and there are regular festivals, celebrating the art of actors or directors, such as Chaplin, Huston, etc. The programmes change often, and are listed in the press.

ARCHITECTURE

Island architecture is noted for its use of the local pinkish limestone, and in the country, in Ibiza, Formentera and Menorca, for the annual whitewashing of houses, and, in Ibiza for the crenellation of walls.

The Arab influence is evident in the use of interior patios and gardens, with a central feature being a well or fountain. The islands have many palaces, churches, castles, monasteries and other architectural wonders for the enjoyment of visitors. Principal among these are Palma's Bellver Castle, Cathedral and Almudaina Palace; Ibiza's D'alt Vila, churches and white exteriors; Menorca's port of Mahón, with its memories of English architecture, the Cathedral at Ciutadella and the Town hall in Villacarlos. Not to mention the prehistoric navetas, taulas and burial grounds, and the windmills on all the islands, used to pump up water.

Finally, there are nature's own sculptures in the face of the landscape, with caves, rocks, peaks and contours which surpass in beauty many of man's creations.

NIGHTLIFE

PUBS & BARS

MALLORCA

Don Gomilo, Plaza Mediterraneo, Palma. Filled with visitors in summer, Lance Callingham's bar is frequented in winter by local residents, mainly English-speaking.

Abaco, San Juan 1, Palma. Truly the most unusual bar to be seen in Palma, Abaco should be visited late at night. The door policy is "no Jeans".

Bar Maritimo, Paseo Marítimo 1, Palma. On the harbour front, large outdoor terrace with local folk dancers.

Cafeteria Loa, Joan Miró 130, Palma. In the Plaza Gomilá nightlife area, Loa offers food and drink from breakfast through the late hours, with the very reasonable prices being charged by partners Andy and Miguel.

Duksa, Paseo Mallorca 10, downtown Palma. Close to the main shopping area, with both indoor and terrace tables for watching the passing scene.

Mam's Bar, Joan Miró 39, Plaza Gomila area, across from Loa's. John and Liz, from Sheffield, England, offer great homemade hamburgers and other solid fare. Cosy fireplace for winter.

El Mecca, Av. Son Matias 22, Palma Nova. Well located near hotels and apartments, beach nearby.

Dickens' Pub, Paseo del Mar 23, Palma Nova. Very popular with British visitors, right on the beach, evening live entertainment.

Mano's Place, Complejo Magasol, Magalluf. Even though Magalluf gets bad press occasionally, Mano's is the place where one can enjoy a noisy night out with friends.

Admiral's Bar, Paseo Marítimo 35, Palma. Right on the harbour front. Elegant, a bit dressy, excellent cocktails and service.

Bar Bellver, Plaza Gomila 10, Palma. The principal bar on the busy plaza, Bernat and his professional staff have one of the top summer sidewalk bars.

Bar Bosch, Plaza Pio XII, Palma. Opposite C & A department store, across from the tortoise fountain in the Borne, this is the favourite downtown sidewalk café.

Bar Guell, Aragón 74, Palma. Noted for its public-spirited owner, Tolo Guell, who annually organises a walking marathon for all-comers, from his bar to the Monastery at Lluch.

La Oficina, Paseo Mallorca 26, Palma. A bar used mainly by local business-people, but Tony, the owner, welcomes visitors for coffee, aperitifs or snacks. Sidewalk tables, to rest after shopping.

La Pollila, Joan Miró 55. Near Plaza Gomila, popular with youth. Passers-by will note the loud music and strange-smelling smoke issuing from windows and door.

Las Verjas, tucked away in a corner of Plaza Mediterraneo, next to the Tai-Pan Chinese restaurant. In the Plaza Gomila area, with genuine Spanish gypsy guitars and singers. Drink the bottled beer and go accompanied, preferably by a local.

Totem, Joan Miró 47, Palma. Near Gomila, this is a topless bar. Prices of drinks increase in proportion to the degree of interest shown in the staff. Many other topless bars exist in the area, but are not listed due to lack of space.

Bar Niagara, Paseo Mallorca 46, Palma. Right downtown, popular with students and local professionals.

Bar Sorrento, at the split in the road in Illetas, just outside Palma. Opposite the elegant Bonanza Playa Hotel, the Sorrento is a pleasant place to relax over a drink.

Club de Mar Bar, Paseo Maritimo, Palma. Very busy with locally-based yacht people, and visiting boaties. Outside terrace, and reasonable prices.

Africa Bar, Teniente Mulet 17, Palma. Near Plaza Gomila, popular year-round with local English-speaking residents. The owner, Maureen McLaughlin, keeps things going with memory-lane music, raffles, stuffed animals all over the walls, and a swear-box to help keep it all clean.

Wellies, at the superb Puerto Portals marina, just outside Palma. Wellies is not cheap, the service is disorganised, yet the best location in the marina ensures it is always full of action. Many other bars and restaurants offer a great choice of where to go within the marina, but are not listed due to lack of space. The best move is to go there and walk around.

Box Office, Paseo Marítimo 33, Palma. Now an echo of its former glory, "El Box", as it is locally known, it still enjoys an excellent location right on the harbour-front, and the staff are nice.

Minim, right on Plaza Gomila. One of the most popular bars with young people; the clients overflow into the square and block traffic, but it is all good-natured fun. Next door is Tito's disco.

El Patio, Plaza Gomila. Formerly a famous restaurant, El Patio is now a yuppie haven, with upmarket decor, service, clients and prices.

Dylans, Joan Miró, opposite the Hotel Borenco. Music bar, mainly for youth. At the back, there's a great big patio and pool table.

Gillen's, Paseo Maritime 3A, Palma. Right on the harbour-front with big John serving man-size drinks and nostalgic food, kippers, bangers...

Zhivago, Teniente Mulet 18, Palma. Near Gomila's action, this live-orchestra bar attracts more mature visitors, who enjoy dancing while holding each other.

Trago Loco, across the street from Zhivago, is for stay-up-lates. Music and videos till sun-up.

Es Trui, next door to El Patio, is popular with a younger crowd who like their background music right in the foreground. Pleasant decor and a nice owner.

Bar Chotis, Calle de Nigul, Plaza Gomila, Palma. Tucked-away in an alley next to La Cocina, Chotis is for youth. Run by Bert and Maruja, and offering a choice of good draught beers, it helps if you like to play space invader machines.

Rustic Bar, across the road from the Don Gomilo, and run by the people from the next-door Hostal Terramar, appeals to local English youth, and has a downstairs pool-table.

Bar Taba, Joan Miró, next door to the Mandarin Chinese restaurant. Good for breakfast, all-day meals or a leisurely sit on their sea-facing terrace.

Waikiki, Plaza Mediterraneo, just past Don Gomilo and The Factory; owner Laval, from Mauritius, serves all-night exotic cocktails, and always seems to have the sexiest apprentice barmaids in town.

Bally Jay (in Spanish, Bali Hai!) next door to Waikiki, stays open late, if not all night, and usually has seductive blondes behind the bar.

As in all resort areas, bars often open trade for a season and are then replaced by other owners, a new name, changed decor, and so on. The above listing could be said to be a list of survivors.

MENORCA

Bar Club Nautico, at Binissafua.
Bar Restaurant Marie and Sybille, Binissafua beach.

Pedro's Bar, Cala Torret.
Joe's Palomino Bar, Binibeca.
Bar Pica Tapas, Cala Corp, Villacarlos.
La Paloma, Ruiz y Pablo 17, Villacarlos.
Chris' Delfin Bar, Carrer Gran 22, Villacarlos.
Georgetown Cocktail Bar, Calapadera 4A, Villacarlos.
Don's Bar and Restaurant, Horizonte, Villacarlos.
Es Plans, Alayor.
El Mirador, Arenal d'en Castell.
Bar Grill Alcalde, Arenal d'en Castell.
Pan y Vino, Torret.

IBIZA

In Eivissa, Ibiza, the preferred bars are those facing the harbour, or along the main square of Vara de Rey. They are all led by the first bar on the front, the **Montesol**. Pleasant bars with a nautical tone can also be found in the latest marina, Botafoch, near Talamanca beach.

In San Antonio:
San Francisco, near Calle Soledad.
Cafe del Mar, not far from the harbour jetty.
New Manhattan, on Calle Soledad.

In Santa Eulàlia:
Sandy's Bar, San Vicente 25. Tel. 330021. Probably the island's best-known bar. Try Tim's Bloody Mary.

Grumpy's Pub and Bistro, San Juan 3. Tel. 332175. HQ of the local cricket fraternity.

Pomelo, Camino de la Iglesia. Tel. 330474. Popular uptown meeting-place.

Bar Miramar, San Juan 27. Tel. 331272. Noisy pub and restaurant run by Eddie and Rosie from Britain.

Fred's Bar, in the main square, next to the Guardia Civil. Living off its former reputation, and the fact of its great location. Off-hand service.

PALMA, MALLORCA

The Ivy House, in the Plaza Gomila area, is run by host Paco. Very white, Greek-style decor, tasteful and well-furnished with comfortable seating. Long a meeting-place for international travellers, **La Yedra** is surrounded by other male-homosexuals' bars, listed below:

Gigolo, also nicely decorated and with a large rear patio. Offers late-night shows, professionally staged. Heteros at the door are turned away.

Querelle, across the street, has the same door-policy and also stages late-night shows, with host Marcos to welcome guests.

Status, just up the street past Plaza Gomila, is tucked away down the stairs next to the Pesebre Restaurant, and has Pepe and Bernardo as hosts.

Milord, also near The Ivy House and next door to the 69 Topless bar, is run by Dino.

Capri is a bar with sun-terrace, along the road toward the Apartsuit building. The only bar in this category to open in the mornings, this is where to go for coffee and croissant at breakfast-time, when host Basilio dispenses sympathy for previous-night tough tales, along with aspirin, if required.

All on its own, and also on Avenida Joan Miró, is the **Sombrero**, which welcomes friends from Lesbos.

EIVISSA, IBIZA

As in Palma, the gay bars in Ibiza town are pretty much neighbours, in the area around the foot of D'alt Vila. Principals are:
Anfora Disco, San Carlos 1, Ibiza.
Angelo's, Alfonso XII 11.
Napoleon, Santa Lucia 21.
Incognito, Santa Lucia.
Bronx, Bulevar, Ibiza.
Mouvi Bar, Mayor 34.
Why Not?, Plaza del Puerto.
Es Caballet Beach, out via the airport road

toward the Salinas salt-flats, is recognised as a gay beach.

DISCOS, NIGHTCLUBS AND CABARETS

MALLORCA

In the El Arenal and Ca'n Pastilla area:

Joy Palace	Zorba's	Yoga's
Oberbayern	Kirofano	Ibiza
Makiavelo	Veronica	Bavaria
Riu Palace	Sky Lab	Scorpio
Eden Park	Flash	Chaplin's
Music Laden	Bolero	Klimbin
Kiss Club	Kiss	

In the Cala Mayor area:

La Bamba	Sun Set	Pepe's Club
La Sirena	Liberty	

In the Port of Alcudia area:

Casablanca	Menta	Princesa
Blocks	Bells	Flipper

In Palma:

Besame Mucho	Jamaica	Nabila
Alexandra's	Indigo	Tivoli
Club de Mar	Victoria	Tito's
The Factory	Villa Rio	Luna
Clan Boite		

In the Palma Nova, Magalluf and Paguera area:

Alexandra's	Stadium	Saxo
Sir Lawrence	Banana	Sinatra's
Mr Moustache	Ali Baba	BCM
Graf Zeppelin	Barrabas	Pigmalion
Kings Club	Sky Club	Mississippi

IBIZA

In the area of San Antonio:

Play Boy 2	Manhattan	Nito's
Extasis	Es Paradis	

In Eivissa town area:

Montesol	Amnesia	Angel
Mar y Sol	Xaloc	Pacha
Torre del Mar	Lola	Glory
Casino Piano	•	

KU, the most famous disco, is in the San Rafael area. The open-air Las Dallas is in San Carlos.

MENORCA

Menorca Jazz Club, at El Casino, San Clemente. Tel. 360053.

Lui, two discos in one, between Mahón and Villacarlos.

Adagio, two discos in one, in Ciutadella.

Pacha, in San Luis.

Cueva d'en Xoroi, a disco in a cave, near Cala en Porter.

SHOPPING

GAMBLING

Both Mallorca and Ibiza have modern casinos. Mallorca's is located ten minutes from Palma, and apart from a gaming room, has a major dinner-show, sports centre, beach club and convention facilities, plus an excellent restaurant.

The casino on Ibiza is close to Eivissa and the yacht marina, and also has a restaurant and entertainment.

Menorca has no licensed casino.

Residents and tourists are required to show identification to get into casinos. In the case of non-residents, a passport is essential. Much underground gambling takes place in the islands, usually in privately-run clandestine card-games, but these are unlikely to be seen by visitors.

The Spanish are very avid gamblers, and slot-machine annual revenues here are highest in Europe. There are several lotteries available to the public, including the visitor. Among these is the daily pool run by the blind peoples' benevolent society, ONCE, a weekly national lottery, a weekly "primitive" (6/49 type) lottery, a football and horse-racing pool, and regional lotteries such as Catalunya's two weekly lotteries.

Tax-free prizes of 300 to 400 million pesetas are not unknown, and the national lottery holds one giant lottery yearly, at Christmas, named "El Niño" after the baby Jesus, and annually runs another, known as "El Gordo", the Fat One, in which huge total amounts are won.

WHAT TO BUY

The islands all produce good leatherware, with footwear factories in Mallorca and Menorca, and nicely-designed leather clothing available everywhere.

Mallorca has artificial pearl and glass-blowing factories.

Menorca has a well-developed costume jewellery industry, and produces excellent cheeses and gin.

Ibiza is known for its Ad Lib fashion, an attractive mix-and-match approach to creating an ensemble, and has a large cottage-industry making bangles, jewellery, etc. The three main islands have branches or franchises known internationally, of the standing of Benetton, Bally, Loews, Charles Jourdan, etc.

Locally produced pottery and ceramics, particularly cooking-vessels, are a good buy on all islands, and there is a choice of good embroidery and basketwork.

Reasonably-priced paintings by local artists are also worth looking at, and these can be seen in galleries, or at lower prices in the flea and hippie markets.

SHOPPING AREAS

Palma has the larger choice of areas, with its Avenida Jaime III, Paseo Mallorca, Paseo Maritimo, Sindicatos, Plaza Mayor, Via Roma and the Saturday flea-market. There are multiple stores, such as C & A and Galerias Preciados, and large super- and hyper-markets, both in and out of town. In the city, there are covered markets for product, meat and seafood, all well worth a visit, although parking nearby can be difficult.

A list of suppliers for specialty shopping, such as antiques, embroidery, jewellery, etc, is issued by the local government and distributed through tourist information offices and hotels. In the high season, most resorts have a good choice of shops open, often till late at night. Menorca has good shopping in Mahón, with most of the same variety of outlets as in Palma. Good buys in artisanwork can be found all over Ibiza. This is particularly the case at the Wednesday Hippy Market at Punta Arabi, near Santa Eulàlia. The weekly market-days in the three main islands are:

MALLORCA

Alaró	Fri/PM
Alcudia	Tue, Sun/AM
Algaida	Fri/AM
Andratx	Wed/AM
El Arenal	Thu/AM
Ariany	Thu/AM
Artá	Tue/AM
Binissalem	Fri/AM
Búger	Sat/AM
Bunyola	Sat/AM
Cala Ratjada	Sat/AM
Calviá	Mon/AM
Campanet	Sat/AM
Campos	Thu/AM
Ca'n Picafort	Tue/PM
Capdepera	Wed/AM
Colonia de Sant Jordi	Wed/AM
Costitx	Sat/AM
Felanitx	Sun/AM
Inca	Thu/AM
Lloret	Mon/AM
Lloseta	Sat/AM
Llubí	Tue/AM
Lluchmayor	Wed, Sun/AM
Manacor	Mon/AM
Maria de la Salud	Fri/AM
Montuiri	Mon/AM
Muro	Sun/AM
Palma	Sat/AM
Sa Pobla	Sun/AM
Puerto de Pollença	Wed/AM
Town of Pollença	Sun/AM

Pont d'Inca	Fri/AM
Porreres	Tue/AM
San Lorenzo	Thu/AM
Santa Eugenia	Fri/AM
Santa Margarita	Tue, Sat/AM
Santa Maria	Sun/AM
Santanyi	Sat/AM
Selva	Wed/AM
Sencellas	Wed/AM
Ses Salines	Thu/AM
Sineu	Wed/AM
Sóller	Sat/AM
Son Servera	Fri/AM

MENORCA

Mahón	Tue, Sat/AM
Ciutadella	Fri, Sat/AM
San Luis	Mon, Wed/AM
Villacarlos	Mon, Wed/AM

IBIZA

Eivissa (summer) at Bahamas Complex	Sat/PM
San Antonio (summer) (Sa Tanca)	Fri/all day
San Miguel	Thu/PM
Santa Eulàlia (Punta Arabi)	Wed/all day

SHOPPING HOURS

Most shops are open on weekdays from 09.30-13.30 and from 16.30-20.00, and usually open mornings only on Saturdays, although a number do stay open all day Saturday.

The multiple stores and hypermarkets do not close at lunchtime, and usually open from 10.00 to 21.00 Monday through Saturday.

EXPORT

Certain shops will undertake to export your purchases on your behalf. For example, the famous Lladró line of china sculptures are usually sold in large boxes, better shipped than carried, and Lladró shops normally take care of this task. Otherwise, export of purchases can be arranged through one of the shipping and customs agents, usually staffed with English-speakers.

SPORTS

COMPLAINTS

Complaints about bad service at many businesses should first be directed to the manager. If this is unsuccessful, go to the local town hall, which issues most business licences. The bigger the town hall, the more the likelihood of finding an English-speaker. In Mallorca, there is an office of the Director General for Consumer Affairs, at La Rambla 18 on the 4th floor, telephone 712729, and an Association for the Defense of Consumers, at Montenegro 8. Both these offices are in Palma.

PARTICIPANT

All three main islands have golf, tennis, scuba, horseriding, soccer, squash, windsurfing and other popular sports available for visitor participation. Formentera, with its location and beaches, tends to specialise in windsurfing and watersports, including underwater.

Hang-gliding, go-karting and other activities, including several fun waterparks are also available. In the islands there are 38 tennis clubs, over 10 golf courses, uncounted soccer and sports grounds, and a large number of other organised sports.

The following list details the name and telephone number of the various sporting and recreational federations in the Balearics:

Scuba	463315
Flying	725313
Chess	465966
Hang-gliding	466821
Athletics	275745
Car racing	205555
Basketball	463309
Cricket (Mallorca)	237053
Bowling	246716
Petanque	246716
Boxing	752061
Bridge	231268
Mountaineering	463315
Motorcycling	312612
Roller skating	271213
Hai Lai	710801
Rugby	717757
Tennis	714934
Slingshot	200314
Sailing	402412
Greyhounds	290012
Hunting	725313
Cycling	208362

Pigeon breeding	752467
Darts	457577
Waterski	675856
Soccer	711171
Five-a-side	467760
Gymnastics	570040
Golf	722753
Horseback	404073
Wrestling	753909
Motorboating	206114
Swimming	287647
Canoeing	463318
Squash	454500
Tabletennis	460267
Horse trotting	464577
Volleyball	463318
Sailing school	402512
Cricket (Ibiza)	330321
Cricket (Menorca)	367145

SPECTATOR

During the winter soccer season there are games all over the islands on Sundays, with even the smaller villages having teams. Tennis tournaments, horse-racing, car and motorcycle races, sailing regattas, handball, basketball, billiards and other competitions all have either paid or gratis entry for spectators. Bull-fighting does not have a popular following on the islands.

SPECIAL INFORMATION

DOING BUSINESS

With its own distinctive laws and regulations, Spain has a business environment where expert assistance is needed to start a business or to buy a property.

A good first step is to call on the Spanish consulate, or, if there is one, the Chamber of Commerce, to explain your intentions. They will usually provide advice and guidance.

Secondly, obtain copies of magazines such as *Balearic Homes and Living, New Projects* or *Lookout*, aimed at English-speaking people living or intending to live in Spain. These magazines' addresses are listed in the section on *Further Reading*.

During a first exploratory visit, it is well to have a temporary base, using the offices of a recommended lawyer or one of the business service organisations (see *Communications* section) and an introduction to the manager of one of the English-speaking banks in order to get an overall local briefing on conditions. Eventually, to start the process of obtaining permits and business licences, you would be advised to use the services of a *gestoria*, who specialises in preparing and delivering official documents, and overcoming bureaucratic hurdles.

For property purchases in the islands, use only the services of a real-estate agent with an API accreditation (College of Real Estate Agents). Many have English-speaking staff to advise you of the legal requirements, such as those affecting the transfer of funds to Spain, etc.

CHILDREN

The Spanish love children, and take very good care of their own. With the increasing number of working mothers, many children are left for the day at a *guarderia*, where they are cared for by trained staff.

Children's schooling for English-speaking families exists in Mallorca at one of the English or American curriculum schools in Palma. There are also Swedish, German and French schools. In Ibiza, there are also at least two English-language schools.

Winter brings seasonal visits by circuses and fairs, and the discotheques run special afternoon sessions for the young during winter, generally on Saturdays and Sundays.

GAYS

The islands of Mallorca and Ibiza have over the years proved to have an agreeable environment for male and female homosexuals, who have found the freedom to live their lives unmolested.

On the two islands, there are businesses run by gays, ranging from hostals, restaurants, through bars and discos and nightclubs. In Ibiza, there is a grouping of such businesses, with most being in the town of Eivissa (Ibiza). In Palma, the centre of nightlife action around the Plaza Gomila is also the centre of gay bars and discos. A list of gay bars and clubs is shown in the *Nightlife* section.

DISABLED

Spain has not traditionally been concerned with providing ease-of-movement facilities for the disabled with mobility problems, although more recently the need for these is becoming increasingly obvious. As a result, hoteliers, architects, airports and governments have now made these facilities a priority, and much is now being achieved.

Among the pressures to accelerate the provision of disabled facilities has been the sponsored holidays provided by some European governments for their disabled citizens. Another has been the need to comply with decisions made in this area by the EEC, which Spain joined in 1986, decisions which need to be implemented by 1992.

Spain has one of the better associations for blind persons, the Organizacion Nacional de Ciegos (ONCE), which supports its work with a popular daily national lottery.

Persons with mobility difficulty who intend visiting Spain need only advise their travel agent or airline, and will find that conditions and provisions in airports and hotels, at least, should be similar to those elsewhere.

The following addresses may be of use:
ASPROM—Association of the Disabled, Pascual Ribot 6a, Palma. Tel. 289052.
Diabetic Association, Aragón 34, 1st floor, Palma. Tel. 457110.
Alcoholics Anonymous, Tel. 405445, 402921, 237752 in Palma.

(In Ibiza Alcoholics Anonymous meet at 18.30 on Thursdays, at the Insalud Building, Santa Eulàlia).

STUDENTS

Students carrying a recognised student-card will generally be able to obtain discounts and reduced entrances to some events. It is not easy for a foreign student to land legal temporary or part-time work in Spain unless these have been pre-arranged, or are part of a summer course. Specialised voluntary work such as an archaeology student helping in a dig is permissible, but permission must be obtained before arrival. Several organisations exist for the arrangement of family exchange holidays, placing a Spanish student in a foreign family's home, with a reciprocal visit to a Spanish family.

PILGRIMAGES

There are no mass pilgrimages in the islands of the magnitude of Lourdes or Santiago de Compostela, but local shrines exist, and attract pilgrims, as well as non-religious tourists.

Particularly favoured is the Virgin of Lluc, in Mallorca, and in Menorca, the Sanctuary at Monte Toro, with many believers climbing the hill on foot.

FURTHER READING

Books on the Balearics can be found at principal in-town bookshops, such as the English Library in Mahón at C. Deià, 2; or the Libreria Fondevila, Arabí, 14, Palma; or at Island Books, Isidoro Macabich, Santa Eulàlia, Ibiza.

Throughout the islands, there are second hand book-exchanges and libraries specialising in English or other non-Spanish language books.

Further reading material in English:

First Eden, David Attenborough, Collins/BBC Books.

Mallorca Observed, Robert Graves and Paul Hogarth, Doubleday and Co., and Cassell.

Winter in Majorca, translated and with comments by Robert Graves, Valldemossa Editions, Mallorca.

Butterflies of the Province, Honor Tracy, Methuen.

The Spaniard and the Seven Deadly Sins, Fernando Diaz-Plajas, Gollancz and Pan Books.

A Stranger in Spain, HV Morton, Methuen.

You and the Law in Spain, David Searl, Lookout.

Here in Spain, David Mitchell, Lookout.

404 Spanish Wines, Frank Snell, Lookout.

Cooking in Spain, Janet Mendel Searl, Lookout.

Gardening in Spain, Marcelle Pitt, Lookout.

IN SPANISH

Boira, Gastao Heberle, Galeria Sargantana, San José, Ibiza. Short stories about Ibiza.

Diccionario de Secretos de Ibiza, Mariano Planells, Editorial Obelisco, Barcelona.

La Gran Guia de la Isla, Studio 30,

Abad y Lassierra 22, Ibiza. Also issued in English and German, one of the best guides to Ibiza.

MAGAZINES

Lookout, Puebla Lucia, Fuengirola, 29640 Malaga.

Balearic Homes and Living, Edificio Neptuno, Plaza Mediterraneo, 07015 Palma de Mallorca.

New Projects, Editora Inmobiliaria Balear, Julian Alvarez 12a-2, Palma de Mallorca.

Note: The books published by Lookout can be ordered from the magazine at the Fuengirola address above.

USEFUL ADDRESSES

TOURIST INFORMATION

MALLORCA

Consell de Mallorca, at airport Arrivals building.

Gobern Balear Tourist Office, Jaime III 10, Palma.

Fomento del Turismo de Mallorca, Constitución 1, 1st floor, Palma.

Palma Municipal Tourist Offices are at Santo Domingo 11, and Plaza España, in Palma.

Other municipalities, such as Calviá, have their own local offices. Some are seasonal, mounted on trailers, and located strategically.

MENORCA

Consell de Menorca, Cami del Castell 28, Mahón, and on the central Plaza Esplanada, 40, Mahón.

IBIZA

Consell de Ibiza, Vara de Rey 13, Eivissa (Ibiza town).

Fomento de Turismo de Ibiza, Historiador José Clapes 4, Ibiza town.

Municipality of San Antonio, Passeig des Fonts, San Antonio.

Municipality of Santa Eulàlia, Mariano Riquer Wallis, Santa Eulàlia.

FORMENTERA

Municipality of San Francisco Javier, Port of Savina. (At the ferry terminal).

The Spanish National Tourist Office has representation in the following cities: Brussels, Buenos Aires, Copenhagen, Chicago, Düsseldorf, Stockholm, Frankfurt, Geneva, Helsinki, Houston, The Hague, Lisbon, London, Los Angeles, Mexico, Milan, Munich, New York, Oslo, Paris, Rome, St Augustine, Sydney, Tokyo, Vienna and Zurich.

CONSULATES

PALMA

Austria, Plaza Olivar 7, Tel. 713949.
Belgium, Paseo del Borne 15, Tel. 724786.
Denmark, Union 2, Tel. 714097 and 727857.
USA, Jaime III 26, Tel. 722660.
Philippines, Marques de la Cenia 35.
Finland, L Fabregas 1, Tel. 452465.
France, Caro 1, Tel. 230301.

Liberia, Amilcar 1, Tel. 264165.
Italy, Pasaje Papa Juan XXII 6, Tel. 724214.
Dominican Republic, Plaza de Santa Pagesa 3, Tel. 200600 and 750776.
Luxemburg, J Cremona 3, Tel. 710987.
Norway, Juan Alcover 54, Tel. 460052.
Netherlands, Tous y Maroto 5a, Tel. 816493 and 726642.
Paraguay, Ctra. Valldemossa, Tel. 202604.
Portugal, Sindicato 42, Tel. 711213.
United Kingdom, Plaza Mayor 3a, Tel. 712445 and 716048.
Sweden, Puigdorfila 1, Tel. 725492, 722381 and 727713.
Switzerland, Paseo Mallorca 24, Tel. 712520 and 714972.
Tunisia, Gremio Zapateros 28, Tel. 209466.
Uruguay, Plaza Mayor 1, Tel. 715569.

IBIZA

United Kingdom, Isidor Macabich 45, 1st floor, Tel. 301818.
Netherlands, Via Punica 2, Tel. 340450.
Germany, Pasaje A. Jaume, Tel. 315763.
(all three in Eivissa [Ibiza town])

ART/PHOTO CREDITS

Eames, Andrew	26, 79, 103, 144, 151, 270/271
Galerie Bischofberger	258
Goodman, Doug	73, 80, 116, 161R, 185, 202/203, 221
Gual, Juame	25, 29, 61, 69, 99, 106/107, 110, 111R, 112, 122, 133, 186, 206, 207, 214, 215, 216, 217, 222, 238, 256/257, 272
Heberle, Jussara	260
Mockler, Mike	115, 234, 235, 237, 239
Murray, Don	3, 31, 32, 33, 34/35, 37, 38, 40, 41, 43, 45, 46/47, 48, 49, 50, 51, 52, 53, 66, 72, 74, 78, 96, 118/119, 120, 121, 123, 126, 130, 132, 135, 136, 138/139, 145, 158, 159, 164R, 166/167, 168, 169, 178, 181, 194, 204/205, 210, 220, 242, 243, 245, 246, 248, 249, 250/251, 252, 254, 255, 262/263, 264/265, 267
Naylor, Kim	36, 59, 101, 102, 104, 127, 128, 131, 134, 165, 200/201, 229, 259, 268/269
Obiol, Walter	76/77, 227, 230, 247
Reichelt, G P /Apa Archive	64/65, 86/87, 88/89
Reuther, Jorg	137, 244
Spectrum	81, 150, 180, 196, 223, 226, 231
Wassman, Bill	9, 14/15, 16/17, 18/19, 20/21, 22, 24, 27, 30, 54/55, 56/57, 58, 62/63, 70/71, 82/83, 84/85, 90/91, 92, 97, 100, 105, 108, 109, 111L, 113, 114, 117, 124/125, 129, 140/141, 142/143, 146, 149, 152, 153, 154, 156/157, 161L, 162, 163, 164L, 170/171, 172/173, 174, 175, 177, 182L, 182R, 183, 184, 187, 188, 189, 190/191, 192/193, 197, 198, 199, 208, 209, 211, 212/213, 218/219, 224/225, 228, 236, 240/241
White, Betty Luton	232

Abbreviations used above: L = Left; R = Right; FR = Far Right; FL = Far Left.

INDEX

A

African Reserve, 133
agriculture, 208
Alaior, 153
Albufera Lake, 153
Alcudia, 117
Alfábia, 266
Almirante Hotel, 148
Almudaina, Artá, 131
Almudaina, Palma, 94-5
Arab Baths, 98-9
Archbishop's Palace, 98
art, 259
Artá, 129

B

Balafia, 177
Banyalbufar, 110
Barceló, Miguel, 127, 259-60, 261
Berenguer III, Count Ramón, 32
Binibeca Vell, 152
Binisalem, 135
birds, 235-8

C

Ca Na Costa, 197
Cabrera, 121-3
Cala Santa Galdana, 161
Cales Coves, 152
Campos, 138
Can Magraner, 254
Can Prunera, 254
Canet, 266
Capicorp Vell, 137
Casa Forteza Rey, 254
Castle of Bellver, 101
Catalan, 37-8
Cathedral, Palma, 95-8, 253

Ceramics Mallorca, 127
Charles, Prince, 75
cheese, 146, 147, 150, 222
Chopin, Frederic, 75, 94, 111, 114
Ciutadella, 159-61
Collingwood House, 148-9
Colomer, 117
Consolat del Mar, 101
Convent of San Bernadino, 130
Convent of San Francisco, 132
Convento de los Mínimos, 135
Cueva d'en Xoroi, 152, 227
Cuevas de Artá, 131
Cuevas del Drach, 128

D

D'Alt Villa, Eivissa, 181
de Montgrí, Guillermo, 42
Deià, 75, 112, 113
Denia, 32, 33
Dragonera, 210

E

Eivissa, 178, 179, 180, 181-3
El Pilar, 198
English, the, 49, 168-9
Es Cavallet, 184
Espalmador, 198
Estang d'es Peix, 195
Estang Pudent, 195
expatriates, 81-3

F

Felanitx, 127
Ferrandell-Oleza-Mas, 27, 28
Ferreries, 163
Fiesta de la Patrona, 216
fiestas, 161, 162, 216
Figueretas, 183
fincas, 243
food, 150, 221-3
Fornells, 165

G

gardens, 265
Gaudí, Antoni, 97, 253, 254
Genoa, 38
Georgetown, 149, 151
Germanía, 44
Golden Farm, 149, 169
Gordiola Museum, 138
Graves, Robert, 112, 113
Grupo Ornithologico Balear (GOB), 210

H

Helium, 188
hierbas, 183, 197
hippies, 152, 178, 188, 197
Hotel Formentor, 77, 117
houses, 243-8

I, J, & K

Ibiza, 175-188
Ibizencos, 62
Inca, 135
Jacobson, Ellis, 261
Jaime I, king of Aragón, 33, 34, 35, 60, 109
Jaime II, 98, 101
Jaime III, 42, 98
Jaleos, 152
Jews, 39-40, 44, 50, 60, 99
Juan Carlos, King, 75
Kane, Colonel Richard, 168, 169

L

La Albufera, 131
La Cartuja, 114
La Granja, 110, 261
La Lonja, 101
La Sabina, 195
language, 37, 169, 179
Las Salinas, 184, 186
Lluc, 115
Lluc, monastery, 254
Llucmajor, 137
Llull, Ramón, 50, 100, 132, 137
Luis Salvador, Archduke, 114

M & N

Macarella, 162
Mahón, 49, 146-8
Mallorquíns, 59, 61
Manacor, 128
March, Juan, 131
Menorquíns, 61-2
Mercadal, 164
Mirador, 95, 96
Mirador d'es Colomer, 117
Mirador de Ses Animes, 110
Monastery of Lluc, 254
Monte Toro, 164
Montesión, church, 99
Moors, 31, 33, 38, 42, 177
Muntaner, Ramón, 40
Muro, 134
Museum of Artá, 129
Museum of Mallorca, 95, 98
Naveta d'es Tudons, 155, 163
nightlife, 227-31

P

Paseo, 180
Palacio Salort, 161
Palma de Mallorca, 94-104
pearls, 128
Pedro, Don, 41, 42
Pereira, theatre, 227
Petrá, 134
Playa de Mitjorn, 197
Plaza del Borne, 159-60
Plaza Santa Eulàlia, 101
Pollença, 116, 215-7
Portal del Mirador, 95, 96
Porto Cristo, 128
prehistoric sites, 27, 28, 137, 155, 163, 197
Puerto de Andratx, 109
Puerto de Pollença, 117
Puerto de Sóller, 111, 113
Puig Major, 114
Punta Arabí, 178, 188
Punta Pedrera, 198

R

Raixa, 265, 266
Rey, Lluis Forteza, 254
Royal Palace of the Almudaina, 94
Royal Palace, Mallorca, 95
Rubió, Joan, 253, 254

S

Sa Calobra, 115
Sa Penya, 182
Sala d'Exposicions del Claustre del Carme, 147
salt, 176, 186, 195
Salvador, Archduke, 75
San Cristóbal, 165
San Francisco, church, 99, 132
San Juan de Misa, church, 162
San Juan, fiesta, 161, 162
San Luis, 151
San Miguel, church, 127
Sand, George, 75, 94, 96, 111, 114
Sant Antoni, 184-5
Sant Ferráu, 197
Sant Francesc Xavier, 196
Santa Eulàlia, church, 132
Santa Eulàlia del Riu, 187-8
Santa Maria, 135
Santa Maria, church, Mahón, 146
Santuario de Nuestra Señora de Puig Randa, 137
Santuario de Nuestra Señora El Toro, 164
Santuario de San Salvador, 127
Santuario de Santa Magdalena, 133
Sanz, Nuño, 34, 37, 42
Serra, José Miguel, 130
Serra, Fray Junípero, 99, 130, 134
Shangri-La, 153
Sierra, Mallorca, 109-17
Sineu, 134
Sóller, 111, 113, 254

Son Bou, 153, 155
Son Catlar, 155
Son Marroig, 113
Son Matge, 27, 28
Son Servera, 133

T

Tagomago, 188
Talati de Dalt, 155
talayots, 28, 154, 155
taulas, 155, 163
Torralba d'en Salort, 155
Torre d'en Gaumes, 153, 155
tourism, 51, 52, 146, 209, 210

V, W, & X

Valldemossa, 114
Vermells Sacristy, 97
Villacarlos, 149, 151, 168
Waters, Neville, 69-71
windmills, 136
wine, 223
Xueta, 60

A
B

D
E
F
G
H
I
J
a
b
c
d
e

g
h
i
j
k
l